THEY WERE WOMEN LIKE ME

They Were Women Like Me

Women of the New Testament in Devotions for Today

JOY JACOBS

WingSpread Publishers
Camp Hill, Pennsylvania

WingSpread Publishers
Camp Hill, Pennsylvania
www.wingpreadpublishers.com

A division of Zur Ltd.

They Were Women Like Me
ISBN: 978-1-60066-108-2
LOC Control Number: 2010929665

Previously published by Christian Publications, Inc.
First Christian Publications Edition 1998
First WingSpread Publishers Edition 2010

14 13 12 11 10 5 4 3 2 1

CONTENTS

Section 3: Preparing My Heart for Discipleship:
"Daughters of Jerusalem, Weep Not for Me . . ."

Section 4: Other Daughters . . .

Section 5: Preparing My Heart for Outreach:
"You will be My witnesses in Jerusalem . . ."

Section 6: Preparing My Heart for Outreach:
"You will be My witnesses . . . in all Judea and Samaria . . ."

Section 7: Preparing My Heart for Outreach:
"You will be My witnesses . . . to the ends of the earth!"

Section 8: Preparing My Heart for Christmas:
" . . . when the fullness of the time was come . . . "

The woman God uses
is the woman God chooses
no matter what others may say . . .

And the woman He uses
is the one He infuses
with power and strength for the day.

FOREWORD

What has been will be again,
what has been done will be done again;
there is nothing new under the sun.
Is there anything of which one can say,
"Look! This is something new"?
It was here already, long ago;
it was here before our time.
There is no remembrance of men of old,
and even those who are yet to come
will not be remembered
by those who follow.
(Ecclesiastes 1:9-11)

The preacher said that there is nothing new under the sun. The elements of life—though endlessly changing in form and variety—remain the same. Flowers flourish multihued, incomparably diversified. Yet they all have leaf, blossom and stem. Music echoes through the centuries in ethnic combinations of chord and melody, rhythm and tone—perpetual modulations of notes that endure incessant rearranging. Snowflakes fall white-patterned—eternal variegations of hydrogen and oxygen.

Humankind is the same. Every person, man or woman, who has ever lived has been unique, individual, a peculiar entity. And yet we are one. We share similar feelings, similar circumstances, no matter the clan or people we find ourselves among, no matter the geographic location where we live upon the earth, no matter the age in which we live.

Sometimes women today feel they have nothing in common with the average woman of Israel two millennia ago. Worlds apart in time and culture, we assume that the stresses we face are unique to our own century, that women of the Bible were a breed apart.

We find, however, in these sensitive portraits of women living during the life and times of Jesus Christ, the startling discovery that what they faced seems uncannily familiar. Joy has transmitted their feelings across the years. And we find great encouragement and comfort realizing that there is an eternality to Christ's relationship with women.

For those of us who are, and those yet to come, it is good to remember.

Karen Burton Mains

PREFACE

My first book, a devotional on women of the Old Testament, was released in 1981, the year I attempted to teach full time as well as mother full time—and continue to be the full-time wife of an evangelist. Finally my kind Christian doctor bluntly told me I had to choose between the middle schoolers and kindergartner at home and the middle schoolers at the local public school.

No one prepared me for the feelings of failure that hit after I quit teaching, but God knew what He was doing—although I certainly didn't. Soon thereafter, Prentice-Hall asked me to write a follow-up to *They Were Women, Too.* The editor in charge of their new Christian line requested "Oh, about thirty chapters, in a similar format on women of the New Testament."

And so a sequel was conceived. I saw this as my chance to be a missionary, with the opportunity to enter secular bookstores where Christian publishers were not invited.

Most readers have little idea of the mental agony, after the initial euphoria, that a writer endures during the gestation period of a book. The mind, rather than the womb, feels bloated, but the inevitable morning sickness often extends into late evening hours, and the labor pains are just as intense. After the book, *They Were Women Like Me,* was finally born in 1985, its early childhood development proved to be traumatic. Prentice-Hall was bought by a conglomerate and overrun by another publisher, and the baby was dropped on its head. Prentice-Hall "dumped" my book, offering me the leftover copies.

Eventually Christian Publications was kind enough to pick it up and promise to take care of it—even understanding its need, a dozen years later, to emerge into a full-grown devotional, a 365-pager like its big sister. Miraculously, the books have now become twins.

Both books are divided into fifty-two units. The introduction to each unit features the character and theme of the chapter as well as a background reading. Following each introductory page are six daily devotionals with key verses and scriptural reading assignments, a poetic comment from the woman being studied and historical/biblical background.

The poetry for each day is meant to reflect the feelings of these women—as perceived, of course, by me. (As I used to tell our sons, it's good to preface statements of opinion with the words, "In my opinion . . .") Since the Bible gives us too few facts, I have taken the liberty of reconstructing some areas of these women's lives in my poetry. I trust that, along with Mary and myself, you will "ponder these things in your heart."

Please keep in mind that the time frame covered in writing has moved from the writer as a mother of young children to an almost-empty-nester grandmother.

But somehow the house never seems empty! A huge thank you goes to my family—including my "adopted" family members—and my friends, my support team! Your love, your support and your confidence that God continues to work through me has kept me writing.

Joy Jacobs

Section 1:

Preparing My Heart for Grace

Week 1

The Scarlet Women of Matthew 1

Do you remember *The Scarlet Letter,* a book written by early American author Nathaniel Hawthorne? In the story, a young woman named Hester Prynne and her daughter were forced to wear a scarlet letter—the letter A—on their clothing. The adulteress and the child of adultery were shunned by the condemning community.

Centuries earlier, in biblical times, the color scarlet had already been associated with a problem past. Scripture tells the "scarlet stories" of women who also experienced rejection by those around them:

- *Tamar,* a shrewd widow who took the law into her own hands in a scandalous way . . .
- *Rahab,* a hotel manager who, over the years, played hostess to many men . . .
- *Ruth,* a young refugee woman, who perfumed herself and lay at the feet of a wealthy landowner while he slept . . .
- *Bathsheba,* the wife of one of the king's top thirty soldiers, who was called to the king's bedroom while her husband was at war . . .
- *Mary,* a teenager who became pregnant while engaged to be married, yet claimed she was still a virgin . . .

Who are these women? Did God condemn them? It might surprise you to know that, in the first chapter of Matthew, the five women named in Jesus' family tree are these scarred or scarlet women.

What was God thinking? Why didn't God choose women who were named "Mother of the Year" . . . or "most likely to succeed"? Why did He choose women with questionable reputations?

If the truth were known, perhaps He chose women like you and me.

Perhaps He was telling some of us that we don't have to wear the letter A for the rest of our lives . . . or pass that letter on to our daughters.

He was saying to all of us that we don't have to stay in the scarlet areas of our lives. That there is a way out. That the vivid scarlet of His shed blood cancels out the blotched scarlet of our sins.

As you read the stories of these women, the words of the prophet in Isaiah 1:18 will have new meaning for you: " 'Come now, let us reason together,' says the LORD: 'Though your sins are like scarlet, they shall be as white as snow.' "

BACKGROUND READING: Matthew 1

1 — Monday

DOES ANYONE CARE ABOUT ME?

"The eternal God is your refuge, and underneath are the everlasting arms." (Deuteronomy 33:27)

Read Matthew 1:3; Genesis 38:1-11

My husband's gone, the one I loved
—his brother too, who hated me—
and now my father-in-law has said
his home's no longer home to me.
The faces of my parents show
a look of disappointment
—and of shame.

—Tamar

According to the Hebrew law of levirate marriage, Tamar was the legal responsibility of her father-in-law, Judah. After all, she had married *two* of his sons! Since both Er and Onan had died without leaving an heir, Judah was required to give Tamar his youngest son, Shelah.

"Return to your father's house for now"—Judah said, eyeing his weeping daughter-in-law uncertainly—"until my son grows up." As she slowly gathered her belongings, Tamar felt the sharp sting of rejection. She went back to her father's house and waited—she had no other options. Would she spend the rest of her life waiting?

Like Tamar, have you experienced loss? abandonment? rejection? loneliness? Does it seem that no one cares what happens to you? Has bitterness crept in to join loneliness? And, since people don't seem to care, have you come to the conclusion that God must not care either—and so you've distanced yourself from Him, from His Church, from His people?

Whether you believe it or not,
God has a plan for your life.

IF GOD HAS A PLAN FOR MY LIFE, WHEN AM I GOING TO FIND OUT WHAT IT IS?

"For it is by grace you have been saved, through faith—and this not from yourselves, it is the gift of God." (Ephesians 2:8)

Read Genesis 38:12-30

A plan, a plan—has God a plan?
A plan for her, perhaps, her friends . . .
but does His care extend to me?
Why is it others have a life
of carefree fun and happiness
while I see only misery?
—Tamar

Tired of experiencing grief, tired of waiting for her brother-in-law to be old enough to marry her, tired of waiting for Judah to take care of her, Tamar decided to take matters into her own hands. If somehow she had Judah's child, he would *have* to take care of her. Once she made her decision, everything fell into place. Disguised as a prostitute, she waited along a road she knew her father-in-law, a lonely widower, would travel. It was a matter of time. . . .

Tamar's plan worked! She conceived twin sons, Perez and Zerah, who became well-known in the tribe of Judah. But was the plan God's "Plan A" for her life?

Have there been times in your life when you felt as desperate as Tamar and did things that shocked—or grieved—those around you? Perhaps you're trying to put those times into the past, but you feel that everyone still remembers. Or perhaps no one knows, but you can't forgive yourself. And you're tired of waiting for God to work a miracle. . . .

It may not be evident to you right now,
but God is at work all around you
to include you in His plan.

DOES GOD KNOW WHAT I'M REALLY LIKE?

"Though your sins are like scarlet, they shall be as white as snow." (Isaiah 1:18)

Read Joshua 2

If you only knew, you wouldn't give
another glance to this sad stare.
If you only knew, you'd pull away
afraid to touch or feel or care.
If you only knew, you'd walk—or run—
avoid my problems, refuse to share.
If you only knew . . . I'm sure you don't . . .
Can't take the chance, my heart's too bare.
—Rahab

When the Israeli spies visited Jericho, Rahab could not hide her identity. Everyone knew Rahab as the leading lady of the local inn. And, because of the scarlet cord hung from her window, so would all of Israel.

Rahab knew right from the start that the God of Israel knew all about her too. Really, it's better that way. It doesn't work to hide anything from God. He is omniscient; He knows everything. He knew *you* when you were in your mother's womb. God can see into your heart.

God also knows when, like Rahab, you realize it's time for a change. She was sick of her sin. She wanted to leave her sin behind and never return to it. She wasn't about to carry a "piece of the rock"—a piece of the wall—with her.

All of us have sinned.

Our sin is an insult against God and causes Him great grief.

Sin is punishable by everlasting separation from God.

Like Rahab, we must see our sin clearly before we recognize our need for a Rescuer.

We cannot save ourselves.

Like Rahab, we must be rescued from Satan's stronghold.

What is your Jericho?

What do you need to turn away from?

GOD WANTS A PERSONAL LOVE RELATIONSHIP WITH—ME?

"Praise be to the L*ORD, who this day has not left you without a kinsman-redeemer." (Ruth 4:14)*

Read Ruth 3-4

They stare at me, stare right through me.
I'm just a nothing—nothing me.
I count for nothing—zero me.
I'm good for nothing—shameful me.
I need a reason to be—me.
Please find a reason to be me.

—Ruth

Ruth must have felt like a nobody. She was a widowed refugee from the hated land of Moab. But she had made a choice to stay with her widowed mother-in-law Naomi—and she intended to follow through on her commitment. God honored Ruth's commitment by sending a "kinsman-redeemer" into her life—Boaz. (Incidentally, Boaz was the son of a refugee named Rahab!) Not only was Boaz wealthy enough to buy back Naomi's land, he was also obedient enough to marry the widow Ruth!

God honors lives lived unselfishly. God's answers to prayer don't always come as quickly as they did in the book of Ruth, but He does answer. And even though His answers aren't instant and His thoughts are not ours nor His ways ours (Isaiah 55:8)—we can count on the fact that He cares equally about each one of us.

God desires to have a personal love relationship with you.

He wants to bring into your life people who fit His plan for you.

Jesus became our Kinsman-Redeemer—He redeemed us by paying for our sin on the cross.

Now He desires to become your "Bridegroom-Protector" and to add to His family through you.

"CREATE IN ME A CLEAN HEART, O GOD"

"According to your unfailing love . . . blot out my transgressions. . . . Let the bones you have crushed rejoice." (Psalm 51:1, 8)

Read Psalm 51

My heart was broken, like the lamb
whose shepherd broke his straying limb,
but broken legs and wills and hearts
can keep a lamb from further sin.
And once the Shepherd's held us close
until the healing can begin
wee lambs have no desire to leave
His heartbeat—or the Shepherd's hand.
—Bathsheba

Sometimes an Oriental shepherd spent so much time in search of a stray from the flock that he was forced to take drastic action. And so he carefully broke the leg of the repeatedly disobedient "black sheep." He bandaged the leg, anointing it with medicinal oil and wine. Then he carried the lamb next to his heart until the leg healed. And it was said that the wanderer never strayed again.

The author of Psalm 51, a song of confession, was King David, who allowed lust to lead him astray. Imagine the shame Bathsheba must have felt—whether she was a victim or a willing participant—after the king engineered the murder of her husband Uriah and she moved into the palace as David's wife. And imagine the palace gossip!

Although God hates sin and must punish it, He loves the sinner. (And He loves a victim too!)

When you repent and confess your sin, God forgives because Jesus took your punishment on the cross.

And so God chooses not to remember your sin.

Remember that it is Satan who accuses us after God has forgiven us.

"WITH GOD, ALL THINGS ARE POSSIBLE"

"I am the Lord's servant. . . . May it be to me as you have said." (Luke 1:38)

Read Luke 1:46-55

I wonder, how can these things be?
How can they happen, Lord, to me?
A child begun in such a way—
Will He ever have a normal day?
And what about my heart, O Lord?
How will I feel the piercing sword?
—Mary

Imagine the emotions with which Mary struggled after the visit of the "annunciation angel"! Did she expect no one in Nazareth to believe her story—not even her own mother—and so turned to her cousin Elizabeth?

God gifted Mary with a great honor—and great responsibility. An ordinary young woman, Mary was being asked to lend her womb to the Almighty One, to bear, to raise—and then to give back to His Father—an extraordinary child who would become the God-man. And along with all that came a promise delivered by the old prophet Simeon: "And a sword will pierce your own soul too" (Luke 2:35). How did Mary feel when her Son asked His Father to forgive those who had humiliated, tortured and finally killed Him? When He cried out that His own Father had forsaken Him?

Do you feel that you or your family members have been treated unfairly? Do you find it hard to forgive? Are you angry at God? Do you wonder where God was when . . . ?

Where was God?

He was watching His own Son hang, in terrible agony, on a cross.

Because God is just, He must punish sin.

But because God is merciful, He put the punishment for sin on Jesus when He hung on the cross.

By recognizing that Jesus took your punishment on the cross, you can experience forgiveness of sin and receive the gift of eternal life.

Section 2:

Preparing My Heart for the Resurrection

Week 2

The Girl at the Gate

A rooster stirred, opened one eye and seemed to stare at the girl who was warming her hands at the small fire in the courtyard. The slight rustle of feathers caught the girl's attention. *Even the birds and the animals seem jumpier than usual tonight,* she thought.

It had been an unusual evening in Jerusalem, this night of April 6, A.D. 30. With people coming and going so frequently, there was little rest for anyone who worked in the house of Caiaphas, the religious leader of Israel, especially for the girl who kept the gate of the courtyard.

Most evenings she considered her job to be monotonous. Often the girl's long, dark eyelashes drooped as she sat by the gate, and she dreamed of leaving the courtyard and meeting more exciting people than the occasional priests who scurried by for a private conference with her master, Caiaphas.

But tonight had been different. In the house of Caiaphas, Jesus of Galilee was on trial.

At least one of tonight's visitors had not been a priest. The girl remembered that the big fisherman who had tried to slip unnoticed into the courtyard both talked and smelled like a Galilean—probably one of the followers of the Galilean who was on trial, she thought. In spite of his physical impressiveness, the big, burly man had appeared to be as frightened as a little boy facing a snarling dog. He had tried to evade the girl's well-practiced questions, although she had asked them courteously; obviously he did not want anyone to know that he was a friend of the Galilean who had caused all the hubbub.

The girl drew her scanty shawl around her and walked with quick, decisive steps toward her seat at the gate. Picking up her lamp, she thought of another, more cunning face its light had revealed earlier in the evening. That man was not nearly as imposing as the big fisherman, but he too had tried to slip by her. At her question, he had mumbled that his name was Judas and that he had business with her master, the High Priest. Later the girl had heard the temple guard mention his name contemptuously as a traitor. The Galilean had been betrayed.

Strange how her thoughts kept coming back to *Him!* Shivering in the raw morning dampness, the Jewish girl reviewed her memories of the man so many had called Master such a short time earlier. Just last week He had ridden into Jerusalem, and multitudes had thrown down palm branches in His path. She had watched from a distance.

Tonight, the servant girl had had the chance to look into His eyes. They were the kindest eyes she had ever seen, yet the most penetrating, and the saddest. As she had watched Him being shoved roughly into the courtyard by the temple guards, He had turned and looked at her, and His eyes seemed to pierce her very soul.

Jesus of Galilee, Jesus of Nazareth: both names of derision to a girl brought up in Jerusalem, the Holy City. "Can anything good come out of Nazareth?" was the old saying. She had heard many conflicting things about this "Master."

Who was He, really?

BACKGROUND READING: Matthew 26:69-75; Mark 14:66-72; Luke 22:54-62; John 18:15-27

2 — Monday

CAN ANYTHING GOOD COME OUT OF NAZARETH?

"In the beginning was the Word, and the Word was with God, and the Word was God. He was with God in the beginning. Through him all things were made; without him nothing was made that has been made." (John 1:1-3)

Read 1 John 3:1-12

Who is that Man?
They call Him
Jesus of Galilee.
His tongue is Galilean
But His eyes still speak to me.
—Caiaphas' servant girl

If you look at a map of Israel, you may realize with a sense of shock that this little country, which hits the news almost every night of the week, stretches only 150 miles north to south and 75 miles east to west. Israel's area is close to that of the state of Maryland. In the time of Jesus, however, approximately 3 million citizens (speaking at least three dialects) lived within the provinces of Judea, Samaria and Galilee.

One unifying influence drew these diverse elements together: Jerusalem was the religious, historic and geographic center of the country. The Jerusalem schools attracted the best teachers and many of the most intelligent students; as a result, the city dwellers tended to look with increasing contempt upon their country cousins, especially the uncultured Galileans, who spoke with a soft slur. Caiaphas' servant girl may have tried to dismiss Jesus as one more simpleminded Galilean.

POINT TO PONDER: Many people still ignore the Man from Nazareth. Can someone from a completely different age and culture have anything relevant to say to us today?

God, life is so confusing sometimes. It's hard to know what to believe. Can You help me?

2 — *Tuesday*

NEEDED: A LEADER

"In him was life, and that life was the light of men. The light shines in the darkness, but the darkness has not understood it." (John 1:4-5)

Read 2 Corinthians 4:3-18; Matthew 12:17-21

Who is that Man?
They brought Him
In bonds
Tied like a slave
And yet His eyes were free
As the winds . . . the clouds . . . the waves.
—Caiaphas' servant girl

The Holy City, during the holy days of the Passover season, was full of *un*holy Roman soldiers. Pontius Pilate, the Roman procurator, always called in additional security during the special Jewish observances, and the Passover was one of the most important of these. As every Jewish heart warmed to the celebration of the exodus from Egypt, each Jewish mind was very much aware that this nation was once again bereft of its most cherished possession: freedom.

How could God allow this to happen to His "chosen people"? Ah, but He had promised a deliverer. "The people walking in darkness have seen a great light. . . . For to us a child is born, to us a son is given, and the government will be on his shoulders. And he will be called Wonderful Counselor, Mighty God, Everlasting Father, Prince of Peace" (Isaiah 9:2, 6).

But where was the promised deliverer? The girl at Caiaphas' gate may have wondered how this Jesus of Galilee could possibly deliver anyone from anything. He couldn't even save Himself—how could He save others?

God . . . I need peace in my heart. I need a Counselor. Is Jesus Christ truly the Prince of Peace? What does that mean? Please show me through Your Word.

2 — *Wednesday*

RECOGNIZING THE LEADER

"He was in the world, and though the world was made through him, the world did not recognize him." (John 1:10)

Read Galatians 3:26-4:7

Who is that Man?
They follow,
The ones who know Him best;
But though they follow,
Fail
To stand by Him in this test.
—Caiaphas' servant girl

Caiaphas' gatekeeper may have heard that twelve men had followed and lived with Jesus for three years as He crisscrossed the land of Israel. Probably none of them were well educated. (Only elementary education was compulsory.)

Several women had also joined the group, an unheard-of thing in those days. Women and men unrelated by blood or marriage simply did not associate with each other openly. Furthermore, women were allowed to learn reading and writing, but the "third R"—religion—was not seen as necessary. What could a woman understand of such things? But women like Mary Magdalene, Salome and Joanna looked back to Old Testament women like Miriam, Deborah and Huldah and broke the rules.

POINT TO PONDER: Jesus welcomed women into a "man's world," and both women and men left everything to follow Him. Some saw Him as a great teacher; others believed Peter's statement: "You are the Christ, the Son of the living God" (Matthew 16:16).

Thank You, Jesus, for Your concern for women. I really do want to believe in You. If You are the Son of God, please make this knowledge a reality in my life.

2 — *Thursday*

REJECTION OF A LEADER

"He came to that which was his own, but his own did not receive him." (John 1:11)

Read Matthew 10:16-31

Who is that Man?
His own friend
Denied He knew Him
Yet . . .
In spite of His aloneness
His face I can't forget.

—Caiaphas' servant girl

Although Peter was trying to avoid questions, the girl at the gate and others in the courtyard asked him if he was a follower of the Galilean on trial. Three times he answered, roughly and negatively.

The restless rooster in the courtyard shook its wings, rose sleepily to its feet as though obeying an unseen command, and crowed. Peter unexpectedly broke into sobs. The men around him seemed as embarrassed as the big fisherman obviously was. They looked away as, pulling his cloak over his face, he ran from the courtyard.

A few minutes earlier, Jesus had been escorted out of the house and back through that courtyard. As He passed Peter, He had lifted His head and looked sadly into the big man's eyes, recalling without words His earlier statement: "Before the rooster crows, you will disown me three times!" (John 13:38).

Jesus, I too have been embarrassed by Your presence. I too have rejected You and denied You by ignoring You. Please forgive me. If You understood Peter, then You understand me as well.

2 — *Friday*

REDEMPTION BY THE LEADER

"Yet to all who received him, to those who believed in his name, he gave the right to become children of God—children born not of natural descent, nor of human decision or a husband's will, but born of God." (John 1:12-13)

Read Philippians 2:5-11

Who is that Man?
He's gone now.
To Pilate He's been led.
The trial's fixed. The High Priest,
It's rumored, wants Him dead.
—Caiaphas' servant girl

If Jesus was the Son of God, then He knew ahead of time everything that would happen to Him. If Jesus was the Son of God, He could have overpowered the soldiers who came to arrest Him. If Jesus was the Son of God, He could have taken over the Roman Empire with a wave of His hand.

Why didn't He?

Imagine that you were trying to communicate with an ant. You watched the little creature for some time and you admired his industrious ways and you wanted to tell him so. You also wanted to give him some helpful hints in a few areas. You lectured in his direction for quite some time, but he paid absolutely no attention to you. Why? Because you were speaking in your language, not Antese. You were not on the same level as that little ant, and he didn't understand a word you said.

God created us (humankind). He yearned to have fellowship with us. He gave Adam and Eve a simple protective set of rules, and they promptly broke His loving heart by their disobedience. He sent the Old Testament prophets with warnings, but for the most part they were ignored and rejected. Finally, He made the supreme effort to come down to our level. He sent His Son to earth to become "ant-size"—our size—to speak our language and to show us how much He cared. "The Word became flesh. . . ." (John 1:14).

Thank You, God, for Your unbelievable caring.

2 — Saturday

RECEIVING THE LEADER

"The Word became flesh and made his dwelling among us. We have seen his glory, the glory of the One and Only, who came from the Father, full of grace and truth." (John 1:14)

Read Philippians 3:7-14

Who is that Man?
I might have
Left all to follow Him
If His friends had told me of Him
While the fire was growing dim.
—Caiaphas' servant girl

We must leave the girl, Caiaphas' gatekeeper, with her memories and her thoughts. She is still sitting faithfully at her post, shivering in the predawn dampness.

The temple guards have left with Jesus. Peter is gone. Anyone else left in the courtyard is probably catching a few well-deserved winks. There is no one to tend the fire.

POINT TO PONDER: As we have asked the question "Who is that Man?" what has been your reaction? Have you acknowledged Him as the Son of God? Is there a fire burning in your heart? Or is it cold and lifeless, like the embers in the courtyard of Caiaphas?

"To all who received him, to those who believed in his name, he gave the right to become children of God" (John 1:12).

God, it's difficult for me to grasp this concept that You sent Your own Son to earth. I don't understand why He was willing to give up so much for so little. Please keep helping me to understand, a little at a time.

Week 3

Claudia

It was a true exercise in futility. Night after night, terrorized by her own guilt, Shakespeare's Lady Macbeth went through the motions of washing the blood of King Duncan from her hands. The imagined spots simply would not "begone."

Claudia Procula, named by historians as the wife of Pontius Pilate, the hated Roman ruler in a Jewish country, tried to spare her husband a similar agony. She urged him, "Don't have anything to do with that innocent man" (Matthew 27:19) and Pilate officially washed his hands of the blood of Jesus Christ.

Several years later, however, Pilate's political life came to an abrupt end; he was banished to the south of France, it is reported, and ultimately committed suicide. Were he and Claudia, like Lady Macbeth, haunted by the what-might-have-been?

A short historical background is in order. There is no record of Pontius Pilate before A.D. 26, when he and Claudia arrived in Caesarea, the beautiful resort city on the sandy banks of the Mediterranean. Pilate's background may have been in government or trade; Claudia had the connections that won Pilate his position as procurator. Some say she was the granddaughter of Caesar Augustus, past ruler of the Roman world.

In any case, Claudia had influence with Sejanus, a counselor to Tiberius Caesar, who not only got Pilate his position, but also won for Claudia the unusual privilege of accompanying her husband rather than staying behind in Rome. She undoubtedly enjoyed acting as hostess in their homes in Caesarea, Jerusalem and Samaria, entertaining both for pleasure and for political reasons.

With all this in mind, we can understand why Claudia felt free to intervene on Jesus' behalf. Although Pilate was known for his hard-nosed cruelty toward the Jewish people, he apparently refused his wife nothing.

Perhaps because of her request, Pilate did not condemn Jesus to death; conversely, he did not save Him from the mob. Although he symbolically washed his hands of Jesus' blood, he may have spent the rest of his life trying to remove the stain of guilt from his mind and heart.

BACKGROUND READING: Matthew 27:11-26; Luke 23:12

3 – Monday

A NEW RELIGION—OR A NEW LIFE?

"So faith comes by hearing [what is told], and what is heard comes by the preaching [of the message that came from the lips] of Christ, the Messiah [Himself]." (Romans 10:17, Amplified)

Read Mark 4:14-20

I, Claudia Procula, let Him die!
Because of pride
I stood back far too long.
My lips said nothing
When they should have testified
My faith in Him.
That week He died
Was not the first I'd heard of Him.
I'd seen Him often in the busy streets.
The city buzzed with talk
Of this great Man.
—Claudia Procula, wife of Pilate

Roman religion was a mixture of practicality and pleasure. There was a god for almost every object in the house (for example, god of the door), as well as many personal events (god of love and fertility, god of death). Emperor worship, a convenient way of justifying the monarch's absolute power, was the new religion of the times, and the nearby Greek influence encouraged sexual promiscuity under the guise of religion. (The temple prostitutes were available to any "worshiper"—for a fee, of course.)

Pleasure seeking, from the emperor on down, was the national pastime. Claudia had probably grown up in an atmosphere of unrestrained immorality; completely opposite were the teachings she heard her servants discussing as they repeated to each other the sayings of "the Master."

I guess you could say my life has been pleasure oriented too. Christianity sounds so martyrlike, although a lot of people who call themselves Christians live the same way I do. There's still a lot I don't understand, God.

3 – Tuesday

A NEW CREATION

"Therefore if any person is (ingrafted) in Christ, the Messiah, he is (a new creature altogether,) a new creation; the old (previous moral and spiritual condition) has passed away. Behold, the fresh and new has come!" (2 Corinthians 5:17, Amplified)

Read 1 John 1:8-10; 2:15-17

As Pilate's wife
I could not walk the streets
Or follow Him
As other women did.
I longed to walk with Him
As did the Magdalene,
Of whom I'd heard
So many lurid, lusty tales . . .
But I dismissed them
When I saw her face-to-face.
—Claudia

The Holy City must have seemed strange to Claudia. Her friends in Rome dressed in expensive silks, linens and furs, with scarves draped across bare shoulders and delicate fabrics for undergarments. A Jewish woman, by comparison, wore a total of five garments (petticoat through outer girdle) and a full scarf to protect her modesty, hiding much of her face. Roman ladies were quite familiar with cosmetics, wigs and manicures, but Jewish women were taught that all this was sinful vanity.

The Roman poet Ovid made this cynical statement: "Pure women are only those who have not been asked." Faithfulness in marriage was a joke to the Romans; Jewish laws concerning adultery were harsh. But Jesus saw the chinks in the armor of the Jewish leaders, pointing out that the commandment against adultery was directed against lust as well and that any man who undressed a woman with his eyes was already committing adultery with her in his heart.

Lust is such a laughing matter in today's world. Is it really wrong? Isn't it just natural? What does the Bible mean by becoming a "new creation"? Is it possible for me to experience that? Please show me, God.

3 — *Wednesday*

THE GOOD LIFE—OR ETERNAL LIFE?

"If any one would serve Me, he must continue to follow Me—to cleave steadfastly to Me, conform wholly to My example, in living and if need be in dying—and wherever I am, there will My servant be also. If any one serves Me, the Father will honor him." (John 12:26, Amplified)

Read 1 Peter 2:21-25

There was a certain look
Each woman had
Who followed in His humble caravan—
A look of wholeness,
Peace, content,
Fulfillment that I sadly lacked.
Yes, I wore silks of purple, crimson, red.
My retinue obeyed my least command
But life was lonely
Even in a crowd.
I would have given all my earthly goods
To feel His smile on me.

—Claudia

Perhaps Claudia was finding that her daily smorgasbord of pleasures left her feeling uncomfortably full but soon empty again. At one time she may have enjoyed the climb on the ladder of political success, but had the journey lost its excitement?

Now Jesus Christ was headed in Claudia's direction. What impact would He have upon her life? What did it mean to follow Christ? The Roman concept of "the good life" had centered around houses, possessions, servants, luxury. The Man of Galilee had none of these; His life was the epitome of simplicity. The people who followed Him, it seemed, had also given up everything.

POINT TO PONDER: What *does* it mean to follow Jesus Christ? Is it to pursue the "good life"? If we "conform wholly" to His example, what does that involve?

Are you asking me to die for You, God? How do I know what You want of me? How do I know how to follow You?

3 – Thursday

THE STAGE IS SET

"For there is no difference between Jew and Gentile—the same Lord is Lord of all and richly blesses all who call on him." (Romans 10:12)

Read Hebrews 11:24-31

Yet pride and fear prevented me
From sharing how I felt.
Pilate would laugh—
A woman of my royal blood
Daydreaming of a Jew!

Then came the night the servants whispered long and loud.
I dreamed of Him, and begged my maid for news.
She finally told me He had been betrayed;
He'd soon be brought to Pilate.
Time was running out!
—Claudia

The Virgin's Fountain and the Pool of Siloam had been Jerusalem's sources of water for centuries. But, tired of the summer water shortages, Pilate decided to build an aqueduct between Solomon's Pools (outside Bethlehem) and Jerusalem—in spite of Jewish protests. In a display of contempt for the Jews, Pilate financed the project with the temple treasury.

Angered to the point of a frenzied demonstration, the Jews were brutally cut down by Roman plainclothesmen who had secretly mixed with them in the temple area. The growing enmity between the Jews and Pilate was complicated by the fact that the dead demonstrators were not citizens of Jerusalem but of King Herod's province, Galilee. Jesus' trial could only intensify the three-way struggle.

Considering all this, it would have been much easier for Claudia to content herself with entertaining than to "worry her pretty little head" with more serious forms of competition. She was taking a chance on arousing Pilate's anger; she had to make the choice between responsibility and the easy way out.

I think You're asking me to make a choice as well, God. I guess I've been holding back from making a responsible decision.

3 — *Friday*

THE CHOICE

"Because if you acknowledge and confess with your lips that Jesus is Lord and in your heart believe (adhere to, trust in and rely on the truth) that God raised Him from the dead, you will be saved." (Romans 10:9, Amplified)

Read Hebrews 11:32-40

I had to act now . . .
Or the crowd would kill!
I knew their hatred for this gentle Man.
I must act now
Or never get the chance
To speak to Him,
To find the secret of His peace.
I wrote a note to Pilate, dispatched it by my maid.
I waited, trembling for her to return.
—Claudia

Claudia was faced with a choice: obey her conscience, or compromise? She had "suffered a great deal" (Matthew 27:19) in a dream about Christ; perhaps the dream had placed squarely on her shoulders the awful responsibility of the verdict. Claudia was sure He was innocent. Was she as sure that He was the Son of God?

Whatever her beliefs, she decided to risk Pilate's displeasure and to use whatever influence she had in an attempt to save Jesus' life. Claudia faced the possibility that, in a fit of jealous rage, Pilate might even accuse her of unfaithfulness. After all, the emperor himself (Tiberius) had been betrayed by his wife Julia.

She must take that chance.

Lord Jesus, I've waited long enough. I admit that I'm a sinner and that I cannot save myself. I repent; I turn away from my sins. I ask You to forgive me for rejecting You and Your lordship over my life, and I believe and place my trust in You. I receive You as my Savior and Lord. Thank You for loving me enough to die for me. Please cleanse my heart and life and make me a new creation (2 Corinthians 5:17).

3 – Saturday

THE DECISION

"Anyone who trusts in him will never be put to shame."
(Romans 10:11)

Read Hebrews 12:1-13

But I had waited far too long!
My husband thought my fears a dream,
A nightmare that would disappear in day.
He washed his hands of innocent blood
Indifferently.
I stood back, powerless.

"Daughters of Jerusalem," the Galilean said,
"Don't cry!
Don't cry for Me, but only for yourselves."
And so I lie here on my queenly bed,
Silken sheets tear-stained.
I waited far too long.
I failed the King of kings.

—Claudia

Pilate's face flushed as he read the note from his wife. He was already irritated by the clamoring Jews in his courtyard and now this—this sentimentalism! He felt closed in between two opposing forces.

At that point Pilate thought he saw a way out. He could outmaneuver these disgusting, screaming Jews, placate his wife and peacefully settle the stalemate between himself and Herod, all in one shrewd move! This Jesus was a Galilean. Let Herod, tetrarch of Galilee, resolve the whole mess. "Take Him to Herod," Pilate said. "It's not my problem."

In Herod's presence, Jesus calmly ignored the tetrarch's questions. Frustrated, Herod dressed the "king of the Jews" in a gaudy robe, mocked Him cruelly and sent Him back to Pilate.

Here He comes again, Pilate! One more chance to stand for the right! Your reply?

"I find no fault in Him," Pilate admitted.

I'm just as weak as Pilate. I'll need Your strength and Your wisdom, Jesus, if my friends and family reject me. Please guide me.

Week 4

Herodias

Jesus' brief trial before Herod Antipas, tetrarch of Galilee, might have had a different ending if the tetrarch's wife, Herodias, had used her influence to plead for the Galilean's life. But Herodias had never been interested in saving lives.

Herodias, the Jezebel of the New Testament, was responsible for the death of John the Baptist. To achieve her goal, she subjected her own daughter (named by historians as Salome) to the lecherous desires of a dirty old man, her second husband, Herod Antipas. She encouraged and even used a relationship with incestuous overtones to further her own purposes.

Why was power so important to Herodias? Why was there no softness, no motherly nature in this strange woman? What were the forces that shaped her life?

Herodias was the granddaughter of Herod the Great who, in his paranoia, killed all the male Hebrew children after he was told by the wise men of the birth of a future king. Herodias' father, Aristobulus, was Herod's son by Miriamne, the first of his ten wives; supposedly Miriamne was the only person Herod ever loved, but he killed her also because she was suspected of a plot against his life.

Herod Philip, Herodias' father's half-brother, was also Herodias' first husband, but Philip was disinherited and exiled to Rome because of the plot against his father, Herod the Great. In Rome with Philip, Herodias entertained another half-uncle, Herod Antipas, who had come to Rome to be invested with the position of tetrarch of Galilee.

Determined to attain a position of power at any cost, Herodias persuaded her uncle Antipas to divorce his wife; in turn, she divorced Philip (evidently a loser in her eyes), and the strange pair left for Tiberias, the capital of Galilee, with Herodias' daughter, Salome.

Power lust breeds murder to survive. It drove Herodias' grandfather to kill the only woman he ever loved and to exile his own children. Herodias inherited that same passion, or learned it; her power lust, like her grandfather's, would not only kill but also twist and cripple those who survived.

BACKGROUND READING: Matthew 2:1-18; Luke 3:1

4 – Monday

GRANDDAUGHTER AND SISTER OF A KING

"God opposes the proud but gives grace to the humble."
(James 4:6)

Read Luke 9:7-9; 13:31; 23:1-11

I could have saved Him,
That Jewish "King of kings"!
I had the power! Had I cared,
I could have figured out a way,
Persuaded Herod to release
That strange, calm prisoner of the Jews.
But somehow I didn't care to stay
Around Him long.
I felt a power in that Man
As though He were a king. . . .
—Herodias

Was Herodias present when the quiet Galilean, the cousin of John the Baptist, was tried by her husband? Neither Scripture nor history tells us of her presence, but can you imagine Herodias missing the event if she were in Jerusalem? Herodias was the type of woman who was aware of *everything*.

History tells us that later Herodias persuaded her husband to ask for the title of king. (Herodias' brother, Herod Agrippa I, had earned that title, and she could not be outdone.) It was a bad move, however; Agrippa brought charges against Antipas, and the would-be king was exiled to Western Europe.

Herodias, since she was Agrippa's sister, did not share the indictment, but surprisingly enough she chose to be exiled with her husband. Had she mellowed with age and actually developed a love relationship with her husband, or was it simply that she had nowhere else to go, no one else to turn to? In those lonely days of exile, did she look back on her days of power and wish she had used her influence differently? Let's review Herodias' life in this chapter.

Father, thank You for helping me to see that my influence on others may be greater than I realize. Please keep reminding me that my vote counts.

4 – Tuesday

POWER LUST

"For where you have envy and selfish ambition, there you find disorder and every evil practice." (James 3:16)

Read Luke 3:19-20; Matthew 14:1-12

I could have saved him too!
I ruled his destiny, not God!
I had the power—I, Herodias,
Daughter of kings and born to rule!
I planned his death. . . .
Yes, even now the hate I felt
Still boils within me.
That John the Baptist, he was called,
Simple of mind as in his dress
Of camel's hair. . . .
The wild man who defied a queen!
—Herodias

"It is not lawful for you to have her," John announced simply to Herod Antipas shortly after he entered Galilee with his new partner. Herodias had struggled long and hard to climb power's ladder; now, just as she had her feet firmly planted on the top rungs, a *nobody* dared attempt to dislodge her. A nobody who lived in the desert, ate unmentionable foods and wore the skins of animals.

POINT TO PONDER: Power lust does not see people as having worth in themselves, only as tools to be used as needed and discarded when outdated. In an age of disposable diapers and fast food, it is easy to drift in and out of convenient relationships when they become *in*convenient. Often, we seriously hurt the people we use in this way, and we damage ourselves and our ability to experience true love in the process.

Evaluate the relationships that you have with people: Do you "use" people? (Ask a trusted friend to think about it and be honest—you might be surprised at the answer.)

Forgive me, Father, for "using" other people You have created, people You love just as You love me. Show me where I need to right relationships.

4 — Wednesday

HERODIAS' HERITAGE

"What causes fights and quarrels among you? Don't they come from your desires that battle within you?" (James 4:1)

Read James 5:1-12

I should have been a queen!
Yes, even as a child
I stood atop Masada in my mind
And out as far as I could see
The land was mine!
I saw the crowds bow to their queen.
The Baptist didn't bow!

—Herodias

I toured Masada shortly after it was featured in the TV movie and found it to be a fascinating place. The Israelis who held out to the end on that natural tower were determined to let the Romans know that they had *chosen* to die! Enough food had been dried and sorted to last for months on end, and the mountain of rock boasted a hidden supply of water. The proud Israelis chose to die rather than fight their brother-slaves, who were forced by the Romans to build the ramp that spelled defeat for Israel.

Herodias' grandfather, Herod the Great (concerned only with his own safety), built a well-protected palace on the side of Masada, but even the stone fortress could not protect him from inner intrigue. To save his own life, he killed the only chance for human happiness he might have known: his first wife, Miriamne.

That same fierce blood ran in Herodias' veins. John the Baptist may have been imprisoned at Masada, but no fortress could keep him safe from Herodias' schemes.

Help me, Father, to face the "inner me."

DOING VS. BEING

"You want something but don't get it. You kill and covet, but you cannot have what you want. You quarrel and fight. You do not have, because you do not ask God." (James 4:2)

Read Romans 8:31-39

He dared to call my name
And shame me publicly,
Tell Herod he'd defied the law
By taking Philip's wife.
And who is Philip?
Just a pawn in power's play—
I am a queen!
I was born to be a queen!
—Herodias

Sigmund Freud concluded that the two basic drives behind human behavior are pleasure and power. We have already discussed the Roman obsession for pleasure. The inevitable by-product of a thirst for power is violence, as evidenced in the life of Herodias. But are there deeper needs within the human "stream of unconsciousness"?

POINT TO PONDER: From Dr. Lawrence Crabb, a Christian psychologist:

> People have one basic need which requires two kinds of input for its satisfaction. The most basic need is a sense of personal worth, an acceptance of oneself as a whole real person. The two required inputs are *significance* (purpose, importance, adequacy for a job, meaningfulness, impact) and *security* (love—unconditional and consistently expressed; permanent acceptance).[1]

A child who grows up feeling unaccepted and unacceptable may base all his or her feelings of personal worth on what he or she can *do* to become significant, rather than on what he or she *is* as a person. Doesn't this sound like Herodias? Do I hear echoes in my own life?

Thank You, Father, for Your promise that nothing can separate me from Your love. If You are on my side nothing else matters.

4 – Friday

IRRESPONSIBLE LIFESTYLES

"When you ask, you do not receive, because you ask with wrong motives, that you may spend what you get on your pleasures." (James 4:3)

Read Romans 8:1-17

I hated Herod too!
After that first sexual urge
The stolen waters were not sweet.
His lust and greed soon sickened me,
But, even worse, his fear!
He feared the Baptist, feared his eyes,
Refused to kill him—
He feared the words
Of a captive man!

—Herodias

Whatever pleasure Herodias temporarily experienced with Herod Antipas was shattered by John's ringing condemnation of their illicit union. Her fury at the prophet's denunciation was probably exceeded only by her disgust at Herod's reaction to the Baptist. *He is actually afraid of that maniac!* Herodias fumed.

People have many strange ideas as to what fulfills their needs for significance (meaningfulness) and security (permanent acceptance). These wrong ideas or philosophies of living dictate wrong patterns of living. When Herodias' plans to achieve significance through power were in danger of being upset by John the Baptist, she had to find a way to deal with the interference. Her method, although shocking, was deliberate and pointed.

We all use our own unique ways of defending ourselves and satisfying our needs. How do I react when I feel insecure and defensive? What do I do when feelings of "nothingness" threaten to overwhelm me? Do I understand the real route to personal worth?

Thank You, Father, for setting me free from the spirit of fear and for adopting me into Your family.

LEARNING WHO I AM

*"For you did not receive a spirit that makes you a slave again to fear, but you received the Spirit of sonship. And by him we cry, '*Abba, *Father.' " (Romans 8:15)*

Read James 4:13-17

I felt no fear—I fear no one!
I plotted slyly for John's death
And laughed when that huge head appeared!
Salome has never been the same. . . .
She's but a child—she will outgrow
Her squeamish feelings and her fears!
I'll train her to become a queen!
—Herodias

Herodias was so convinced of the necessity of John's death that the grisly banquet scene mentioned in Matthew 14:1-12 probably did not bother her in the least. Her philosophy of life, her need for significance through power, told her that John had to go—the sooner the better.

POINT TO PONDER: As Lawrence Crabb points out, Jesus Christ presents to us a completely opposite philosophy of life from that of Herodias. My significance results from an understanding of who I am in Christ—a child of God. I will begin to feel significant as I have an eternal impact on others in God's family (the body of Christ) by serving and ministering to them. My Father promises to enable me to do this, and as I become more and more like His Son, I will better understand true significance and enjoy it more completely.

For me, that means that being an author cannot take precedence over my family and friends. A letter from a discouraged divorcée or a phone call from a rescue mission needing a low-budget speaker for their kaffeeklatsch may seem to usurp the time I had planned for research and writing—but who knows what new material may be unearthed in being sensitive to God's leading? What opportunities is He presenting to me today?

Abba Father, thank You for the many opportunities You will present to me to minister to other members of my new family.

Week 5

Joanna, Wife of Chuza

Like his father Herod the Great, King Herod Antipas loved to build. About 25 A.D. he built his capital, Tiberias, choosing a spot just a few miles from the small town of Magdala—more importantly, a spot that faced the Sea of Galilee. It was an area noted for its healing hot springs; tourists can still view a "bathing hut" dating back to antiquity. Perhaps "that fox," as Jesus called him, deliberately built the town over an ancient cemetery, avoided by orthodox Jews as unclean, so that he would not be bothered by the Jews and their laws.

The houses of Tiberias covered one of the many hillsides that sloped gently downward toward the sea. Possibly Jesus delivered His "Sermon on the Mount" near Tiberias, probably facing a natural amphitheater close to the sea as He spoke. If it was a clear day, perhaps the snow-covered tip of Mount Hermon was visible. In spring, when all of Galilee was in bloom and the sea reflected the billowing clouds, Tiberias was a beautiful place to be.

And the rulers of Tiberias may have been "beautiful people"—but not in spirit! They would not have understood the words Jesus spoke in that sermon: "Blessed are the poor in spirit, for theirs is the kingdom of heaven" (Matthew 5:3).

In the previous chapter you discovered that Herodias, the power-hungry granddaughter of Herod the Great, left her first husband, Herod Philip (her father's half-brother) for her half-uncle, Herod Antipas. When Herod Antipas visited Rome, instead of bringing some Roman souvenirs back to

Tiberias for his wife, Herod brought home another wife—and her daughter, Salome.

Herod lived to regret that decision. His furious father-in-law, King Aretas of the Arabian city of Petra, never forgot the insult to his daughter. Aretas took revenge, years later, by marching against Herod and humiliatingly defeating him.

In later years, Herodias prodded Herod to demand the title of king from the emperor. But the emperor had grown tired of this reckless playboy-tyrant and his pushy wife. Herod was removed from power in 39 A.D. About fifteen years after his building spree, he was banished to Gaul, in Western Europe, where he died.

Can you imagine being a servant in the house of King Herod? The Bible tells us that Chuza was Herod's "steward" or head administrator. I picture Chuza as a quiet but very efficient man. Had he been anything else, he probably would not have survived.

And Joanna, his wife? The Bible simply tells us that she was one of the women who followed and ministered to Jesus—after Jesus had healed her.

BACKGROUND READING: Matthew 14:1-12

5 – Monday

A HEART THAT DEVISES WICKED SCHEMES

"The LORD hates . . . a heart that devises wicked schemes. . . ."
(Proverbs 6:16, 18)

Read Mark 4:1-34

Tiberias,
on the Sea of Galilee . . .
Herod took advantage of a spot
so rich in peace and natural beauty—
and yet
investing all his riches
he built a place bereft
of human peace,
devoid of human love.
—Joanna, wife of Chuza

Before she met Jesus, Joanna may have been acquainted with the woman Mary from nearby Magdala. Now called Mejdel, the town was noted for its weaving and its fishing. Joanna and Chuza may often have walked the three miles that lay between the towns, enjoying the view of the Sea of Galilee, bringing back with them the salted fish for which Magdala was noted. Or perhaps they bought material out of which Joanna made their clothing.

On those visits, did they see the woman the villagers called "the wild one"? Did Joanna feel sorry for this one who had been sinned against so much that her mind and emotions could no longer handle her grief? Perhaps she had been wronged by the Roman soldiers who must have swarmed the little outpost of Magdala. Or by Herod himself, who openly lusted after his own stepdaughter.

POINT TO PONDER: It is easy to discern and define faults in others—and yet deny our own. God hates a heart that thinks up wicked schemes.

Lord, please check my life for things You hate.

5 – Tuesday

ANOTHER WORLD

"But when John rebuked Herod the tetrarch . . . he locked John up in prison." (Luke 3:19-20)

Read 1 Samuel 10:1-13

My first mistress, daughter of Aretas
the Nabatean king just to the south of us . . .
Her memories were of happier days
riding her Arabian horse beside her father's
Into a palace carved from rocks of rose,
a home where she was loved and cherished
—the ancient city, Petra.
She had no acquaintance with
the evils of King Herod's court.
—Joanna

The ancient city of Petra is still a fascinating place today. Hewn out of a mountain of rose-colored rock, the only entrance is the same low arch through which the daughter of King Aretas probably left the city and came back to it 2,000 years ago. Windows of caves are carved out of this uniquely beautiful rock, caves that served as homes of both kings and commoners. Was it a true "open house," a loving community where the princess was adored by her subjects as well as her family?

If so, why did she leave? Was Herod entranced by her beauty, or was the marriage simply to increase Herod's power and guarantee peace between Judea and Arabia? Whatever the attraction between Herod Antipas and the daughter of King Aretas, it was short-lived. Herod was incapable of faithfulness.

And Joanna? As the wife of Herod's chief administrator, was it her job to acquaint Herod's new wife with the luxuries of his court, to escort her to his healing hot springs? Did a friendship grow between them? Did Joanna teach the princess not only her language, but also her belief in the Master whose teachings were inspiring waves of new hope—as well as ripples of approaching disaster—around the Sea of Galilee?

Make me aware, Lord, of whatever opportunities a servant spirit may offer.

5 — *Wednesday*

HANDS THAT SHED INNOCENT BLOOD

"They said, 'Moses permitted a man to write a certificate of divorce and send [his wife] away.' 'It was because your hearts were hard that Moses wrote you this law,' Jesus replied." (Mark 10:4-5)

Read Luke 3:1-20

As if vile Herod were not vile enough,
he took unto himself
a second wife
with scorpion bite
and heart of stone.
Return to Petra, daughter of Aretas!
Your father-king will wreak revenge on Herod!
Your broken heart and trust will heal
in healthier surroundings,
once more protected by the walls of rose.
—Joanna

If a friendship had grown between Joanna and the princess, imagine Joanna's feelings when Herod returned from Rome with a new wife and daughter. Imagine her grief when her mistress was sent back to her home in Petra. Imagine Joanna's fear and hatred of Herodias. Imagine her disgust and terror when Herodias forced her own daughter to dance before the eyes of drunken lustful men.

Was Joanna present in the court of Herod, awaiting the choices of Herodias for dinner, on the night Salome danced? Was Joanna in attendance the evening that the head of the now-stilled baptizer was served on a platter? Did a voice whisper to Joanna that the gory vision would be forever, indelibly imprinted on the screen of her mind? That her mind would never know peace again? Perhaps Joanna's nightmares did not end with the morning light. And perhaps Chuza feared that Herod was not the only one who had lost a wife.

You know, Lord, the memories with which I struggle. I ask for Your healing touch upon my head and heart.

5 – Thursday

MAD MARY'S MASTER

"Some Pharisees came to Jesus. . . . 'Leave this place. . . . Herod wants to kill you.'
He replied, 'Go tell that fox, "I will drive out demons and heal people today and tomorrow, and on the third day I will reach my goal." ' " (Luke 13:31-32)

Read Mark 6:14-29

I cannot go with you, my princess . . .
I have a husband here
and I must stay
but Chuza bids me find a healing touch as well
for fear that lurks within my heart
a paralyzing, deadly fear that lurks within my heart.
—Joanna

Joanna may have heard of the healing of Mary of Magdala. Stories must have flooded the entire area of Galilee. The "wild one" was now clean and clothed, in her right mind, speaking the words of peace she had heard from Jesus! Mary of Magdala had a new Master, a Master who cared enough about her to allow her to become a follower, to travel with Him. It was unthinkable—and wonderful!

If there were hope for Mary, there was hope for Joanna. Possibly it was just that thought that enabled Joanna to say a "shalom" to Chuza that meant "farewell . . . for now." Perhaps it gave her courage to leave the house of Herod during the night, to slip past the Roman guards, to find the place in the wooded hillsides surrounding the Sea of Galilee where Jesus and His followers were camping. Perhaps it was Mary of Magdala—a peaceful, glowing Mary—who came out to meet Joanna and introduce her to Jesus.

POINT TO PONDER: How would you feel about being introduced to Jesus by a woman like Mary Magdalene? Would you be afraid of a relationship with the Master of "mad Mary"?

Dear Jesus, thank You for reminding me that You love each of us—equally.

5 – Friday

PARALYZED OR PROTECTED?

"Herod said, 'I beheaded John. Who, then, is this I hear such things about?' And he tried to see him." (Luke 9:9)

Read Luke 9:1-9

The fear is gone! He touched my heart!
Compassion chased the fears away
and trust replaced anxiety.
I'm paralyzed no more by fear.
The tightening cord no longer binds my throat
and takes my breath.
I feel protected
liberated
safe.
—Joanna

And so Joanna was healed. It was just that simple. She met Jesus—and the "night terrors" were gone, along with the panic attacks of each day, and the fears of tomorrow.

Could she go back to the house of Herod to tell Chuza? Or had her husband encouraged her to simply follow Jesus, wherever that path might lead? Did Chuza also trust in Jesus—especially now that everyone was telling the story that Mary *and* Joanna had been healed of their infirmities?

At one time, people whispered about those who were considered to be "mental cases." Today understanding, help and counseling are much more readily available. But have you noticed that church lists of prayer requests are filled with physical needs, with very little said about "emotional infirmities"? In our "hurry-up-and-wait" culture, those who have suffered grief and loss are often advised: "Snap out of it—get on with your life!"

Help me, Father, to offer Jesus' kind of compassion.

5 — Saturday

STRANGE BEDFELLOWS

"Jesus said, 'My kingdom is not of this world. If it were, my servants would fight to prevent my arrest by the Jews. But now my kingdom is from another place.' " (John 18:36)
"That day Herod and Pilate became friends—before this they had been enemies." (Luke 23:12)

Read Luke 22:66-23:12

My Chuza watched as Herod questioned Jesus.
He answered nothing to "that fox,"
so Herod mocked Him with an elegant robe
and sent Him back to Pilate.
"I find no fault in Him," said Pilate,
but dressed Him yet again in purple robe,
a crown of thorns upon His head . . .
the evil rulers now fast friends,
too blind to see
the royal color is becoming
to the King of kings.
—Joanna

Perhaps Joanna did not see Chuza again until that fateful morning when their eyes met in the court of the winter residence of Herod—in Jerusalem. Joanna had followed Jesus from the court of Caiaphas to the palace of Pilate to the house of Herod. For the third time that terrible morning, Jesus was put on trial.

And since Jesus refused to answer Herod, "that fox" sank to the depths of his wicked scheming. Herod mocked the dignity he could only mimic. He ridiculed the sanctity he had raged against. He ordered his soldiers to jeer at Jesus, to robe Him with fake royalty, to spit on His sovereignty.

How did Joanna react? How did Chuza react? If you had been in the court of Herod, how would you have reacted?

Jesus, You are my King. To You, and You only, do I owe my allegiance.

Week 6

Salome, Wife of Zebedee

Family businesses can be great. They allow family members with the same basic set of values to work together with a mutual understanding of each other's needs and capabilities.

Sounds good (on paper!), but family businesses also have their own set of special problems. Just ask almost anyone involved in a family business. Tolerance levels for others' idiosyncrasies are often lower than in other relationships because past (even childhood) conflicts tend to creep into and complicate present problems.

Family members, like square pegs, may be forced into "round-hole" positions for which they have no taste, talent or training. (For example, my husband, once a tenor, began singing bass in the family singing group because no one else could get the low notes. Fortunately, he *enjoys* the "low spot" on the totem pole.)

Peter seems to have fit into the "big fisherman" category quite naturally, but what about other fishermen like John, brother of James, son of Zebedee? It is easier to picture this "beloved disciple" as a lad, sitting quietly for hours at a time by the Sea of Galilee, than as a net mender with rough, calloused hands.

John seems to have been a familiar figure to the household of Caiaphas, the High Priest; he was able to slip into the courtyard and gain admittance for his friend Peter as well. Perhaps Caiaphas' household manager had bought fish from the family of Zebedee for years. Zebedee apparently had a thriving family business, since he had hired people (Mark 1:20), a mark of prosperity. The fishing was done in Bethsaida, a village on the Sea of Galilee, but the business probably had its major market in Jerusalem.

John may have been his mother's younger favored son. She seemed to understand his relationship with Jesus . . . but did Father Zebedee?

BACKGROUND READING: Matthew 4:12-22

6 – *Monday*

COUSINS OF JESUS

"They pulled their boats up on shore, left everything and followed him." (Luke 5:11)

Read Luke 5:1-11

My husband didn't like it
When they left with Mary's son;
He blamed it all on me because
Our sons were on the run,
He says they all are "ne'er-do-wells,"
This band of Jesus' men—
But if they stayed at home and fished,
Would he be happy then?

—Salome, wife of Zebedee

Some Bible scholars suggest that Zebedee's wife, Salome, was a sister or cousin of Mary, Jesus' mother. If this is true, Zebedee may have felt a very natural reluctance to recognize Jesus as anything more than a roving teacher. (How could you acknowledge your wife's nephew as divine, as the Messiah?) Zebedee's sons James and John were busily mending the family's nets with their dad when Jesus came along one day and said simply: "Come with Me and I'll show you how to fish for men!"

Ol' Zeb may well have thought that to be the most irresponsible statement he had ever heard, but his sons, the "sons of thunder," his assistants whom he had been training to take over the family business, were gone, never to resume a "normal" life! The old man had been a powerful figure in the community, but suddenly he felt powerless. I can hear him thundering to the unresponsive sea: "They're nothing but a bunch of vagabonds and gypsies! How could they leave me with these unmended nets?" Did Ol' Zeb take out his frustrations on his wife? How did she react?

You do work in mysterious ways in our lives, Lord, to get Your messages through to us. Teach me to thank You deliberately even when I do not feel the slightest bit thankful.

6 – Tuesday

SONS OF THUNDER

"Fathers, do not irritate and provoke your children to anger—do not exasperate them to resentment—but rear them [tenderly] in the training and discipline and the counsel and admonition of the Lord." (Ephesians 6:4, Amplified)

Read Psalm 127

They never seemed to please their dad,
No matter what they did.
Even when the boys were little
And came running at his bid,
He always said their noise was sure
To scare the fish away.
So they stopped playing near their dad . . .
A little less each day.

—Salome

I keep a little note on my refrigerator door, a note by an unknown author: "Shouting at your children to make them obey is like using your horn to steer the car." The Living Bible paraphrases Ephesians 6:4 in this way: "Don't keep on scolding and nagging your children, making them angry and resentful. Rather, bring them up with the loving discipline the Lord himself approves, with suggestions and godly advice."

But no matter how many methods I use to remind myself to keep calm, inevitably the times come when some little thing becomes the "last straw" and I hear the voice of a fishwife. Can that be me? Surely not! But it is.

POINT TO PONDER: Butterflies have become my favorite symbol of metamorphosis, of my realization that we *can* change—not in our own strength, but through Christ's enablement. As I recognize God's love for me, just as I am, it helps me to accept my family members, just as they are. I also remind myself that butterflies don't yell.

Thank You, Father, for the serenity that comes only from a right relationship with You.

6 — *Wednesday*

FUTURE RULERS?

"Do nothing from factional motives—through contentiousness, strife, selfishness or for unworthy ends—or prompted by conceit and empty arrogance. Instead, in the true spirit of humility (lowliness of mind) let each regard the others as better than and superior to himself—thinking more highly of one another than you do of yourselves." (Philippians 2:3, Amplified)

Read Philippians 2:1-11

I know this friendship with their cousin
Helped them to mature.
They'd never been away from home,
But they were very sure
They were called to follow Jesus.
I'm glad they felt that way!
He may be Israel's leader
And they too may rule someday.

—Salome

Apparently Salome, Zebedee's wife, recognized Jesus' leadership abilities right from the start. (If she was related to Mary, possibly she knew and believed the story of Jesus' conception and birth.) She herself followed Jesus, ministering to Him and probably supplying money to support Him and her two sons.

"Following Jesus" involved a lot more than the familiar phrase implies today. It meant leaving a comfortable home with servants, perhaps smooth stone floors covered with oriental rugs, for the life of a persecuted wanderer. It meant raised eyebrows and condemning stares directed toward one who had once been a pillar in the community.

Perhaps Salome's years with Zebedee, however, had hardened her to insulting remarks. Salome was a woman who knew what she wanted, and no one could keep her from it. Any problems were worth the effort, if it meant that her sons might someday rule Israel.

I know the meaning of a servant spirit, Lord; now please help me to live out the meaning. Help me to discern my true motivations for doing Your work.

6 – *Thursday*

PROMISES AND PURPOSES

"Whoever wants to become great among you must be your servant." (Matthew 20:26)

Read Matthew 20:20-28

I wonder if my nephew's noticed
All of their potential.
They've followed Him almost three years
Through drought and rain torrential!
In the kingdom James and John deserve
The very highest places;
The day will come when everyone
Will recognize their faces!
—Salome

Yes, Salome knew what she wanted, and it seems her primary goal in life was to see her sons become successful, by her definition of success. Evidently she had few, if any, qualms about their leaving the family fishing business, but she did want their close relationship with Jesus to result in extra prestige and special honors.

Foolish woman, we say. *Didn't she realize Jesus' immediate destiny was not a throne? Wasn't she listening to anything He said?*

POINT TO PONDER: Do *we* realize that? Doesn't American Christianity, along with our friend Salome, look for a blanket insurance policy guaranteeing avoidance of all ills? Our friend Rev. Ken Schuler, who experienced all the complications of a kidney transplant, said it well: "His promises are mixed with His purposes—and God's purpose is to conform us to the image of His Son!" Ken is now experiencing the fulfillment of God's promise—eternal life and eternal health.

Thank You, Father, for the growing pains, for the rain that helps my life to blossom and bring forth fruit.

6 – *Friday*

THE SUPREME SACRIFICE

" 'You don't know what you are asking,' Jesus said. 'Can you drink the cup I drink or be baptized with the baptism I am baptized with?' " (Mark 10:38)

Read Mark 10:35-45

He answered me so strangely,
Disappointed in a way.
"You don't know what you ask!" He said,
But I'd planned it many days.
What did He mean by baptism?
We'd been baptized by John.
He talks as though His work on earth
Could be already done.

—Salome

In the story told in Matthew 19, the rich young ruler had come to Jesus asking what he must do to have eternal life. He was willing to obey the Ten Commandments, but not to make what for him was the supreme sacrifice—selling all his possessions and giving the profits to the poor.

After the young man sadly made his exit, Peter compared the disciples' sacrificial spirit to the ruler's: "We left everything to follow you. What will we get out of it?" (19:27, TLB). Jesus answered that the first would be last and the last first and went on to illustrate His answer with the parable of the workers in Matthew 20. The parable ends with a reemphasis of the need for a servant spirit.

We ask: Where was Salome when Jesus pointed out, "The first shall be last"? Perhaps Salome was like me: Even while Jesus was speaking, her mind may have been running ahead to her next question. Even with an attentive, respectful look on her face, she wasn't listening.

Teach me, Lord, to listen for Your *answers to my questions.*

6 — *Saturday*

SALOME AND SERVANTHOOD

"For even the Son of Man did not come to be served, but to serve, and to give his life as a ransom for many." (Mark 10:45)

Read Matthew 20:1-16

My sons don't always understand
The parables He speaks.
He's talking of betrayal
In Jerusalem—next week?
What's happened to the kingdom
That we've all been waiting for?
Can it be that His words are true?
Then what could lie in store?
—Salome

Immediately following the parable of the workers, Jesus clearly outlined to the disciples the tragic events that lay ahead in Jerusalem: betrayal, trial, condemnation, persecution, crucifixion. He longed for them to understand.

But His carefully selected words were as unheeded as the prediction of a record-breaking cold snap at a summer swimming party. Nobody wanted to hear it. Salome seemed oblivious to whatever her sons may have tried to share with her, if indeed they heard Jesus' words. Salome had waited, perhaps for years, for the opportunity to ask Jesus this super-important question, and now, before they became immersed in the hubbub of the city, now was the time.

Can you imagine Jesus' inward reaction? I've often felt like asking, "Didn't you hear anything I just said?" Instead, He patiently stressed the need for a servant spirit in His answer to Salome: "I have no right to make that decision—it is my Father's. I did not come to be served, but to serve, and to give my life for others."

It was so hard for Salome to learn the lesson of servanthood. It's also a difficult lesson for me. Sometimes I wonder if I will ever really learn it. Thank You, Jesus, for the example of Your patience.

Week 7

Mary Magdalene: The Misunderstood

Way back in the early '80s, I was invited to speak at two weekend retreats in Oregon. At the time, I was overwhelmed that this group actually wanted to fly me cross-country—and *pay me for speaking as well!*

For over a year I prayed about what my Father wanted me to present at those two weekend retreats. And in one session in that pine tabernacle in Oregon, I felt led to explain the difficulty many women have when they confuse the attributes of their heavenly Father with the actions of their earthly fathers. I shared my earlier resentment toward my own father and the results of allowing the roots of bitterness to take hold. It had been a difficult topic to handle, one that I had held back from, but one that I knew my heavenly Father wanted me to present in a completely honest and straightforward way.

After the Saturday evening message, an altar call was given. To my amazement, twelve women responded! Other counselors were ready, and so I was able to sit on the platform and "watch and pray." I particularly noticed one woman about my age who wept and prayed with a counselor for quite some time. Her heartrending sobs became understandable the next morning, however, when she handed me this note:

> I'm praising God for you and your obedience to Him tonight. If you had not shared your bitterness with your

dad, I wouldn't be free from the same bitterness and resentment toward my dad. I've been carrying it around and didn't realize he was involved. I've been confessing and asking for forgiveness pertaining to other things and other people—Pop has been the root of all of it. I was molested, dominated, put down by him for many years. . . .

I longed for Jesus to be Lord of my life—in my heart and life, not just in my head—to be able to trust Him completely, in and with everything. There was a blockage there and I didn't know what it was. Perhaps I should add here that I have been going to a counseling center for nine months. By the Lord's grace and help I feel I've made tremendous progress, as last July I was really on the bottom . . . thinking about suicide, the whole bit. Anyway, we got over or through many barriers, but this one with my dad was buried so deep it wouldn't surface. (At least I wouldn't let it—why should I? He is dead; what did it matter?)

Praise God, my eyes were opened and my ears opened and it's all forgiven! I feel pounds lighter! There is nothing between me and my Savior tonight! I might clarify one thing—Pop gave his heart to the Lord a year before he died. . . .

(Incidentally, the author of this letter is now a professional counselor!)

We will now be studying Mary of Magdala, a woman whose name is mentioned fourteen times in Scripture. Obviously, she was an important personage to the Gospel writers, yet before she met Christ her life was in a sad state of affairs.

What was the root of Mary's problem?

BACKGROUND READING: Luke 8:1-3; Matthew 12:22-30

7 — *Monday*

ROAMING ROMANS

"Do not be afraid of those who kill the body but cannot kill the soul. Rather, be afraid of the One who can destroy both soul and body in hell." (Matthew 10:28)

Read John 10:1, 16-33

I remember how it started long ago . . .
Oppression came and lingered like a cloud,
A cloud so thick and dark it smothered me.
I'd lie there looking at the walls without a sound,
But inside I was screaming, long and loud!
I was ashamed to let my friends and family hear
The tortured noises of my inner soul,
Expression of my agonizing fears.

—Mary of Magdala

Magdala, home of Mary, is thought to have been a small village presently named Mejdel on the western shore of the picturesque Sea of Galilee. Apparently it was known by two other names, Magadan and Dalmanutha (Matthew 15:39; Mark 8:10) and was located about three miles north of Tiberias, where Herod Antipas, ruler of Galilee, had his capital. The name Magdala is derived from the word "migdol," which meant "a tower" or "watchtower." Perhaps the town was considered an outpost that could alert Herod of any surprise attack.

These facts may give us some hints of Mary's life before she met Jesus Christ. The Scriptures simply tell us that she had been possessed by seven demons—no more, no less. What were the natures of the seven demons? The question is not answered for us, but there may be some clues. A town so close to Herod's capital must have been constantly visited by soldiers, Roman soldiers far away from friends and family. Mary may have caught their attention early in her life; perhaps she was even taken to Herod who, as we discussed earlier, was known for his lust. Whatever the causes of her tortured emotions, her personality must have resembled the Sea of Galilee on its troubled days, when the wind swept its waters into a raging tempest.

Abba Father, You know all about the tempests in my life . . . and I know that You can still the winds and the waves.

7 — *Tuesday*

CONTEMPORARY CULTURE

"For our struggle is not against flesh and blood, but against the rulers, against the authorities, against the powers of this dark world and against the spiritual forces of evil in the heavenly realms." (Ephesians 6:12)

Read Matthew 5:27-30; 9:12-13

For no one seemed to hear what I could hear
And no one ever saw the things I saw.
They pressed in on me through the days and night,
So rough they left me bleeding, bruised and raw.
My bruises weren't the kind that could be seen;
They too were in the spirit and the mind—
Emotions long repressed, too long held back,
Emotions that could crush and my soul blind.
—Mary of Magdala

In early 1984 the U.S. Justice Department designated $800,000 to evaluate juvenile response to pornographic films and magazines in an effort to determine whether exposure to pornography causes juveniles to become juvenile offenders. The effort was admirable, but is there any doubt as to the effects of pornography—on juveniles or adults?

A *Decision* article by Karen Mains provides clear answers:

> We live in a culture that is pervaded with a demonic spirit of lust because the culture has given itself over to unnatural affections. Even more, this culture of ours has called this spirit out. It invites lust, toys with it, loves it. This culture of ours under the false name of sexual freedom has become the inventor of unimaginable sexual evil. In order to stand against it, we must be prepared. Ignorance will protect us no longer.[1]

Lust is not a new word. The "I want what I want *now*" attitude it describes was also present in Mary Magdalene's day. Who knows what damage local soldiers—or Herod himself—might have inflicted on her body and emotions?

Father, I too fight this demon of lust. And sometimes I too have toyed with it . . . please cleanse my life.

THE BELT OF TRUTH

"Therefore put on God's complete armor, that you may be able to resist and stand your ground on the evil day [of danger], and having done all [the crisis demands], to stand [firmly in your place]. Stand therefore—hold your ground—having tightened the belt of truth. . . ." (Ephesians 6:13-14, Amplified)

Read John 14:6-29

One day no longer could they be repressed . . .
Explosion! Tiny pieces flew all 'round.
I stood as others cried and laughed,
My heart and life in pieces on the ground.
No one could understand the truth,
I tried explaining, but they looked away,
Their eyes averted from me, calm and cold,
Their eyes expressing what they did not say.
—Mary of Magdala

I distinctly remember several times in my life when I was shocked by news of a suicide attempt or a nervous breakdown or a divorce. I thought, *But I didn't even realize anything was wrong!* As Christians, we must be aware that a war is being waged on the battleground of life and that weapons are a necessity.

POINT TO PONDER: The belt of truth is the first item on the "must" list. Truth means confessing our past sins to God, and perhaps going further than that. Look back into the mirror of memory and ask God to show you where *you* may have been responsible for scars on someone else's life. Look into the mirror of God's Word as well and ask God to do His cleansing work in your life.

Face the truth about your past. Recognize, as in Mary Magdalene's life, that there may have been situations where you were used or abused by others. Refuse to carry false guilt any longer. Resist the devil by realizing the extent of his influence on your thinking and attitudes. Meet him on the battleground, face him—and stand firm!

Thank You, Jesus, for being the way and the life because You are also Truth.

7 — *Thursday*

BREASTPLATE AND FOOTGEAR

"Stand firm then, with the belt of truth buckled around your waist, with the breastplate of righteousness in place, and with your feet fitted with the readiness that comes from the gospel of peace." (Ephesians 6:14-15)

Read Ephesians 6:10-13

"She's mad!" the whispers went around the town.
"She's mad!" the whispers echoed in my ears.
I screamed, but no one seemed to care.
Again . . . again . . . but no one seemed to hear.
I tried to take my life. They tied me down
With cruel ropes that bit into my skin.
Now everyone could see my cuts and scars,
The marks of what they often called my sin.
—Mary of Magdala

I remember from my high school days a song called "A Town without Pity." Like many small-towners, the people of Magdala probably showed little sympathy for the "crazy woman" who lived among them. "Stay away from her!" they may have warned their little ones. There were few, if any, prayers said for her by the religious leaders in the synagogue.

But Jesus said, "Unless your righteousness surpasses that of the Pharisees and the teachers of the law, you will certainly not enter the kingdom of heaven" (Matthew 5:20). In Isaiah 64:6 we are told that "all our righteous acts are like filthy rags" (one commentator called them "menstrual rags") and, in Jeremiah 17:9, "The heart is deceitful above all things and beyond cure. Who can understand it?"

That's why it's so important that our hearts be covered with the breastplate of God's righteousness, not our own, and that our feet be fitted with the gospel in order to be ready for battle. Feet have two kinds of problems: they tend to get cold and refuse to go where they should, or they trespass into forbidden territory. (They can even make their way into our mouths.)

Thank You, Father, that I am "accepted in the beloved" (Ephesians 1:6, KJV). That assurance motivates me to go wherever You ask me to go.

7 — *Friday*

HELMET, SHIELD AND SWORD

"In addition to all this, take up the shield of faith, with which you can extinguish all the flaming arrows of the evil one. Take the helmet of salvation and the sword of the Spirit, which is the word of God." (Ephesians 6:16-17)

Read Ephesians 6:14-18

I could not tell them where the sin began;
I could not speak of wrongs once done to me.
I couldn't express the fears from childhood days;
I could not ever hope to make them see.
Sins of the fathers, I had heard, stayed on
To visit in their children's lives and souls.
What better proof of this than I?
I had no hope of being cleansed and whole.
—Mary of Magdala

Some time ago one of our sons acquired a nasty brush burn on his leg in a slide to third base. Later that same week, while wrestling with a friend, the abrasion began to bleed. Normally the pressure caused by the wrestling hold would not even have been noticed, but the injuries had piled up.

So perhaps it was with Mary of Magdala. The hammers of rejection mercilessly drove the stakes of previous abuse even deeper into her hurting heart. The "flaming arrows of the evil one" may have been aimed by so-called "friends," the bow pulled and released by family members. The wounds may have become so intense that death seemed a welcome respite.

POINT TO PONDER: Mary had not yet met the Master. She did not have access to the helmet of salvation, the shield of faith or the sword of the Spirit. Each piece of battle gear, however, is available to us as Christians; do we use them for their intended purpose? Like a sword, our ability to use God's Word must be kept sharp and ready for use by consistent honing and practice of our skills. If my Bible is dusty, my sword is rusty!

And do we have compassion for the wounded and fallen on the battlefield?

Thank You, Father, for the helmet, the shield, the sword. Please help me to learn to use them effectively.

ARMOR NEEDS OIL

"And pray in the Spirit on all occasions with all kinds of prayers and requests. With this in mind, be alert and always keep on praying for all the saints." (Ephesians 6:18)

Read 2 Corinthians 10:4-5; 13:3-5

And then one day the whispers changed. They told
Of One whose power touched all who could believe!
His name was beautiful—at once I knew
Jehovah God had sent this Man to me!
I can't explain what happened, how I knew
That Jesus was the Christ, the Son of God.
My past, my present disappeared and fled!
I looked into the eyes that understood.
—Mary of Magdala

Unlike Mary, we cannot physically talk with Christ, but we can communicate with Him continually. (Note the "all" in Ephesians 6:18.) We cannot spend all day on our knees, but we can be in the spirit of prayer. That means having our hearts cleansed of sin on a continuous basis, immediately confessing a lustful or greedy or bitter thought as soon as it finds a chink in our armor. Prayer is the oil that lubricates our armor.

Karen Mains writes:

> Christ has given us a remarkable tool to combat the spirit of unnatural affections that pervades our age. . . . The state of our mind, not the state of our heart . . . is the battlefield where we must gird ourselves in order to stand against an age which is keynoted by sexual lust.[2]

Discipline yourself to turn off the TV when a bedroom scene sparks your imagination. Pitch the magazine that causes your thoughts to linger on "beefsteak" that does not belong in your oven. Quit listening to the ear-tickling song that encourages your mind to jump the fence into the greener grass of your neighbor's bed (and I'm not talking about flower beds).

Thank You, Jesus, for cleansing Mary's life . . . completely. Help me to learn to "take captive every thought," to make them obedient to You (2 Corinthians 10:5).

Week 8

Mary Magdalene: Love vs. Lust

What comes to your mind when you think of Mary Magdalene? A physically beautiful woman with flowing red hair? A temptress? A prostitute?

Over the years Mary of Magdala has been pictured as a seductress. Edith Deen points out, however, that since medieval times, Mary Magdalene has been one of the most unjustly accused women in the New Testament. Scholars of an earlier period identified her with the unnamed sinful woman of Luke 7:36-50. Their accusations became popular, though never accurate.[1]

The twentieth-century musical *Jesus Christ Superstar* revived the tradition. A haunting melody spells out the confused emotions of a woman who had always known how to "love" men until she met the Man of Galilee.

In today's world there are many who would like to bring Jesus Christ to the same level as the humans He created. Implications of a sexual relationship between Jesus Christ and Mary Magdalene would be an easy way of doing just that. Others have portrayed Christ as being involved in homosexual relationships with His disciples. Why do people level these accusations?

Karen Mains writes:

> I have become convinced that we live in an age of unnatural affections. Those chilling passages in the first

> chapter of Romans describe our age perhaps better than any others in Scripture: "Therefore God gave them over in the sinful desires of their hearts to sexual impurity for the degrading of their bodies with one another. They exchanged the truth of God for a lie, and worshipped and served created things rather than the Creator" (Romans 1:24-25).
>
> Other cultures worshiped idols, hand-made gods who represented the supernatural that man could not understand. But our world is a man-centered world. Man, human ideas, human personality, human reason, is the god of this century. We worship ourselves. We have transplanted the Creator with the human.
>
> We are living in a time when the very atmosphere is so polluted by a spirit of unnatural affections that the Christian can be swept into the personality of the culture before he knows what is happening to him. Consequently, the Christian must prepare to defend himself from a culture whose major spirit is the spirit of lust.[2]

Certainly this spirit is reflected in television programming, many popular movies and the best-selling literature of our day. Think about the meaning of that song from *Jesus Christ Superstar.* Did Mary know how to love Him? Do we? What does love really mean? How is it different from lust?

BACKGROUND READING: Matthew 5:27-30; 17:14-21

8 – Monday

UNCARING OF THE COST

"If I [can] speak in the tongues of men and [even] of angels,
but have not love [that reasoning, intentional, spiritual
devotion such as is inspired by God's love for and in us],
I am only a noisy gong or a clanging cymbal."
(1 Corinthians 13:1, Amplified)

Read Colossians 3:1-17

I followed Him uncaring of the cost.
Some said I was still mad, some laughed, some cried.
Some tried to talk me out of going on.
Some said, "This woman should be set aside."
It was unheard of, that He cared for me!
I knew He loved me, knew He understood.
And every man that I had ever met before,
By contrast to Him, seemed so rough and rude.
—Mary of Magdala

The natives of the small town of Magdala must have been thoroughly shocked when Mary left home to follow Jesus. It was one thing for men to become His disciples—but a woman? Women were to stay in their homes, unless they were needed in the fields, and definitely off the streets. To be seen talking with a male nonfamily member (if judged as flirtatious) was an offense worthy of divorce. The fact that Jesus allowed, probably even encouraged, Mary to join His followers may have been the final straw in the eyes of the Jewish leaders.

To quote Evelyn and Frank Stagg, "It probably does not do justice to Jesus to say that He was a 'woman liberator.' He came to liberate the human being."[3]

Thank You, Father, that I too am "accepted in the beloved" (Ephesians 1:6, KJV).

8 – Tuesday

LOVE = C.I.A.

"Love endures long and is patient and kind; love never is envious nor boils over with jealousy; is not boastful or vainglorious, does not display itself haughtily."
(1 Corinthians 13:4, Amplified)

Read Ephesians 2:17-22

No man had ever looked straight in my heart,
There was no lust involved; His eyes were true.
He looked at me—I felt no guilt or shame.
All that had been was in the past, He knew.
And so I followed, though the people talked,
Content to follow Him in this new role.
Whatever I could do to serve my Lord
Was my ambition. Life had found a goal!
—Mary of Magdala

Mary was learning the difference between a lustful glance and the eyes of love. One cares only about personal pleasure, the other cares about the person. One is easily satisfied at another's expense; the other is willing to pay the price, share the cost. One gluts itself, then walks away; the other one is constant and dependable. Lust wants what it wants when it wants it; love waits patiently and takes responsibility for its actions.

Jesus Christ was (and is) the embodiment of love, and as she followed Him, Mary Magdalene began to realize the meaning of love. Jesus' commitment to His Father's will involved commitment to others as well, and that meant service.

Love=C.I.A. Love is Commitment In Action.

POINT TO PONDER: "Submit to one another out of reverence for Christ" (Ephesians 5:21). That's not easy, is it? We live in a "do-your-own-thing" kind of world that advises us to "look out for Number One!" The word submission has been misused, overused and generally abused, but we need to remember that Christ was submissive to His Father's will.

Open my eyes, Lord, to the true meaning of these important words—love and submission.

LOVE IS EMPTYING WHISKER WATER

"[Love] is not conceited—arrogant and inflated with pride; it is not rude (unmannerly), and does not act unbecomingly. Love [God's love in us] does not insist on its own rights or its own way, for it is not self-seeking; it is not touchy or fretful or resentful; it takes no account of the evil done to it—pays no attention to a suffered wrong." (1 Corinthians 13:5, Amplified)

Read Philippians 2:1-11

Still the men murmured who were followers too—
Judas especially would have bid me leave—
But other women (Joanna, Mary too),
Left all to follow Him, their fears relieved.
Those who had worried learned what trust can mean;
Those who were doubters left their doubts behind;
Those who were angry gave Him all their rights.
He loved us all! With all He freely dined.

—Mary of Magdala

Myron and Marj Bromley are a husband and wife who chose to give up wealth in civilized areas of the world to serve the Lord in an uncivilized region—Irian Jaya, Indonesia. Despite unquestionable dedication to God's will in both their lives, they still live with the same kinds of irritations every couple, Christian or otherwise, undergoes in marriage.

Marj once told about the day she decided she had emptied Myron's "whisker water" for the last time. They had no running water, so it was a daily pain to clean his whiskers out of the basin. Myron insisted, when confronted, that he "nearly always" did it himself. Systematic Marj decided upon a solution: she would mark on the calendar each day she had to take time from her own duties (Marj is an MD) for this chore. Shortly after the momentous decision, the mailbags came in—a time for celebration—and Marj recognized with elation that a new Bible translation had arrived. Opening the Word, her eyes caught these convicting words: "Love keeps no record of wrongs."

Mary Magdalene had no past as far as Jesus was concerned. Love lives in the present, not the past.

Help me, Jesus, to burn my mental ledger sheets.

COMMITMENT ISN'T EASY

"It does not rejoice at injustice and unrighteousness, but rejoices when right and truth prevail. Love bears up under anything and everything that comes, is ever ready to believe the best of every person, its hopes are fadeless under all circumstances and it endures everything [without weakening]." (1 Corinthians 13:6-7, Amplified)

Read John 12:20-36

Relaxing in His presence, yet we knew
The time would come when this must surely end.
And tension lines formed circles 'round His eyes
As knowledge of the future He must lend.
"No, Lord!" we'd say. "You are our future King!
You've come to save us from the Roman rule!"
Yet as I looked into His knowing eyes
I'd see the pain that often filled them full.
—Mary of Magdala

Early one Memorial Day morning I walked along the waterfront at Sandy Cove Ministries, a retreat center in Maryland, reading the poignant conversation between Jesus and Peter in John 21. I found myself wishing that I could look up from my little New Testament and see Jesus standing in front of me, that I too could talk to Him face-to-face, that I could touch His hands and look into His eyes.

As I experienced the intensity of that longing, I began to realize what Mary Magdalene's reaction must have been when she first heard Jesus speaking of the future, of His death. How difficult it must have been to bite back the words of protest that flew to her lips, for she of all people would have understood the terrible, quiet pain in His loving eyes.

POINT TO PONDER: As much as she would have liked to protect Him, Mary was learning to trust, to hope, to persevere. She was learning that because Jesus was committed to the will of His Father, He would obey His Father even though another course would have been easier.

Thank You, Jesus, for the "always" in Your love.

BACK TO MAGDALA?

"Love never fails—never fades out or becomes obsolete or comes to an end. . . . Our knowledge is fragmentary (incomplete and imperfect), and our prophecy (our teaching) is fragmentary (incomplete and imperfect). But when the complete and perfect [total] comes, the incomplete and imperfect will vanish away—become antiquated, void and superseded." (1 Corinthians 13:8-10, Amplified)

Read John 14:1-14

And then the terrors of that awful week,
Too vivid even now to call to mind—
Our Friend betrayed by one who called Him Lord,
Our Friend betrayed by one of our own kind.
Who could He trust if not one of His own?
Could I too turn against my Lord?
Would I betray Him in a moment's fear?
Regain the past if threatened by a sword?
—Mary of Magdala

Perhaps a background of insecurity helps us to be more dependent on the Master. With Mary's past in mind, I can't imagine her ever becoming cocky, overly sure of herself and her own reactions. I can't imagine her ever saying (as Peter did): "I would never deny You, Lord!" She had given her entire life to the Master, but she must have wondered what would happen if she lost her beloved Leader.

Looking back, we realize that when Jesus left the earth, He sent His Holy Spirit to comfort His disciples—then and now—but those early disciples had no understanding of that fact. He had assured them that He would not fail them, that He would not leave them "as orphans" (John 14:18), but what was life without the Master? Surely Mary couldn't go back to Magdala again.

POINT TO PONDER: Sometimes Jesus wants us to do just that—to go back to our Magdalas, to our "towns without pity," to the roots we ran away from. Is He beckoning you back?

Thank You, Father, for Your love that never fails, even when I fall flat on my face because I've followed my desires instead of Yours.

THAT FIRST GOOD FRIDAY

"When I was a child, I talked like a child, I thought like a child, I reasoned like a child; now that I have become a man, I am done with childish ways and have put them aside. For now we are looking in a mirror that gives only a dim (blurred) reflection [of reality as in a riddle or enigma], but then [when perfection comes] we shall see in reality and face to face! Now I know in part (imperfectly); but then I shall know and understand fully and clearly, even in the same manner as I have been fully and clearly known and understood [by God]."
(1 Corinthians 13:11-12, Amplified)

Read John 14:9-27

I stood before the cross, not knowing how
To comfort Mary in her time of need.
She stood there, loving as a mother does;
A cruel sword had pierced her heart, indeed.
We all were overwhelmed by grief and loss;
The One we loved most, Jesus, now was gone.
How could we hope to serve our Master now?
How could we even face another dawn?
—Mary of Magdala

Even knowing the part the cross played in God's eternal purpose and plan, it is difficult for us to face the terrible agony of the cross. We turn our heads rather than look on the lacerated, bleeding body of Jesus Christ; we pull our fingers away from the first prick of a thorn and cannot comprehend a crown of such material pressed upon a human head.

If your reactions are similar to mine each Good Friday as you contemplate the cross, imagine Mary's feelings that first day—a day marked by earthquakes and terrible storms. Oblivious to the fury of the elements, Mary stood before the cross, aware only of the great loss she was suffering.

What comfort Paul's words could have given her: "Now I know in part; then I shall know fully, even as I am fully known" (1 Corinthians 13:12). What comfort those words give us! Someday we will understand.

Thank You, Father, for that promise.

Week 9

Mary Magdalene: Attic Treasure

Before and after: Mary Magdalene's personality had resembled the Sea of Galilee, wind-tossed and troubled into a raging tempest; Jesus Christ had quieted those winds and calmed the storm. But now the Master of the elements was gone.

Another Mary—Mary of Bethany—had come crashing down from a mountaintop experience to the gloomy valley of her brother's death and had remained there in a paralysis of grief until Jesus came. Mary of Bethany now had brother Lazarus to lean on again, a living reminder of the reality of resurrection power, but Mary of Magdala had no one. Luke tells us that the disciples thought she was telling a "fairy tale" (Luke 24:11, TLB) when she said Jesus had risen. That says a lot about her relationship with them.

The Gospel writers differ somewhat in their telling of the story, but in each account Mary Magdalene's name stands out. Unlike Mary of Bethany, she was not immobilized by her grief; it seems she was even able to minister to the other women. How was this possible? Her life had been changed.

This was reemphasized to me one sizzling June day when I ascended my attic steps to find picnic supplies and found a sadly sagging Christmas candle.

Bent
Misshapen
My forgotten candle lies
In attic's summer heat.
Last winter's glow extinguished,
Purposeless
Its beauty gone
It waits for rediscovery,
Its twisted body
Giving forth
A fragrance—
Bittersweet.

Words from a song
Heard long ago:
"Remold us,
Make us like Thee. . . ."
Only then are we able
To survive
Life's attic heat.

Mary's life had not been remodeled, but remolded!

BACKGROUND READING: Matthew 27:56, 61; 28:1; Mark 15:40, 47; 16:1, 9; Luke 24:10; John 19:25; 20:1, 11, 16, 18

9 — *Monday*

MARY THE "APOSTLE"

"Whoever wants to become great among you must be your servant, and whoever wants to be first must be slave of all. For even the Son of Man did not come to be served, but to serve, and to give his life as a ransom for many." (Mark 10:43-45)

Read John 15:1-8

They laid Him in the tomb so tenderly,
His broken body needed loving care,
But Jewish law said we must wait until
The Sabbath ended—stay we did not dare.
On Sunday morning, early before dawn,
We hurried through the streets toward His grave.
We did not think what could become of us.
I only knew I was His love-bondslave.

—Mary of Magdala

As I read through Matthew, Mark, Luke and John and relived with them the crucifixion and resurrection, one name stood out in almost every account.

At the cross . . . Mary Magdalene was there. When Jesus' lifeless body was taken down from the cross and laid in the tomb . . . Mary was there. When the first rays of post-Sabbath sunlight penetrated the garden's gloom . . . never thinking of her own safety or reputation, Mary was there.

Mary came to the tomb with a broken heart. She had not bargained for a position in kingdom leadership; she had not lobbied for women's rights in the kingdom. She was content with the lowest place, the unpleasant task of caring for Jesus' dead body. But she was the first to see Him alive.

Because Mary had seen Him, she could bear witness to the reality of the resurrection. We could call her the apostle ("sent one") to the apostles, because Christ sent her first: "Go to my brothers!" (His brothers were, incidentally, a very skeptical audience.)

Thank You for this beautiful example of selfless love.

9 – Tuesday

PROBLEMS AND PRINCIPLES

"This is love: not that we loved God, but that he loved us and sent his Son as an atoning sacrifice for our sins."
(1 John 4:10)

Read John 16:1-16

We wondered how we would remove the stone
Or if the guards would keep us from our Lord,
But then we found the stone was rolled away
And knew there was no need to fear the sword.
The Roman guards fell into a dead faint!
An angel told us women not to fear:
"I know the One that you are looking for,
Jesus the crucified—but He's not here!"
—Mary of Magdala

Although Mary pleased her Master with the persistence of her search for Him, we realize that she was searching mistakenly. She was looking for a corpse, for the human remains of the Person she had loved so dearly.

Like Mary and Martha of Bethany, Mary believed mentally in Christ's resurrection power, but her heart and emotions had not absorbed its reality. Like many of us, she had to hit bottom before she could turn her face completely upward.

POINT TO PONDER: What crisis will it take in my life to turn my philosophy of life into a possession of the heart? When will I be able to apply the principles I've learned to my everyday problems? When will I stop worrying about the stones of doubt and fear and realize that Jesus' power has rolled them away?

Your power is incredible, Lord. Help me to absorb its full meaning.

9 — *Wednesday*

PRISONS AND CHAINS

"I came that they may have and enjoy life, and have it in abundance—to the full, till it overflows." (John 10:10, Amplified)

Read John 16:17-32

"Go, tell—forever tell the news:
Christ is not here—He's risen from the dead!"
My mind could not absorb this truth.
I only heard "He's gone!" and then I fled.
I went to Peter and, of course, to John—
They'd understand! but I saw in their eyes
The glimmer of a doubt . . . has she gone mad?
Did her old problem come back when He died?
—Mary of Magdala

Several years ago I heard Gloria Gaither, a well-known Christian musician-writer, share a poem in which her daughter thanked her parents for giving her "a mind that knew no prisons and a heart that knows no chains." How I wish that could be true of every child—and every adult! Because of the wages of sin, the chains and prisons do exist, but in the realization of Christ's love, they can be left behind.

Mary Magdalene understood this, I'm sure, but did the disciples, perhaps even the other women who followed Jesus? Those around us may remind us of what God has already forgiven . . . only God buries the past completely.

And that is part of the meaning of the abundant life Christ offers, a life that is not crippled by memories and guilt from the past. Oh, the scars may remain to remind us how far we have come, but the wounds have been healed by love. The chains have been broken, the prison doors have opened.

Jesus, You are the key.

9 – Thursday

NO ROOM FOR DOUBT

"And now, little children, abide (live, remain permanently) in Him, so that when He is made visible, we may have and enjoy perfect confidence (boldness, assurance) and not be ashamed and shrink from Him at His coming." (1 John 2:28, Amplified)

Read John 17:1-12

And what I saw reflected in their eyes
Began to haunt me—had I gone insane?
Had I imagined what I thought I saw?
Had seven devils returned their home to claim?
No, no, it cannot be—I'm healed!
He is my Lord and Master, and He cares!
He will protect me as He always has:
I will go back to seek His spirit there!
—Mary of Magdala

Imagine Peter and John's reaction to an emotionally distraught woman. Mary was probably crying and laughing at the same time, perhaps screaming the good news at the top of her lungs or perhaps only repeating the good news over and over again, "He's alive! He's no longer in the tomb!" Despite her conviction, Peter and John must have exchanged glances that said, *Has she come apart at the seams?*

Why didn't they realize what was going to happen? They were aware of the Old Testament prophecies, and Jesus Himself had told them that He would be killed and would rise again the third day. After all the time they had spent with Him, why didn't they understand?

POINT TO PONDER: We too have biblical prophecies available for study. We have seen the Lord come once as a baby; when He comes again it will be as King of kings and Lord of lords. Yet many times we are embarrassed to confess Him openly as Master, and we live as though He had left earth permanently.

Forgive me, Father, for taking Your Word and Your promises for granted.

9 – *Friday*

I NEVER SAID GOOD-BYE

"Praise be to . . . the Father of compassion and the God of all comfort, who comforts us in all our troubles, so that we can comfort those in any trouble with the comfort we ourselves have received from God." (2 Corinthians 1:3-4)

Read John 17:13-26

I went back to that empty, empty tomb.
I wept because I could not say good-bye,
I'd wanted to at least bind up His wounds,
Prepare the grave clothes where His head would lie.
The angels, watching, asked me why I wept.
I answered them, then turned away to see
A man I did not recognize at first.
I didn't realize who had come to me.

—Mary of Magdala

Have you ever lost a close friend without having had a chance to say good-bye? Perhaps she left town suddenly while you were on vacation; perhaps he was killed in a traffic accident. Perhaps she didn't survive what you thought would be a fairly routine surgery. You may have pictured her face or stood by his casket and wept to yourself. *We never said good-bye to each other . . . I never told her how much I valued her friendship . . . I never let him know how much I loved and respected him.*

Was Mary experiencing these emotions as she stood once more before the tomb? In those last hectic days, probably there had been no quiet times to spend with her Master to assure Him of her loyalty, to thank Him for the love that had changed her life. If only she had at least been able to care for His dead body, to say good-bye in that small way.

With all these thoughts filling her mind, it is no wonder that Mary did not recognize the figure behind her. Her face was red from weeping, her eyes bloodshot and full of tears—she probably did not look directly at Him. Even when He spoke to her, her mind was so obsessed by her grief that it was not capable of functioning normally . . . until He spoke her name—"Mary!"

This story says so much about how much You care, Jesus. If You cared that much for Mary, You care that much for me.

9 — *Saturday*

LOVE IS MEANT TO BE SHARED

"But thanks be to God, Who gives us the victory—making us conquerors—through our Lord Jesus Christ." (1 Corinthians 15:57, Amplified)

Read Mark 13:1-27

I needn't have returned to doubt and fear.
He understood me as He always had
For, resurrected from the dead, He came
To find me grieving, desolate, brokenhearted, sad.
He came to me, a woman first of all!
Thus proving, once again, His love for me
And for the many others He prepares
A place, with Him, for all eternity!
—Mary of Magdala

As He does with us today, Jesus Christ stood ready to comfort Mary in her heartbreaking grief. He surprised her with His presence but He did not allow her to be possessive of His presence for even a moment. Immediately He sent her out to share the wonderful news: "Go to my brothers!"

POINT TO PONDER: When we clutch a blessing to ourselves, we begin to stagnate. God has given me the desire and ability to write; as long as I use it for His purposes and His glory, He continues to provide opportunities for writing and speaking. The moment I begin to grasp and to hold onto the "glory" that belongs to Him, it turns to ashes in my hands.

When I think back over the years to the lonely, left-out child I felt myself to be, constantly moving and changing schools, and then think of the many friends God has given my husband and me over the years—not to mention three bright, healthy sons—I can only say, "To God be the glory!"

Thank You, Lord.

Week 10

The Wife of Simon of Cyrene, the Mother of Rufus

"Greet Rufus, chosen in the Lord," Paul wrote, "and his mother, who has been a mother to me, too" (Romans 16:13). In a long list of salutations in the sixteenth chapter of Romans—a letter carried to Rome by Phoebe, a deaconess of the church at Cenchrae, near Corinth—this is the only woman described as a mother. Paul seems to have had a spiritual relationship with this lady, who was probably by that time an older woman in the early Christian Church, well respected by younger women (Titus 2:4), as well as by her son Rufus.

Does the Bible tell us anything about this woman's earlier life? Since her name is not given, probably not.

But historians tell us that the Simon of Cyrene who was volunteered to carry the cross of Jesus had a son named Rufus and also a son Alexander (see Mark 15:21), and that both young men became well-known members of the Christian community.

Some sources state that since Simon was from Cyrene, in North Africa, probably he was a Jewish pilgrim fulfilling a lifetime dream of attending Passover in Jerusalem. Was Simon's holiday ruined when the Roman guards forced him to carry Jesus' cross? To the contrary, Simon was so affected by his short-term relationship with Jesus that he became a believer.

Other sources say that Simon had been born in Cyrene, but that he was a long-time resident of Jerusalem, a farmer, returning to the city from his fields to celebrate the Passover with his family. Perhaps his wife had been shopping for some last-minute items to add to the lamb and unleavened bread—bitter herbs for the sauce, the wine—when she was caught up in the crowd surging through those cobblestone streets. They would become known as the Via Dolorosa, the Way of Sadness, the Way of the Cross. (Tradition assigns a total of fourteen "stations" or stops made by Jesus in His sad final journey.)

Certainly that day of preparation for the Passover turned out differently than Simon's family had planned. . . .

BACKGROUND READING: Matthew 27:20-33

10 — Monday

THE MANY FACES OF HATE

"Then Pilate took Jesus and had him flogged. The soldiers twisted together a crown of thorns and put it on his head. They clothed him in a purple robe and went up to him again and again, saying, 'Hail, king of the Jews!' And they struck him in the face." (John 19:1-3)

Read Exodus 21:2-6; Leviticus 25:8-12, 47-55

They've sentenced Him, this angry crowd
Their hate is written on their face:
the face of hate,
the face of greed,
the face that has no room for love—
and yet they'll soon eat Passover.
—Mrs. Simon of Cyrene

"The Romans brought my husband here from Cyrene, in Africa, as a slave, but Simon was bought by a relative. His 'kinsman-redeemer' set him free in the Year of Jubilee, but Simon loved his master so much that he stayed on as a love-bondslave for another seven years.

"Simon's told me all about the Roman whippings on that long, long trip from North Africa to Jerusalem. Ah, it hurt me just to hear about it. They strip the clothes from the prisoner's body, then tie him to a post and lash him with a whip, a whip with cruel pieces of lead on the ends of it. All the while they are mocking him, spitting on him. And of course no one ever wipes the spittle away. It dries on the prisoner's face.

"I heard that Jesus' trial started dreadfully early this morning. Whatever sleep He got last night, if any, was in what they call 'The Pit' in the basement of the High Priest Caiaphas' house—chained to those cold stone walls, no mats or blankets provided, I'm sure. They sent Him from the High Priest to Pilate, and then to Herod, and then back to Pilate again, mocking Him, putting elegant robes on Him, with a crown—a crown of thorns—pressed hard into His scalp."

Lord Jesus, may I never forget.

10 — *Tuesday*

TAKE UP YOUR CROSS AND FOLLOW ME

"Finally Pilate handed him over to them to be crucified. So the soldiers took charge of Jesus. Carrying his own cross, he went out to the place of the Skull (which in Aramaic is called Golgotha)." (John 19:16-17)

Read Isaiah 53:1-6

He clutched it to Himself,
the cross,
As a young mother hangs her child upon herself,
He held it to His body. . . .
He could not bear for it to touch His bleeding back.
—Mrs. Simon of Cyrene

"As soon as I saw Jesus this morning, I could tell that His back had been ripped apart, that His flesh was on fire, just the way He cringed when anyone bumped against Him. In this crowd, it's been happening time after time. He couldn't carry the cross beam on His shoulder, the way a man normally would; with injuries like that, you couldn't stand to even touch the area, much less lay wood on it. So He had to drag His cross, in a sort of shuffle, moving His legs slowly, pulling one after the other.

"And there's blood in your breathing from the whipping, in your mouth and nose, so it makes every breath a labor, like a mother in the midst of childbirth. And every time you stumble, a soldier yells at you. Or hits you, or kicks you.

"I can't stand to watch. But I can't stand *not* to watch, as though—as though I'm protecting Him somehow, by staying with Him."

Lord Jesus, may I never forget.

10 — *Wednesday*

WOMEN WHO MOURNED

"A large number of people followed him, including women who mourned and wailed for him." (Luke 23:27)

Read Isaiah 53:7-12

My heart breaks with His mother's heart
—I also have two sons.
They're with their father in the fields,
soon to be home for Passover . . .
I watched His body sag and fall
once to the ground
and yet again . . .
Will not they call someone to help?
He cannot bear the weight of it.

Ah, it's late . . . I must complete my shopping,
prepare the food,
prepare my home for Passover.
—Mrs. Simon of Cyrene

"This Jesus . . . He's just a few years older than my sons, my strong young sons. I'm sure He was strong too—before today. I've heard that His father was a carpenter in Nazareth. He must have worked hard, thrown lots of heavy beams over His shoulder, as He was growing up. Their weight probably seemed like nothing to Him then.

"Now He's cradling one end of this incredible weight under one arm, bumping its other end on the cobblestone street. Each stone must seem like a mountain He has to cross.

"The beam is sticking between two stones. Jesus just dropped to His knees, dropped the beam completely. His skin must be screaming, but He simply groaned. The sad, sad sound seems to just hang in the air . . . above all the yelling. . . . I can still hear that groan."

Lord Jesus, may I never forget.

MUST JESUS BEAR THE CROSS ALONE?

"As they led him away, they seized Simon from Cyrene, who was on his way in from the country, and put the cross on him and made him carry it behind Jesus." (Luke 23:26)

Read Matthew 26:17-30

I see my husband's head above the crowd!
My husband's back inside the city walls,
on his way home for Passover.
Oh Jehovah-God . . .
They've called him, called my Simon
to bear the cross on his strong back.
My heart says 'tis an honor—
yet I must ask
what this will mean beyond today . . .
Now I must surely go
to see the end of it.

—Mrs. Simon of Cyrene

"That centurion—did he know my Simon? Was he perhaps one of the soldiers who found Simon in Cyrene, who brought him back to Rome? Will that Roman ignore the fact that Simon is now a freedman?

"No, no, I cannot let my mind go on so. I must concentrate on Jesus and simply pray for my Simon. My husband is strong, and the open cuts of the whip on his back healed long ago . . . but the marks will always be there. Every night they remind us of how much we can thank Jehovah for.

"Jesus is up now. The lamentations stopped for a moment, but now the wailers have begun again. A woman handed Him her handkerchief, and He is wiping His brow with it. How bloody it is! He hands it back with an apology, I think. How can He be so gracious in such a time as this!"

Lord Jesus, may I never forget.

WEEP NOT FOR ME

"Daughters of Jerusalem, do not weep for me; weep for yourselves and for your children." (Luke 23:28)

Read Isaiah 54:1-14

"Women of Jerusalem," He cries,
"weep not for Me, but for yourselves. . . ."
He cares for women, even now
as His life bleeds upon the ground. . . .
He cannot bear the cross, and yet
He bears our needs upon Himself—
the needs and hurts of women
who've been oppressed since Tamar's day.
—Mrs. Simon of Cyrene

"Jesus turned for just a moment and looked at the wailers. He was shaking His head. 'Daughters of Jerusalem,' He almost yelled, in a hoarse voice, 'don't weep for me. Weep for yourselves and for your children. For the time will come when you will say, "Blessed are the barren women, the wombs that never bore and the breasts that never nursed!" ' (Luke 23:28-29).

"And I thought of Tamar, the virgin daughter of David, the one who was raped by her half brother and lived as a desolate woman from that time forth. Was He calling her blessed?

"The wailers were surprised by the strength of His voice . . . and the strength of His words. The women hushed, and the streets were strangely quiet for a moment. Then the wailing began again. The centurion—even the soldiers had stopped and listened—gave a command: 'Enough of that! Let's be going!'

"Now that my Simon, with his long legs, was carrying the cross, the soldiers were forcing Jesus into a faster pace. I had to struggle to keep up. I wove between shoppers, doing a little dance at times to avoid spilling their purchases. I had to keep my husband's head in view. When I could not see his head, I told myself he was bent over, talking with Jesus. I will ask Simon what they said."

Lord Jesus, may I never forget.

10 — Saturday

THE SACRIFICE

"Then he said to Thomas, 'Put your finger here; see my hands. Reach out your hand and put it into my side. Stop doubting and believe." (John 20:27)

Read Mark 14:32-41

They throw Him down upon the cross.
He bleeds anew
They mock His pain.
He looks into their faces as
they penetrate His body now.

It's Passover . . .
My meal's undone, my heart is raw . . .
Yet somehow, seems my heart's prepared
for Passover.
The sacrifice is made.

—Mrs. Simon of Cyrene

"It's only 9 in the morning, but it seems like the end of the day. The drizzle has turned to rain; my shawl is soaking wet. We're reaching the gate in the city wall. There's the hill by the side of the road, and—oh, the poles are already in place, ready for the cross beams. Simon is putting the beam down, carefully, waiting for further orders. Simon, can't you steal away? Now, while the centurion is handing Jesus something—probably wine mixed with myrrh, to deaden the pain. But Jesus shakes His head, refuses it. Jesus, why *not* deaden the pain?

"They're stripping Him, down to the loincloth. My Simon's eyes are riveted to Him. The memories must be as painful as . . .

"Two more men with cross beams. *They* didn't refuse the wine. Now all three of them are stretched out, in the dirt, beside their crosses. They're lifting Jesus onto the cross. Oh, Jesus—Your open back on that harsh wood! They're just yanking Your arms, left and right, palms up. Oh, that awful sound—hammer on metal! I cannot bear to watch anymore . . .

"Oh my Simon, please hold me. *Yes*, I want to go home . . .

"You want to stay? You feel like His—His love-bondslave?"

Lord Jesus, may I never forget.

Week 11

Mary: At the Cross

"Blessed are the poor in spirit, for theirs is the kingdom of heaven. Blessed are those who mourn. . . ." (Matthew 5:3-4)

Perhaps Mary, Jesus' mother, wondered about the meaning of those words when Jesus first spoke them that beautiful day on the hillside. She felt so blessed, so happy that day as she watched the crowds of people gather near the picturesque Sea of Galilee to hear her Son. Blessed . . . her cousin Elizabeth had declared her blessed more than thirty years earlier: "Blessed are you among women, and blessed is the child you will bear!" (Luke 1:42).

Elizabeth's greeting had confirmed the words of the angel Gabriel: "Mary, you have found favor with God" (1:30). His voice had rung with authority. As Mary listened to her Son speak to the eager crowds, His voice reminded her of Gabriel's.

But all of these were memories. Now another crowd had gathered—a shouting, gesticulating crowd, a crowd bent on taking the life of her Son. Thirty-three years earlier *that* had been predicted also, by an old prophet named Simeon: "This child is destined to cause the falling and rising of many in Israel, and to be a sign that will be spoken against, so that the thoughts of many hearts will be revealed. And a sword will pierce your own soul too" (Luke 2:34-35). The "sword" had hung over her head through all those years.

Now, as she stood between the angry mob and the three roughly hewn crosses, she knew the meaning. She felt as though the point of that sword were pressing against her throat, inhibiting her ability to weep or even speak. Her emotions had been crumpled by the pressures of the past week into a tight, tortured mass that defied exploration or expression.

Then the words began, so softly at first that they could have come from Mary herself. But Mary, incapable of words, could respond only in her thoughts and feelings to the Speaker—the broken, lacerated Man her eyes had never left from the first time she had faced that ominous Skull Hill.

His words must have brought back more memories . . . the beginnings of healing . . . and perhaps even a measure of understanding to her weary heart.

The words have been called her Son's "seven last sayings." Scripture does not tell us, but perhaps Mary responded as follows.

BACKGROUND READING: Read Isaiah 53

11 — Monday

"FATHER, FORGIVE THEM . . ."

"An angel of the Lord appeared to Joseph in a dream. 'Get up,' he said, 'take the child and his mother and escape to Egypt. Stay there until I tell you, for Herod is going to search for the child to kill him.' " (Matthew 2:13).

Read Luke 23:1-34; Matthew 2:13-23

He is my Son—and yet divine!
The Babe I bore, this Child of mine
Calls God His Father . . . and forgives
The ones who've ruled He cannot live.
All through His life He's been pursued,
Mistreated and misunderstood.
When He was just a child, we fled . . .
And Egypt's road to Calvary led.
—Mary

Mary remembered the journey so well. What a tiring trip for her little Son; and what did Mary think about during those long hours? Was she worried about the unknown in a strange country, afraid of the future and what faced the little family upon their return to Israel? Perhaps, but she also pondered over things in her heart; the loving watch-care God had shown to her in revealing Himself in a dream to Joseph, and the blessing God had given to her and her little Son in the person of caring, supportive Joseph, who had risked so much to marry her.

And even as Mary thought of all the difficult times she had experienced, she thanked God once again for the one He had given her to share those times—her beloved Joseph. The exercise of thanksgiving lifted her heart just enough to raise her downcast eyes once again—to the cross.

Thank You, Lord Jesus, for teaching me the value of a thankful spirit.

"TODAY THOU SHALT BE WITH ME IN PARADISE . . ."

"Blessed are you among women, and blessed is the child you will bear! But why am I so favored, that the mother of my Lord should come to me? As soon as the sound of your greeting reached my ears, the baby in my womb leaped for joy. Blessed is she who has believed that what the Lord has said to her will be accomplished!" (Luke 1:42-45)

Read Luke 23:35-45; 1:39-56

He always thinks of others first.
Even on the cross; as He is cursed
By all the passersby, He sees
And reaches out to fill their needs.
Elizabeth, my dearest friend,
If I had known His life would end
In such a bitter, shameful way,
Could I have lived to see this day?
—Mary

For a moment Mary was back in Elizabeth's joyous embrace, experiencing the warmth of their close friendship, feeling the inspiration of the Spirit. Her eyes closed, she whispered: "My soul glorifies the Lord, and my spirit rejoices in God my Savior" (Luke 1:46-47).

A taunting comment from someone in the crowd around her awakened Mary to grim reality: "He saved others . . . but he can't save himself!" (Matthew 27:42). A shudder swept her body as she opened her eyes to the horror of the cross. Yet the memory of Elizabeth had given Mary new hope. God had provided an understanding friend and a place of refuge for her, years earlier, when she had needed it so desperately. Could He give His own Son less?

Thank You, Lord Jesus, for showing me the value of the true friend You have provided.

11 — Wednesday

"I THIRST . . ."

"Dear woman, why do you involve me? . . .
My time has not yet come." (John 2:4)

Read John 19:28-29; John 2:1-12

"I thirst," He cries—and suddenly
"What have I to do with thee?"
Memories of Cana flood my mind:
Another thirst, another time.
I didn't understand Him then;
I didn't ask Him why or when.
I didn't need to understand. . . .
My Son had become God-man.
—Mary

Bright, joyous wedding memories—and the family's embarrassment because there was not enough wine! They had all turned to Mary: "Tell Jesus!" And Mary had simply given the news to her Son.

"I can't help you now. . . . It isn't yet my time" (John 2:4, TLB).

He simply meant, Mary mused, *that it wasn't yet His time for miracles. And yet the miracle took place. . . . Why?*

Mary drew her robe about her to shut out the chill in the air that had suddenly become noticeable.

How dark it's getting, she thought. *Looks like a storm's coming. God, are You going to let it storm while my Son is still alive, still hanging there on that wretched cross?*

I trusted Him. I simply told the servants, "Do whatever He tells you to" (John 2:5, TLB). And He supplied the need, as He always had, He told me years ago that He had to do the will of His Father. He always has done Your will, Jehovah God. He was always obedient to Joseph and me and to You—why is this happening to Him now?

Thank You, Lord Jesus, for Your example of obedience to Your Father.

11 — *Thursday*

"MY GOD, MY GOD, WHY HAST THOU FORSAKEN ME?"

"O my God, I cry out by day, but you do not answer. . . ." (Psalm 22:2)

Read Matthew 27:26-49; 12:46-50; Luke 2:40-52

His words keep ringing in my ears,
Recalling earlier times and fears.
He was about Your business then,
Explaining Your commands to men.
I would have torn Him from the cross
And saved the world from this great loss,
Had I the power. But You left Him there!
You are His Father—don't You care?
—Mary

"Joseph, we've lost Him! We've lost Jesus!" Once again Mary felt the urgency of that experience on the road leading out of Jerusalem. Adrenalin reached even her tired, dusty feet as she realized that no one had seen Jesus all day. They must find Him quickly before harm came to Him in the city.

There was another day when *she* had felt like the lost child. She had waited to see Jesus, waited patiently until He had finished speaking, waited for a warm welcome and embrace. She heard Him say, "Who is my mother? Who are my brothers?" Expectantly standing on tiptoe so He could see her, smiling proudly at first, she watched Him point to His disciples as He said, "Anyone who obeys my Father in heaven is my brother and sister . . . and mother."

The words had stung her mother-heart, until she remembered the eyes of a twelve-year-old boy-man looking into hers as He asked: "Don't you understand that I must be about my Father's business?"

But why wasn't He calling His Father "Abba" now? My God, why have You forsaken Him? The darkness was increasing, becoming thicker. . . .

Thank You, Lord Jesus, that Your Father is my "Abba" also.

"IT IS FINISHED . . ."

"Mary was greatly troubled at his words." (Luke 1:29)

Read John 19:30-37; Luke 1:26-38

It is finished, as it began:
A mystery now, a mystery then,
My heart was torn with joy and fear
When first I sensed the angel near.
He called me "highly favored one"
And told me I would bear a Son.
He said that Son would always reign
He didn't tell me of the pain.
—Mary

The sponge had been soaked in sour wine and held to Jesus' lips, as a fulfillment of prophecy (Psalm 69:21—"For my awful thirst they offered me vinegar," TLB).

But Mary was remembering the prophecy that the angel Gabriel had spoken to her: "He will be great and will be called the Son of the Most High. The Lord God will give him the throne of his father David . . . ; his kingdom will never end" (Luke 1:32-33).

What had happened to that prophecy?

Someone broke through the crowd, reporting breathlessly that the veil of the temple, separating the Holy Place from the Holy of Holies, had been torn in half.

As the earth began to quake and cries of terror were heard in the deepening darkness, the familiar word of the prophet Isaiah came ringing through the centuries to Mary's heart: "He was pierced for our transgressions, he was crushed for our iniquities. . . . It was the LORD's will to crush him. . . . He bore the sin of many, and made intercession for the transgressors. . . . We all, like sheep, have gone astray, each of us has turned to his own way; and the LORD has laid on him the iniquity of us all" (Isaiah 53:5, 10, 12, 6).

Thank You, Lord Jesus, for Your terrible suffering that paid the price of my redemption.

11 — *Saturday*

"FATHER, INTO THY HANDS I COMMEND MY SPIRIT . . ."

"Your attitude should be the same as that of Christ Jesus: Who, being in very nature God, did not consider equality with God something to be grasped, but made himself nothing, taking the very nature of a servant, being made in human likeness. And being found in appearance as a man, he humbled himself and became obedient to death—even death on a cross! Therefore God exalted him to the highest place and gave him the name that is above every name, that at the name of Jesus every knee should bow, in heaven and on earth and under the earth, and every tongue confess that Jesus Christ is Lord, to the glory of God the Father." (Philippians 2:5-11)

Read Luke 2:21-39; Matthew 27:26-54

He's given You His spirit now
And I recall a sacred vow . . .
I gave Him to You long ago,
Not dreaming what I now know.
As You prepared old Simeon's heart
To see His Lord, and then depart,
In Your own time, in Your own way,
So take Your Son—and mine—today.

—Mary

What was it old Simeon had said? "Sovereign Lord, as you have promised, you now dismiss your servant in peace. For my eyes have seen your salvation" (Luke 2:29-30).

Mary was beginning to understand. Because Simeon was a servant, he had recognized Jesus, even as a babe in arms, as the suffering Servant-King. The Messiah-King would reign—but in His own time!

For now, the cross was the Father's plan for Mary's Son—and as He bowed His head for the last time on earth, His mother raised her head to the sky.

Thank You, Lord Jesus, for giving up Your place in heaven for a time to come to earth for me.

Week 12

Salome, Wife of Zebedee: Questions of Easter

"Men of Galilee, . . . why do you stand here looking into the sky?" (Acts 1:11).

James and John looked at each other. Yes, they were men of Galilee. Obviously the men asking the question—the men dressed in white—knew who they were. But the two young men known as the "sons of thunder" had no reply.

The mother of the men of Galilee stood at a slight distance, feeling her sons' embarrassment along with them. But it was good to see her sons looking to each other again. The events of the years had often separated them, seemed to polarize them. But her sons had changed over the past months. The whole atmosphere of things had changed. Life was totally different.

I'm *really the one who has changed.* The thought caught Salome off guard, but she did not reject it. *Yes, I've changed. For the first time in my life, I'm open to change. I can admit when I'm wrong. I can stop defending myself and just say, "Yes, I was wrong."*

It was a refreshing new feeling—still a little scary, but good.

There's something you need to do. A soft, tender Voice—not the harsh voice she had heard so often in the past—was nudging her gently. *Go to your sons. Ask their forgiveness for your pushiness in the past, for your demanding ways, for your in-*

sistence that they always "take leadership." That's what you called it, but it was really your own need to take control, projected through them. You knew it was impossible to control Zebedee, ol' Thunder himself, so you controlled your sons—as long as you could—and then gained pleasure from pushing them into places of power.

But you still have a chance to change. Go to your sons . . . now.

Whose was this voice? Salome knew it was speaking truth. She knew she needed to obey while there was still time. Amazingly enough, she *wanted* to obey.

Salome heard movement all around her. She raised her head to find her sons, only to be caught in their embrace.

The same Voice must have been speaking to them, she thought. *He really hasn't left us! He's still here! He's alive!*

BACKGROUND READING: Acts 1:9-11

WHO WILL ROLL AWAY THE STONE?

"When the Sabbath was over, Mary Magdalene, Mary the mother of James, and Salome bought spices so that they might go to anoint Jesus' body. Very early on the first day of the week, just after sunrise, they were on their way to the tomb and they asked each other, 'Who will roll the stone away from the entrance of the tomb?' " (Mark 16:1-3)

Read Matthew 20:20-28

I didn't believe that He would die
yet, much less, rise again!
How many words did I reject, tune out, say:
"No, that can't be true!
I know the way these things will happen . . .
After all, He's still so young.
I'm old enough to be His mother—
I should know . . ."
—Salome

Before the events of this unbelievable week, Salome had relied on her "gut feelings" from years of experience—both as a mother and a citizen of Capernaum—to guide her in her dealings with Jesus. After Easter, Salome had to admit she had been all wrong.

It wasn't that Jesus hadn't tried to explain to her. She had been indignant when He said, "You don't know what you are asking. . . . Can you drink of the cup I am going to drink?" (Matthew 20:22). She remembered thinking, *I brought my own cups along with me when I left home to follow You. You've been drinking from* my *cups.*

Aware of her sons' embarrassment, Salome avoided Jesus' eyes. But when she looked up again, His intense eyes pierced her heart once again with the question: *Can you be baptized with the baptism I am baptized with?* Again she felt confusion. She compared her own baptism in the Jordan with His—yes, it had been at a different time of year, but . . .

Now she realized that she had completely missed what He was trying to tell her.

Father, I need the mind of Christ.

"WHY DO YOU LOOK FOR THE LIVING AMONG THE DEAD?"

"In their fright the women bowed down with their faces to the ground, but the men said to them, 'Why do you look for the living among the dead? He is not here; he has risen! Remember how he told you, while he was still with you in Galilee: "The Son of Man must be delivered into the hands of sinful men, be crucified and on the third day be raised again." ' " (Luke 24:5-7)

Read Mark 10:17-34

Looking back, I see surprise upon those faces—
those who sat beside the tomb.
Was it a man?
or angel?
I know not
but I will not forget his words:
"Why do you seek the living
here among the dead?"
He is not here—He's risen!"
—Salome

"What was I thinking when Jesus was saying—yes, I remember His very words—'We are going up to Jerusalem, and the Son of Man will be betrayed to the chief priests and the teachers of the law. They will condemn him to death and will turn him over to the Gentiles to be mocked and flogged and crucified. On the third day he will be raised to life!' (Matthew 20:18-19).

"I was so sure He was wrong. I was so sure that He would be the One to lead our people against those impostors, the Romans. I felt He had the excitement, the charisma, the touch that the people loved, the power that the people would follow. And I was sure my sons—practical, faithful James, loving, sensitive John—would add just the balance needed for leadership.

"And I was the one who was so wrong. Why didn't I listen to His words? Why didn't I try to understand?

"Why did I seek the living among the dead? I was more deaf and blind than the many afflicted ones He healed."

Father, I need the humility of Christ.

12 — *Wednesday*

"WOMAN, WHY ARE YOU CRYING?"

"Then the disciples went back to their homes, but Mary [Magdalene] stood outside the tomb crying. As she wept, she bent over to look into the tomb and saw two angels in white. . . . They asked her, 'Woman, why are you crying?' " (John 20:10-13)

Read John 20:1-18

She said they asked her the same question
He had asked . . .
and I resented that He'd come to her—
that He had chosen her to be
the very first to see Him.
Why had He not appeared to me?
or to His mother?
Why to someone not even in His family?
—Salome

"Mary . . . I always thought she was still a little crazy. I didn't like the fact that He allowed her to travel with us. It didn't do anything for His reputation. It irritated me, the way she hung on His every word. I didn't think she could possibly understand Him. I guess she understood a lot more than I did.

"I had to admit that she certainly was faithful. She stayed there with Him, through the crucifixion, right up to the very end, when the sky was so terribly black and violent. Maybe I expected her to go back to her old patterns, the ones the villagers of Magdala told us about. But even at the crucifixion, she didn't have that wild look about her, the way I expected. As a matter of fact, even through her terrible sadness, she seemed to have more of a sense of peace about her than I had.

"She loved Him. And He loved her. I never doubted that. At times I doubted the kind of love she had for Him . . . but I was wrong on that as well."

Father, I need the faithfulness of Christ.

12 — *Thursday*

"HOW FOOLISH YOU ARE!"

"Now that same day two of them were going to a village called Emmaus. . . . They were talking with each other about everything that had happened. As they talked and discussed these things with each other, Jesus himself came up and walked along with them; but they were kept from recognizing him. . . . He said to them, 'How foolish you are, and how slow of heart to believe all that the prophets have spoken!' " (Luke 24:13-16, 25)

Read Luke 24:13-33

And when our two friends shared with us
that He'd appeared
and talked and eaten
in their midst,
I felt the hurting for my sons. . . .
Why hadn't He come to them?
Did He not know the grief John felt
—John, who'd been so close to Him?
—Salome

"At least I was comforted by the fact that there were others who didn't seem to understand. Like those two friends of ours from Emmaus. Even after the resurrection, Jesus appeared, walking right beside them, talking with them, and they didn't recognize Him!

"They told us how foolish they felt after He was gone. I knew just how they felt. All those times I've said, 'I know, I know, I believe'—and I had no idea!

"I guess none of us wanted to hear about suffering . . . or persecution . . . or death. We wanted to hear about rebellion . . . and resistance . . . and winning battles against Rome! We wanted instant answers to our prayers. We wanted Him to be the answer—*our* kind of answer. And yet our prophet Isaiah told us long ago that Jehovah's thoughts are not our thoughts, and Jehovah's ways are not our ways."

Father, I need the perseverance of Christ.

"WHY ARE YOU TROUBLED?"

"While they were still talking about this, Jesus himself stood among them and said to them, 'Peace be with you.' They were startled and frightened, thinking they saw a ghost. He said to them, 'Why are you troubled, and why do doubts rise in your minds?' " (Luke 24:36-38)

Read Luke 24:34, John 21:1-24

I also heard that He'd appeared to Peter.
Again I felt the hurting deep within my heart.
The boisterous one, bold Peter,
the loud and noisy one—
and not my John
my sensitive, loving, caring, gifted John . . .
But as we talked there
He appeared.
"Peace . . . *be with you," He said.*
My children—sons—thought it a ghost
but He was speaking to my heart.
—Salome

"That wasn't the first time they thought they saw a ghost. Once, when Jesus was exhausted after ministering to a crowd, He needed some quiet time with His Father. He said He was going up on the mountainside by Himself to pray. He told them to go on ahead of Him to the other side. They were part-way across the Sea of Galilee—and having a hard time of it because of a nasty wind pushing them back—when they saw this Presence, walking toward them on the water. 'It's a ghost!' someone yelled. They were all paralyzed by fear. Jesus tried to reassure them by saying, 'Take courage! It is I. Don't be afraid.'

"Of course Peter would have to show off. James and John said he got out of the boat and walked a step or two on the water—until the wind hit him, hard, and he went down. I didn't know what to believe when I heard that story, but I do know that Jesus caught him. Now if it had been one of my sons walking to Jesus, I might have believed it. . . ."

Father, I need the compassion of Christ.

12 — *Saturday*

"WHY DO YOU STAND HERE LOOKING INTO THE SKY?"

"[Jesus] was taken up before their very eyes, and a cloud hid him from their sight. They were looking intently up into the sky as he was going, when suddenly two men dressed in white stood beside them. 'Men of Galilee,' they said, 'why do you stand here looking into the sky?' " (Acts 1:9-11)

Read Acts 1:1-14

"I tried to tell you"
—He looked my way—
"that prophecy must be fulfilled.
The law has become grace in me.
You all are witnesses of these things.
Stay here," He added. "In this place,
My Father's promise, beloved,
is true.
He speaks, and I fulfill His Word.
His power is Mine . . . and will be yours."
—Salome

"Even after the resurrection, we were still hoping that Jesus would turn out to be the Messiah, our Deliverer from the Romans. One of the times we met with Him, while we were eating, He told us not to leave Jerusalem, because the Father was sending us a gift—His Holy Spirit. We weren't sure what He meant by that.

"One of the men even asked Him if, when the Father sent the gift, would that be the time when He would restore the kingdom to Israel. Jesus was talking about power, and it sounded as though there still might be hope.

"He answered with one of those elusive statements again: 'It is not for you to know the times or dates the Father has set.'

"But then He gave us His word, His promise: 'You *will* receive power when the Holy Spirit comes on you; and you *will* be my witnesses in Jerusalem, and in all Judea and Samaria, and to the ends of the earth' " (Acts 1:8, emphasis added).

Father, I need the power of the Holy Spirit.

Section 3:

Preparing My Heart for Discipleship: "Daughters of Jerusalem, Weep Not for Me . . ."

Week 13

Daughters of Zion

The group of dark-haired, weeping young women caught my eye. They were mourning a tragic death, the assassination of Israel's leader, Yitzhak Rabin.

It was only a picture in a news magazine, but it moved me deeply. Many times over the years I wondered, *Have Jewish women unconsciously obeyed the words of Jesus: "Daughters of Jerusalem . . . weep for yourselves and for your children" (Luke 23:28)?*

The name in the magazine headline—Yitzhak or Isaac, meaning "laughter"—was reminiscent of the Old Testament story of a once-barren woman, Sarah. On Mount Moriah, the future temple site, Sarah's beloved son of promise narrowly escaped death.

Other sons were not spared. Jeremiah, the "weeping prophet" of the Old Testament, predicted the agonizing grief of Rachel, the archetype of the Jewish mother who has lost her children: "A voice is heard in Ramah, mourning and great weeping, Rachel weeping for her children and refusing to be comforted, because her children are no more" (Jeremiah 31:15).

Jeremiah's prophecy had two meanings.

Ramah was the birthplace of Samuel, another son of promise, whose mother Hannah gave him back to God when he was only a small child. It was also one of the towns through which the conquered, enslaved people of Jerusalem passed on their way to exile. "By the rivers of Babylon we sat and wept," they said, "when we remembered Zion. . . . How can we sing the songs of the LORD while in a foreign land?" (Psalm 137:1, 4).

Jeremiah's prophecy, repeated almost word-for-word in Matthew 2:18, was fulfilled in King Herod's massacre of the infants. An angel intervened, and Herod's attempt to kill one special Baby was foiled. But again, many Jewish mothers—many Rachels—lost their sons.

The Child missed in Herod's massacre became a Man. One Friday on Mount Calvary, His side was pierced as another prophecy to another mother was fulfilled: "A sword will pierce your own soul too" (Luke 2:35).

The sad saga continues. Years later, on Masada, a mountain fortress overrun by Romans, Jewish fathers took the lives of their own wives and children. Rather than submit their families to Roman brutality, the fathers did what they did as an act of love. Then the men committed suicide.

Knowing what was about to happen, did the weeping mothers derive some comfort from the fact that their families died in each others' arms, in their homes, together?

The Masada death scenes were the forerunners of the Holocaust. But in the death camps of Germany, there were no arms of loving protection, no sense of family togetherness in death.

The years have gone by. Israel's wars have been many, and mothers have wept through every one of them. Until the enmity between the woman and the serpent is finally resolved, and the offspring of the woman completely crushes the serpent's head, man's inhumanity to man is doomed to continue.

Until then, we as women will continue to weep.

But someday we will enjoy our full privileges as grafted-in daughters of Zion, and God Himself will wipe away every tear from our eyes.

BACKGROUND READING: Jeremiah 31:1-20

13 — Monday

THE GIFT OF MERCY

"When Herod realized that he had been outwitted by the Magi, he was furious, and he gave orders to kill all the boys in Bethlehem and its vicinity who were two years old and under, in accordance with the time he had learned from the Magi. Then what was said through the prophet Jeremiah was fulfilled, 'A voice is heard in Ramah, weeping and great mourning, Rachel weeping for her children and refusing to be comforted, because they are no more.' " (Matthew 2:16-18)

Read Lamentations 1:1-22

We heard the cries of terror,
the sound of women screaming
as though their very hearts
were being torn from them.
The babies' cries were but brief whimpers.
They left their mothers' arms
to nestle snugly in the arms of God.

—A mother in Israel

God gives the gift of mercy to the daughters of Zion.

The senseless crimes we hear about daily make conscientious young people wonder if they should bring children into the world. Yet as we visualize the events of Herod's historic "massacre of the infants," we realize that brutality is not exclusive to our day.

The cold-blooded murder involved in legalized abortion, however, is exclusive to our time. Be assured that God will bring vengeance on those who transgress His law—"Thou shalt not murder"—if they have not confessed their sin and experienced His forgiveness. We must remember, however, several things . . .

Daughters of Zion are called to minister to women who are being lured by the subtle trap of abortion. Daughters of Zion are called to minister to women entangled in the cruel memories of this invasion of their bodies. And daughters of Zion are called to minister to single moms who have made some wrong decisions—but also a right decision—and now need support.

Thank You, Jehovah-rapha, for ministering healing in my own life. Help me to share that healing with other hurting people.

THE GIFT OF PRAISE

"The next day the great crowd that had come for the Feast heard that Jesus was on his way to Jerusalem. They took palm branches and went out to meet him, shouting, "Hosanna!" . . . Jesus found a young donkey and sat upon it, as it is written, 'Do not be afraid, O Daughter of Zion; see, your king is coming, seated on a donkey's colt.' " (John 12:12-15)

Read John 11:32-44

Hosanna,
Hosanna in the highest!
Hosanna
to the Son of David!
Blessed is He who comes
in the name of the Lord!
Blessed is the King of Israel!

—A daughter of Zion

God gives the gift of praise to the daughters of Zion.

The word "hosanna!" means "save!" It is also a word of praise. The daughters of Zion felt no fear of this King who rode into Jerusalem on a donkey. They had heard many stories of His miracle-working power, but this evidence of His humility inspired praise in their hearts.

The gift of praise replaces the spirit of fear.

Praise strengthened the people's faith as they recognized the fulfillment of Old Testament prophecy: "Rejoice greatly, O Daughter of Zion! Shout, Daughter of Jerusalem! See, your king comes to you, righteous and having salvation, gentle and riding on a donkey" (Zechariah 9:9).

Through praise we too become aware of Jesus' presence and demonstrate His power.

Through praise we can overcome Satan and his strategies to discourage us.

Through praise we learn to profit from our trials.

Through praise we bring glory and pleasure to God.

Help me, Lord, to praise You when I don't feel like it—"the sacrifice of praise."

13 — Wednesday

THE GIFT OF GRIEF

"A large number of people followed him, including women who mourned and wailed for him. Jesus turned and said to them, 'Daughters of Jerusalem, do not weep for me; weep for yourselves and for your children.' " (Luke 23:27-28)

Read Matthew 23:37-39

We weep for Him,
but He looks on us
with those eyes of love
and tells us to weep for ourselves
and for our children.
He understands the depth of our great grief.
—A daughter of Jerusalem

I can choose to let a life-shattering loss shake my faith. Or I can choose to make it a time to get to know God better.

"I want to know Christ and the power of his resurrection *and the fellowship of sharing in his sufferings . . ."* (Philippians 3:10, emphasis added).

Losses remind us to stop focusing on meaningless trivia. To live more deeply. To reflect on the true meaning of life.

Sorrow refines my soul. It prioritizes my life. It makes me homesick for heaven.

> Praise be to the God and Father of our Lord Jesus Christ, the Father of compassion and the God of all comfort, who comforts us in all our troubles, so that we can comfort those in any trouble with the comfort we ourselves have received from God. For just as the sufferings of Christ flow over into our lives, so also through Christ our comfort overflows. (2 Corinthians 1:3-5)

I have confidence, Lord, that someday You will use my healed sorrow to comfort someone else. Right now it's hard to imagine, but I believe in Your promise.

THE GIFT OF NURTURING

"Near the cross of Jesus stood his mother. . . . When Jesus saw his mother there, and the disciple whom he loved standing nearby, he said to his mother, 'Dear woman, here is your son,' and to the disciple, 'Here is your mother.' From that time on, this disciple took her into his home." (John 19:25-27)

Read Lamentations 2:1-22

Behold thy Son!
I remember when I sang a lullaby
and then realized
this child was my Lord . . .
and wondered how I'd feel the sword.
Behold thy Son!
As His life ends,
He gives new life to us, His friends.
My motherhood must end today
yet it begins in a whole new way.
—Mary, mother of Jesus

God gives the gift of nurturing to daughters of Zion. Sometimes, due to geographical or emotional distance, we may feel we have almost lost a child. During these times, God may call on us to "mother" another mother's child, to give to someone a bit of—or a lot of—desperately needed nurturing.

The "adoption" may be a totally joyous experience for both people involved. But it can be exhausting or threatening, and we may pull back. "I feel like I've already lost a child, God," we may say. "I don't know if I have enough energy or time for this. I don't know if I can take a risk like this again."

Let me assure you that it's worth taking the risk! Our relationships with our "adopted" children have brought more happiness into our lives than they will ever know. (One of them reminded me that, since he was in college when we met him, I experienced the joys of mothering him without ever having to change his diapers.)

Thank You, Father, that as You have nurtured me, You now give me the opportunity to nurture others.

THE GIFT OF PROPHESYING: PREACHING AND TEACHING TRUTH

"Brothers, choose seven men from among you who are known to be full of the Spirit and wisdom. . . . They chose Stephen, a man full of faith and of the Holy Spirit; also Philip." (Acts 6:3-5)

Read 1 Corinthians 14:1-5

I am the oldest of the daughters four.
My father says I am like Deborah,
a leader and perhaps a judge
Like Jael and Deborah,
we sisters work together well.
Like Barak, men sometimes resist
the call of God
and women take their place.

—A daughter of Philip

God gives the gifts of wisdom, discernment and leadership to daughters of Zion to be used as He wills, particularly during crucial times. He also gives gifts of truth-speaking.

Philip, one of the seven deacons appointed to administer the business affairs of the apostles and the growing church in Jerusalem, probably had homes in both Jerusalem and Caesarea (Acts 21:8). Since Philip's job description included the distribution of relief to the poor, the elderly and the widows, his daughters probably assisted him in those areas.

Philip's evangelistic ministry began with another deacon named Stephen. Philip's daughters probably knew Stephen well. Imagine their grief when Stephen died by the cruel death of stoning! Were they present the day Stephen was stoned? Was Stephen's martyrdom a spiritual turning point in their lives? And how did they react to a man named Saul, who looked on as Stephen was stoned? Did they have difficulty forgiving him? (In later years, he may have stayed in their home.)

Our reactions to losses in our lives leave us *bitter*—or *better.* But we can only speak God's truth when we allow Him to cleanse resentment, hatred and bitterness from our hearts.

Thank You, Father, that because of Your unconditional love, so freely given, I can make the choice to be better, not bitter.

13 — Saturday

THE GIFT OF WAITING

"Rejoice greatly, O daughter of Zion! . . . Return to your fortress, O prisoners of hope; even now I announce that I will restore twice as much to you." (Zechariah 9:9, 12)

Read Lamentations 3:1-24

Most days I am content to minister to others,
to wait in patience for my call from God.
But there are days when it seems all the world
is moving on.
And I am left behind.
I find it hard to wait—so hard.

—A daughter of Philip

God gives the gift of waiting to see God's plan unfold.

"I never brought a child to birth, but I thank the Lord for using me to bring some to rebirth. That is the greatest joy for a Christian. Perhaps this was a bit of losing my life for Jesus and therefore winning it."[1]

Those were the words of Corrie ten Boom, described by Billy Graham as "one of the most amazing lives of the century." She learned about dying to self early in life. At fourteen, Corrie fell in love with a ministerial student who returned her interest. His parents, however, expected him to "marry well," so the romance ended. Through wise words from her earthly father, Corrie was able to surrender her wounded heart to her heavenly Father. When blocked love causes pain, her father said, you have two choices: either kill the love, or ask Christ to help you change your love to a heavenly kind of love. Although her internal struggle was fierce, God gave her victory and peace—and the strength that would take her through her future experiences in Nazi Germany.

Years after her release from a Nazi "death camp," Corrie was speaking to a group of people. To her dismay, she realized that one of her former Nazi guards was there. He approached her afterward and put out his hand. In that instant, Corrie had to decide whether or not she would forgive him. She hesitated, and then extended her hand—and her forgiveness.[2]

Let me never forget, Abba Father, what a privilege it is to be a daughter of the King, a daughter of Zion.

Week 14

The Cana Bride

What was Jesus like as a child . . . a boy . . . an adolescent? There are few similarities between the lives of our teenage boys and His life. His world was very different from ours.

Jesus, like other Jewish boys, was probably taught the Law at age five, including catechetical instruction in synagogue schools. By the age of twelve, when Jesus' parents lost Him and later found Him in the temple, Jewish boys were on the threshold of manhood and were expected to obey the Law. At thirteen they became "of age" and, from that point on, traveled to Jerusalem three times a year for the Passover and the other great festivals.

It might be difficult for our children to identify with those years in Jesus' life, but as a mother of three sons, I can imagine Mary's tangled emotions as her Son began to grow away from her. Perhaps she began to realize His unusual nature that day in the temple, when He asked her why she didn't understand His need to be involved in His heavenly Father's business.

Did she bite her tongue to hold back the words, "But your father is a carpenter!"? Had she almost forgotten who He was?

Our next glimpse into their relationship shows Mary's awareness of Jesus' power, but even that understanding was incomplete. When she asked Him to use His power at the wedding in Cana to which Mary, Jesus and His disciples had been invited, her Son had to remind her that she was rushing things a bit.

The conflict between the desire to slow things down and, on the other hand, to rush other things along is a constant problem for us women, isn't it? I can remember practically pressuring our older boys to learn to walk and talk and all those exciting things. Now I wish our youngest would have stayed age eight all his life! Some days it seems as though nothing is running at the right speed: either nothing happens or everything happens all at once; either we feel lonely and deserted or the phone, the doorbell and the kids all scream for our attention at the same time.

What about the other important woman at the wedding in Cana—the bride? Unlike Mary, she did not have the advantage of years of experience; she must have been full of questions about the future. How did she react to the embarrassing situation she encountered at her wedding?

BACKGROUND READING: John 2:1-11.

ANTICIPATION!

"Though you have not seen him, you love him; and even though you do not see him now, you believe in him and are filled with an inexpressible and glorious joy." (1 Peter 1:8)

Read Matthew 25:1-13; 1 Thessalonians 4:15-18

Today—it was my day,
The day I'd dreamed about,
The day that he would come for me,
The day I'd hear his shout!
My attendants all were ready,
My wedding garments white. . . .
I heard his voice! He'd come!
My heart leaped at the sight.
—the bride at Cana

Betrothal was similar to but more binding than a modern engagement. Betrothal, in Jesus' time, meant that two people promised to marry each other but did not live together until after the wedding. Usually the bride was chosen by the groom's parents. (In Old Testament times he did not see her face until he lifted her veil during the wedding feast week.) Betrothal was legally binding and gifts were exchanged to mark the occasion.

Often a year passed before the wedding feast, a year of separation and preparation. The bride prepared her wedding garments, the household linens and other items; the groom prepared their home and possibly built their furniture. When all was in readiness, the groom dressed in his finest garments and, with his friends, walked to the bride's home to escort her to the wedding feast, which lasted from seven to fourteen days. Can you imagine the mixture of anxiety and anticipation the young (often teenaged) bride must have felt?

Do we feel that same anticipation for the day our heavenly Bridegroom will come for us? This is the time of separation, when we prepare for when our Bridegroom "will come down from heaven, . . . [and we] will be caught up . . . with them in the clouds to meet the Lord in the air" (1 Thessalonians 4:16-17).

It's almost overwhelming, Father, to think that You planned all of this.

14 — Tuesday

PROFILE OF THE GROOM

"I delight greatly in the LORD; my soul rejoices in my God. For he has clothed me with garments of salvation and arrayed me in a robe of righteousness, as a bridegroom adorns his head like a priest, and as a bride adorns herself with her jewels."
(Isaiah 61:10)

Read Psalm 19

As in a dream I walked
Back to his father's home,
Longing for the time
We'd finally be alone.
I had so many questions—
They'd waited for so long!
And now, this was our day,
The beginning of our song . . .
—the Cana bride

What were a young bride's thoughts on that long-anticipated walk to her new home? Her face was covered by a veil, but she could see his. Probably she had watched him often at a distance, but now he was beside her, his arm was touching hers, and I'm sure she took advantage of every opportunity to study the outlines of his profile, the darkness of his hair, the way he set his shoulders, the way he carried himself. Did he appear to be confident or nervous? Was he kind and considerate of her feelings, or was he trying to impress her with his manliness? And most of all—for he was studying her too—she wondered if he liked what he saw. Was he pleased with his father's choice? What would he think when he saw her face?

POINT TO PONDER: What does my heavenly Bridegroom see when He looks at me? That bride of long ago may have worried about an annoying blemish on her face. Am I as concerned about sin's blemishes on my life? Are my wedding garments white?

Thank You, Father, for Your robe of righteousness that covers all my inadequacies.

THE BEST FOR THE GUESTS

"I promised you to one husband, to Christ, so that I might present you as a pure virgin to him." (2 Corinthians 11:2)

Read Matthew 22:1-14

The feast was well in progress—
So many people there,
Each giving us their wishes
For freedom from all care.
But something had gone wrong,
The women were in tears.
They went to one named Mary
And shared their dismal fears.
—the Cana bride

The one- or two-week wedding feast gave the young couple an opportunity to get to know each other and each other's families, but how difficult it can be to get to know someone when others are constantly watching and interrupting!

In addition to feasting, there was entertainment in the form of dancing, singing, games and contests. Everyone looked forward to these occasions, and if the family could afford the expense, usually most of the villagers were invited. (Perhaps some of the guests brought food or a "covered dish" as we Pennsylvania Dutch would say.) The family, however, was expected to provide the wine, and the quality of the wine was determined by the financial status of the family. Each family tried to provide the very best they could afford, in abundance; less than the very best diminished the splendor of this joyous occasion.

Is something throwing a shadow over your happiness? Perhaps it's a major problem, physical or emotional, or possibly just a series of little things. Perhaps you're facing a full-scale rebellion from one of your children that is separating you and your husband, or perhaps that invisible barrier is simply a lack of communication between the two of you. Have you "run out of wine" in your relationship with others, and with Jesus Christ?

Yes, Father, I've been seeing problems in at least one relationship. Help me to recognize the under-the-surface signs of strain.

14 – *Thursday*

AN EVIL OMEN

"Come to Me, all you who labor and are heavy-laden and over burdened, and I will cause you to rest—I will ease and relieve and refresh your souls." (Matthew 11:28, Amplified)

Read John 14:1-14

It was an evil omen!
Our marriage would be cursed,
The wedding feast be ruined—
The women feared the worst.
We had run out of wine
So early in the day;
The guests would all feel cheated
And each would go their way. . . .
—the Cana bride

Did the young bride know Mary, the motherly figure to whom the women were unburdening themselves? Possibly not. Mary may have been a friend only of the groom's family. Perhaps the young bride wondered who Mary was: A wise woman, the daughter or wife of an influential man? Why did the women go to her with their problems? How could she provide a solution for this embarrassing situation?

To run out of wine at a wedding was considered to be a breach of hospitality. Perhaps the young bride wondered how her in-laws could have let this happen. Perhaps she wished she could become a carefree girl again, away from the pressures and responsibilities of adulthood and marriage. "I wish someone would tell me how to cope with all this—I'm not ready for it!"

Don't we all have that feeling at times? In times like this, do we withdraw into a shell, fiercely protective of our "secret" problems, or do we share the battles with the skeletons in our closets, so that others may be encouraged?

Thank You, Father, even for those ugly skeletons. Show me how those "dry bones" can bring glory to You.

14 – Friday

A STRANGE COMMAND

"His mother said to the servants,
'Do whatever [Jesus] tells you.' " (John 2:5)

Read Matthew 9:14-17

Then Mary found her Son
And whispered, "All is well!"
Instructed all the servants
To do as He would tell.
I'd been upset, bewildered
At this unexpected need,
Unsure which voice to listen to,
Confused which voice to heed.
—the Cana bride

How did the servants react to Jesus' command to fill the stone waterpots? There they stood in the corner of the room, six large containers holding perhaps twenty to thirty gallons each. Ordinarily they were used only for ceremonial purposes, but now they were to be filled with water. "Why?" the servants must have asked. "That's a lot of trips to the well!"

Can't you just hear the servants mumbling to one another: "Who is this Jesus, anyway? Just because His mother thinks He knows what He's doing—well, my mother loves me too! What's He going to do, throw some grapes into each waterpot and serve instant wine?"

Perhaps, behind her veil, the bride was now studying Jesus' face. Why did they call this man "Master"? What kind of power did He have?

Help me, Father, to tune out the wrong voices that clamor for my attention. Help me to turn off the TV and the radio and listen for Your still, small voice.

14 – Saturday

JOY RESTORED

"As a bridegroom rejoices over his bride, so will your God rejoice over you." (Isaiah 62:5)

Read John 15:1-6

How many times in later years
We would recount the time
When He walked into both our lives,
Turned water into wine.
He took the little that we had
And made it into much,
He took the simple stuff of life
And blessed it with His touch.

—the Cana bride

There had probably been lots of rumors going around Cana concerning Mary's Son. Recently He had left Nazareth and had spent a mysterious month in the desert—forty days in all. When Jesus made His first public appearance at the wedding in Cana, He would have been deeply tanned and probably quite thin from a prolonged time of fasting, but in good physical condition from all the walking over the rugged terrain.

Jesus went forty days without food, was ministered to by angels and then walked into a week-long feast. He could have reacted negatively to this very human celebration, but He did not condemn the feasting and frolic. Although marriage was not in His Father's plans for Jesus, He who had helped to create the one-flesh relationship understood its joys and the sorrows. Jesus turned their tears into gladness, their water in wine.

POINT TO PONDER: If *we* can just understand what this story says to us! Our heavenly Bridegroom loves us as we are, accepts us as His Father's excellent choice for His Bride, yet desires a Bride who is pure and spotless, who has kept herself set aside (sanctified) for Him. He is divine, yet He understands our human needs and imperfections. As He manifested His power in Cana that day, so He still walks among plain, simple people and brings them joy.

Thank You, Father, for the true joy You have given me. Help me to share it spontaneously with someone today.

Week 15

Mrs. Simon Peter: The Big Fisherman's Wife

In Cana, Jesus had told His mother that His hour had not yet come.

In Samaria, however, Jesus stated openly to the woman at the well that He was the Messiah.

Now, in Capernaum, Jesus' time had come. And for those around Him, this was the hour of decision.

For the first period of His ministry, Jesus' travels would revolve around the freshwater lake called the Sea of Galilee (also the Lake of Tiberias, Lake Kinnereth, Lake of Gennesaret). The famous Jordan River, where Jesus' cousin John had baptized Him before John's imprisonment by Herod, passes through this inland sea, which lies 686 feet below sea level. To the east and the west the landscape rises sharply; from the southern shore the town of Safed can be seen perched on the peaks of Mt. Canaan, the modern "city on a hill" (Matthew 5:14). To the north rises snow-covered Mt. Heron.

Fringing the northwestern shore of the Sea of Galilee are the remains of the village of Capernaum. It was this small but thriving fishing village that Jesus chose to use as His headquarters for His Galilean ministry.

Why Capernaum? Probably the town's location influenced Jesus' choice. Capernaum had been built at an important intersection of two trade routes; it lay on the border between the territories of Herod Antipas and his brother Philip, with a customhouse and a garrison of soldiers keeping a close watch on all town activities.

In Capernaum Jesus rubbed shoulders with many more different types of people than He would have encountered in Nazareth. They were also more responsive, as became obvious when He went back to visit His hometown.

So Jesus settled in the small fishing village of Capernaum, probably in a fisherman's home. In an area of Capernaum only 200 to 300 feet from the sea of Galilee, modern tourists are still able to see the remains of a fifth-century church built on the site of Peter the fisherman's home. (For many years after Peter lived there, his home must have been used by Christians. Inscriptions calling Jesus the Lord, the Most High God—in four languages—were found there.)

And, of course, when I stood on the site of the fisherman's home, I wondered about the woman who lived there. How did *she* feel about their Visitor, their fairly permanent Guest—especially when her husband left town with Him?

BACKGROUND READING: Luke 4:16-32

15 — Monday

NO VISIBLE MEANS OF SUPPORT!

"The Spirit of the Lord is upon me; he has appointed me to preach Good News to the poor; he has sent me to heal the brokenhearted." (Luke 4:18, TLB)

Read Luke 4:14-30

I gave him to You, Lord,
He's Your disciple only . . .
But in the summer evenings
I get so very lonely.
I gave him to You, Lord,
I gave him to You fully . . .
Yet sometimes in the night
My heart can ache so cruelly.
—Mrs. Simon Peter

It's 7 a.m., and as I write I am expecting my husband to walk in the door at any time. He will be very tired, having left New Hampshire late last evening after a concert there.

My husband has been involved in a musical ministry since I met him in 1963, and so I have become accustomed to the "waiting game." This time, however, it has been more difficult than usual to wait calmly for his return, since our youngest son accompanied his father on this trip, and the roads have been covered with ice most of the week. Just after they left, there was a two-car accident in front of our house, which increased my apprehension.

POINT TO PONDER: Trust! An easy word to say, but not so easy to carry through. In times of crisis and aloneness, we find out whether we have learned its meaning. Peter's wife probably learned the lesson of dependence on God the same way I did—and do—when all her "props" were pulled out from under her.

Now *I can understand some of Your purposes, Father, and thank You.*

15 — *Tuesday*

GROWING PAINS

"Do not let your hearts be troubled (distressed, agitated). You believe in and adhere to and trust in and rely on God, believe in and adhere to and trust in and rely also on Me." (John 14:1, Amplified)

Read Matthew 18:23-35

And when the children fight
I wish that he were here
To settle arguments
And wipe away the tears.
His word is always law—
While mine gets argued with
And everything goes wrong.

—Mrs. Simon Peter

When my husband and I underwent the unique maturation experience of living with teenagers, we learned the "facts of life" all over again. One of the most definite facts seemed to be that even the "family who prays together" . . . fights!

Once a friend asked if one of our teenagers could baby-sit. I left the choice to them and one of them said quite agreeably, "If we can't both go" (the most desirable option), "I'll stay home. I have some things to do in my room." When the time actually came, however, the stay-home volunteer wanted to go. Trying to teach him the need to stay firm in a decision that affects others, I said no. His immediate reaction was: "It's not fair! Nobody told me I couldn't change my mind!"

"It's not fair!" was an everyday term in life with our three sons. An older saint in our church with five grown (and exemplary!) children encouraged me one day when she said emphatically, "Even children in the *best* Christian homes fight—it's normal!" (Especially when Dad's not at home!) And I'm sure Peter's kids were no exception.

Thank You, Father, for continued sanity—and, yes, sometimes even serenity—in the midst of struggle.

15 – Wednesday

THE CALL

"Simon Peter . . . fell at Jesus' knees and said, 'Go away from me, Lord; I am a sinful man!' " (Luke 5:8)

Read Luke 5:1-11

And yet when he was fishing
He wasn't satisfied.
He wouldn't admit it to me;
He always had his pride.
But I knew deep inside him,
Behind that burly frame,
He wanted something better . . .
Then Jesus called his name!

—Mrs. Simon Peter

I was in the kitchen putting the finishing touches on a meal and, at the same time, trying to hear what my husband was saying to our guest in the living room. Our visitor, a young mother of four, was asking, "Don't you ever wish you had a 9-to-5 job?" My husband's answer rang out loud and clear: "I don't really waste time thinking about it, because I'm sure this is where the Lord has called me!"

Most days I say "Amen!" to that; but to be honest, there are days when I've grumbled to myself, "That's easy for *you* to say!" Countless hours of running kids to baseball practice, church youth activities, band practice, football games, piano lessons, skating parties, trumpet lessons and quiz meets stretch behind me and attending church alone is still a weekly reality.

But one of my greatest satisfactions in life—like Peter's wife, I imagine—comes when my husband says, "Honey, you're really an encouragement to me! I could never make it without you!"

Thank You, Father, for the supreme satisfaction of living within Your will.

IN-LAWS OR OUTLAWS?

"The first thing Andrew did was to find his brother Simon and tell him, 'We have found the Messiah.' " (John 1:41)

Read John 1:29-42

Andrew was first to meet Him,
The Christ, anointed One;
But Andrew looked for Peter,
Just as He'd always done,
And brought him to the Master
Who that day changed his name.
My husband's life changed also,
It never was the same.

—Mrs. Simon Peter

In her book *God Called—a Family Answered,* Marti Hefley tells the heartwarming story of the Hagerstown (Maryland) Rescue Mission. The book was especially interesting to me because we too work within a family organization. As I look back over the years, I would have to say that some of our deepest joys—and at the same time, our greatest frustrations—are due to that fact.

How did Peter's wife feel about Andrew? Probably the same way each of us has felt toward family members: by turns supportive, embarrassed, loving, angry, close, at arm's length, thankful, jealous, proud. . . .

Was Andrew married? Did Peter's wife have a sister-in-law with whom she could share life's problems and joys? I thank God for sisters-in-law who have been sisters-in-love; I hope Peter's wife was just as blessed.

Thank You, Father, for the special people You have sent into my life.

A FISHER OF MEN

"Jesus replied, 'Blessed are you, Simon son of Jonah, for this was not revealed to you by man, but by my Father in heaven.' "
(Matthew 16:17)

Read Matthew 17:24-27; Mark 10:17-31

I knew he'd found his calling
When I saw him again.
He was a different person,
Not just a different name
He had so much to tell me . . .
At first I was afraid
And frightened of the future—
How would the bills be paid?
—Mrs. Simon Peter

Fishing has never been an easy occupation, and a fisherman's life on the Sea of Galilee was as unpredictable as the inland sea itself. Like an oversized mixing bowl full of water in the midst of the surrounding hills, this picturesque sea can be whipped to a frenzy by the winds that descend quickly and powerfully to its surface, 686 feet below sea level.

Perhaps one of these frightening storms had occurred the morning before Peter found it necessary to fish all night. Discouraged and exhausted, Peter returned to shore with an empty boat, possibly wondering how his wife would take the news. Busy washing his nets, Peter may not have been too enthusiastic about Jesus' request to use his boat as a floating platform. What a nuisance, all these crowds of noisy people! No wonder the fish were scared away!

Perhaps Peter's wife was in the crowd. Perhaps she witnessed the miraculous catch later. Perhaps she said to herself, *Now, finally, Jehovah's blessing is upon us, and things will go well from this day on.* And perhaps she was bitterly disappointed when her husband left the fishing business to become a fisher of men.

Thank You, Father, for the lessons I've learned through the discipline of disappointment.

15 — Saturday

ANOTHER SUPPORT SHAKEN

"Jesus looked at them and said, 'With man this is impossible, but not with God; all things are possible with God.' " (Mark 10:27)

Read Matthew 18:1-14

The day I met the Master
I thought my heart would break.
First I had lost my husband
and now . . . one more heartache.
My mother had the fever;
If she died, I would lose
My husband and my helper.
Could I the Lord refuse?

—Mrs. Simon Peter

Peter's wife may have admired and even followed Jesus from a distance, but how did she react the day Simon (the name she had always called her husband) quit the fishing business? I would imagine she reacted as any normal woman would have—she probably panicked!

Remember, Jesus had come to Capernaum from Nazareth, where His hometown fan club had tried to kill Him because of jealousy and their inability to believe that He was who He said He was. After all, they had known Him since childhood! Certainly news of the attempted lynching had spread to nearby Capernaum (about twenty to twenty-five miles away), and Peter's wife must have wondered just what her husband was getting involved in.

And now, the one person on whom she could still rely, her mother, was very sick with a high fever. Medicine was very crude in those days, with little understanding of the causes of sickness, and doctors could help very little. How helpless Peter's wife must have felt!

Sometimes, Lord, it is necessary for me to come to the point of desperation in my life before I fall on my knees before You.

Week 16

Mrs. Simon Peter: A Fisherman's Future

One of my favorite memories of Israel is crossing the Sea of Galilee, with snow-covered Mt. Heron in the distance, listening to my husband sing "The Stranger of Galilee." Although, of course, the boat was very different from that of Jesus' day, as were the people around me, it is easy to imagine that "Stranger" resting in the bow of a boat as He calmly watched the approach to the little village of Capernaum.

Actually, Capernaum was the largest of about thirty fishing towns around the sometimes serene, sometimes stormy sea. In the ruins of Capernaum can still be seen the remains of a beautiful synagogue, built on the ruins of the synagogue of Jesus' time. As was traditional, the place of worship was built on the highest point in town, near water, with the entrance facing the east and the seats arranged so that worshipers would face Jerusalem when praying.

Houses in Capernaum were made of basalt stone with doorways leading into the street; they were single story, with roofs of mud mixed with straw. Peter was not wealthy, but prosperous enough to own his own home in the most important neighborhood in town. How did his wife react to the thought that the day could come when she, like Sarah of old, might leave her comfortable home to follow her husband and this Stranger? Where, God only knew!

I prayed as I planned the course of my life.
I prayed for His presence, His peace. Noise and strife
Entered in, and I heard my Lord say;
"I will determine, and you must obey."

"But Lord," I protested, "how can this be of You?
These people around me block You from my view!
I need time alone to read and to pray!"
"I will determine, and you must obey."

And so strife continued within my own soul;
I wanted His will, yet I wanted control.
Interruptions kept coming each hour of the day.
He would determine; I had to obey.

Then my Lord showed me, if His peace I'd know;
His love I must share in a strong healing flow.
As I gave to others, He'd give strength for each day.
Now He truly determines . . . I simply obey.

BACKGROUND READING: Genesis 12:1-9

16 — Monday

THE MASTER IS HERE!

"And [now] I am no more in the world, but these are in the world and I am coming to You. Holy Father, keep in Your name [in the knowledge of Yourself] them whom You have given Me, that they may be one, as We [are one]." (John 17:11, Amplified)

Read Mark 1:16-38

But when I met the Master
And looked into His eyes,
I found myself just trusting
And giving Him my why's.
He asked about my mother,
Then took her by the hand.
As He rebuked her fever
He told her: "Rise and stand!"

—Mrs. Simon Peter

How often I've wished I could physically look into the eyes of Jesus! It seems as though immediate understanding would have been available to Peter's wife just by looking into the face of the Master—but perhaps it was not so easy.

Have you ever felt so annoyed or angry at someone that you did not want to see his eyes? If Peter's wife was upset about their new ratings in community status, it may be that she had avoided even being in the same room with this outcast from neighboring Nazareth.

But this day she was ministering to her mother, perhaps trying to feed her, when Peter burst excitedly into the sick room. "He's coming, Jesus is coming!" And as she looked up to quiet Peter's voice, *He* was there. His eyes met hers—lovingly, pleadingly, firmly—and as Peter's wife watched her mother rise, her own spirit rose also, never to sink into the depths of doubt and desperation again.

Lord . . . stop my ranting and raving . . . and reveal Yourself.

A NEW PERSPECTIVE

"While I was with them, I kept and preserved them in Your name. . . . I do not ask that You will take them out of the world, but that You will keep and protect them from the evil [one]." (John 17:12, 15, Amplified)

Read Luke 4:31-44

Before our eyes, she changed
From lying at death's door
To loving, giving, living,
The way she'd been before.
I couldn't believe the change
And then I realized that
The Master never takes
Without His giving back.

—Mrs. Simon Peter

The Gospel writers tell us that after Peter's mother-in-law was healed, she arose and ministered to them. Perhaps she said, "Go take a walk with your wife, Simon! She's been working too hard, and you two need some time alone. I'll make supper—I feel great!"

I can visualize Peter and his wife following the path down to the Sea of Galilee, then walking along the shore as they discussed the ways in which their lives would change. Perhaps they sat on a rock that had been a favorite rendezvous since childhood, and Jesus Himself, refreshed by the meal that had been prepared for Him so willingly, may have met them there.

"Your husband has great potential," Jesus may have said to Peter's wife. "If I can just harness all that energy and direct it properly, He will be a dynamo! But he needs to know it's all right with you before he can give Me his best."

Please continue to help me, Jesus, as You did Peter's wife, to let go . . . to give You the director's chair.

PETER'S NEED FOR ATTENTION

"Then Peter began to speak and said to Jesus, Lord, it is good and delightful that we are here; if You approve, I will put up three booths here, one for You and one for Moses and one for Elijah." (Matthew 17:4, Amplified)

Read Matthew 17:1-13

Well, after that had happened
I never was surprised
At the other miracles
I saw with my own eyes.
When Peter shared with me
The power and the glory
He'd seen upon the mountain,
I didn't doubt his story.

—Mrs. Simon Peter

How quiet the house must have seemed when Jesus and Peter were gone! Enthusiastic, even boisterous—we might describe someone like Peter as a person who "opens his mouth to change feet."

In the stories in the Gospels, it seems Peter *always* has something to say. Even during the Transfiguration, after having climbed a high mountain (possibly Mt. Hermon—the traditional site, Mt. Tabor, was occupied by a walled city during Jesus' time) and having witnessed the glory of God, Peter had a suggestion. Even in the presence of such legendary figures as Moses and Elijah, Peter vied for Jesus' attention: "It's good we're here, Lord; I'll build you a temporary shelter from the sun and weather."

POINT TO PONDER: God personally rebuked Peter for his thoughtless chatter, well-meaning though it was. "This is My Son, My Beloved, with Whom I am [and have always been] delighted. Listen to Him!" (Matthew 17:5, Amplified).

Father, as I huff and puff up the Mount Hermons of my life, teach me to keep my eyes upward . . . and my mouth shut.

16 – Thursday

A QUIET SPIRIT

"Instantly Jesus reached out His hand and caught and held him, saying to him, 'O you of little faith, why did you doubt?' " (Matthew 14:31, Amplified)

Read Matthew 14:22-36

Yes, even when he said
He'd walked upon the sea,
I could believe him then!
There was no doubt in me.
I laughed a little when
He told me of his fear.
My Peter's still a man
And that makes him more dear.
—Mrs. Simon Peter

When Peter addressed women in his first epistle, he urged them to "fit in" with their husband's plans (1 Peter 3:1-5, TLB), probably remembering how valuable his own wife's cooperation had been to him. As the wife of a fisherman, she had never been able to dress extravagantly, with jewels or gold, but her true beauty shone through a peasant's garb—the beauty of a gentle and quiet spirit.

POINT TO PONDER: I believe that Christ's power, evidenced in Peter's boatload of fish, had conquered his wife's tendency to worry, just as her mother's miraculous healing had conquered fear and doubt. Jesus' compassion for the multitudes, and especially His affection for her impetuous, hard-to-live-with husband, had given her an example to follow for the rest of her life.

And Peter kept learning too. He cautioned men, in the same chapter of that first epistle, that a man and wife "are partners in receiving God's blessings," and that if a wife is not treated lovingly, her husband's prayers "will not get ready answers" (3:7, TLB). Sounds like the voice of experience, doesn't it?

Jesus, I see myself in these familiar characters. Help me to learn from their examples, but most of all, from Yours.

16 — Friday

A SUPPORTIVE WIFE

"Jesus commanded Peter, 'Put your sword away! Shall I not drink the cup the Father has given me?' " (John 18:11)

Read Matthew 26:31-35; John 18:1-11

But my heart sank within me
When I heard of the night
Peter denied our Master
In fear and doubt and fright.
What had happened to the kingdom?
Why didn't the Master fight?
Why had Peter been rebuked
When he was in the right?

—Mrs. Simon Peter

We know that several women followed Jesus during His earthly ministry, but Peter's wife is not mentioned as one of them. She may have needed to stay in Capernaum, at least while their children were small (if they had children) or to care for her aging mother.

A few years later, the day must have come when she heard of Peter's denial of the Master. Perhaps she heard it from her husband's own lips, when he returned to Capernaum after the resurrection. Peter cried when the cock crowed in Caiaphas' courtyard, and he may have cried again when he told his wife of his cowardice. Perhaps it was the first time she had ever seen her robust husband break down.

Peter probably told her also of his effort to protect Jesus by thrusting a sword at the high priest's servant in the Garden of Gethsemane. It had been such a confusing, unnerving, frustrating evening, and he, Peter, had completely failed the test. I can picture his giant shoulders shaking with sobs as he recounted the terrible events, and I'm sure she comforted him as only a wife can. Yet she may have felt like a mother with a much-loved but disobedient child: "But Peter, it's all over now . . . and He is risen!"

Lord Jesus, curb my tendency to continue a rebuke when compassion and comfort are needed.

TRUSTING ALL THE WAY

"Again He said to him the second time, Simon, son of John, do you love Me—with reasoning, intentional, spiritual devotion, as one loves the Father? He said to Him, Yes, Lord, You know that I love You—that I have a deep, instinctive, personal affection for You, as for a close friend. He said to him, Shepherd (tend) My sheep." (John 21:16, Amplified)

Read John 21:1-22

My Peter was impulsive,
Sometimes conceited too . . .
And yet he loved the Master,
Desired His work to do.
As well as I know Peter,
The Master knew him best.
Peter would serve much better
After he'd failed the test.

—Mrs. Simon Peter

Peter had mellowed and matured, but even in the last chapter of John's Gospel his personality comes through. Just as Peter had denied Jesus three times, so Jesus questioned Peter three times concerning his love, then predicted Peter's type of death. Typically, Peter responded: "What about John?"

POINT TO PONDER: In Acts 5:29, however, we see a man who is no longer concerned about what others are thinking or doing: "We must obey God rather than men!" The difference? Peter had been filled with the Holy Spirit at Pentecost, and it was an ever-present reality with him, a day-by-day dying to self, a day-by-day infilling (Acts 4:8).

The apostle Paul mentions in First Corinthians 9:5 that Peter's wife accompanied her husband on his missionary endeavors. Staying at home may have been difficult, but traveling with one's husband, especially in those days, would have demanded an even greater flexibility. Church tradition relates that Peter and his wife died together (crucified upside down) and that he comforted her with these words: "Remember the Lord."

Thank You, Father, even for the weaknesses in our own nature that force us to depend on You.

Week 17

The Woman with the Bleeding

I have been told that my book on Old Testament women, *They Were Women Too,* has been read by men. Well, men, if you are reading *this* book, this section is not for you!

This week we will be discussing the woman who suffered an issue of blood for twelve years. Only another woman can even imagine the absolute wretchedness of such a condition. Even with today's potassium supplements, vitamins complete with iron dosages and constant innovations in feminine care that compete with each other in convenience, absorbency and scent—let's face it, a twelve-year problem of this sort would be enough to drive anyone to despair. Then imagine yourself facing it without running water or disposable feminine aids.

As if that were not enough, a woman with a problem like this was practically ostracized from community life. Jewish laws concerning menstruation were very definite: the woman was in a state of theoretical "uncleanness" or ceremonial defilement during menstruation and for seven days afterward. (We'll go into more detail concerning ceremonial defilement later.) A woman who continued to hemorrhage was continually defiled or "unclean."

Unclean was a dreaded word. Victims of leprosy were also termed "unclean"—they could not associate with family or friends but had to live in a leper colony at a distance from any settlement. They were obliged to call out "Unclean!" to anyone approaching.

And so our friend must also have felt like an outcast from society. Was she married? If so, life would have been more difficult than if she were single, for she would have had a husband's frustrations to deal with as well as her own. Possibly he would have taken a second wife who could meet his needs and bear him children.

Perhaps she was single and had spent all her own resources on doctors who could not cure her. Probably they had no sympathy as well as no cure.

Don't you admire this woman for having enough courage to brave the crowds? Jesus commended her for her faith; how could she have had any faith left after twelve years of physical misery and emotional rejection?

> Consider it wholly joyful, my brethren, whenever you are enveloped in or encounter trials of any sort, or fall into various temptations. Be assured and understand that the trial and proving of your faith bring out endurance and steadfastness and patience. (James 1:2-3, Amplified)

BACKGROUND READING: Mark 5:22-43

17 — Monday

TABOOS AND TURTLEDOVES

"When she is cleansed from her discharge, she must count off seven days, and after that she will be ceremonially clean. On the eighth day she must take two doves or two young pigeons and bring them to the priest. . . ." (Leviticus 15:28-29)

Read Leviticus 15:19-30

All those years . . .
You know how long they were?
Twelve long years . . .
Seems like half my life—and more.
The constant drain and weakness,
The constant soil and mess,
The washing and the cleaning,
The airing and the sunning . . .
A cycle never ending
Through all those years.

—the "unclean" woman

The word *unclean* applied not only to the menstruating woman, but also to anything her body touched in any way. Also, anyone touching her bed or other furniture would be ceremoniously defiled and was required to wash his or her clothes and bathe—and still remain defiled until the evening. Sexual intercourse, of course, was not allowed during the time of ceremonial defilement.

It's important to understand the context of these laws. During the time Leviticus was written Israel was on an extended "camp out" in the wilderness, and attempts at health and cleanliness were very difficult problems. Some would call the Levitical laws a form of ancient "taboos." (In other cultures women were forced to live in "menstrual huts" for four days and could be punished if their flow continued longer.) But if all facts were known, I believe God had good reason for laying down His sanitation laws.

Aren't you glad that we live under grace, not law—otherwise we'd have to shop for turtledoves once a month!

Thank You, Father, for being omniscient, all-knowing. Help me to trust when I do not understand.

17 – Tuesday

SHUNNING THE SADDENED

"Love one another with brotherly affection—as members of one family—giving precedence and showing honor to one another." (Romans 12:10, Amplified)

Read Romans 2:17-29

All those years . . .
I was unclean, unclean!
My husband could not touch me
Lest he be unclean too.
I felt just like a leper;
Outcast by those about me.
The feeling of rejection
Was more than I could bear,
A circle closed, unbroken
Through all those years.

—the "unclean" woman

Man has always done very well at taking God's good laws and enforcing them in a painful rather than loving way.

What may have originally been God's sanitation laws for wilderness campers grew into a cruel form of rejection ("shunning," as some would call it). This poor woman, who had suffered from hemorrhaging for twelve years, had undoubtedly undergone one humiliation after another simply because of a physical problem.

POINT TO PONDER: We pride ourselves on living in more enlightened times, but how often do I ignore the handicapped and their special needs? Oh, sure, everyone loves "beautiful people" like Joni Eareckson Tada—but what about the not-so-beautiful people she represents? How often have we rejected people with emotional problems simply because we were too busy or too impatient to be bothered with them? "She has problems . . . stay clear of her," we might say.

Precious Father, I need Your compassion.

17 — *Wednesday*

RETAIN OR REJECT

"As it is written, None is righteous, just and truthful and upright and conscientious, no, not one." (Romans 3:10, Amplified)

Read Psalm 32

All those years . . . I sought for help in vain.
Each doctor had a potion,
A new astringent, tonic.
Each one was guaranteed
Until we paid the price
And when it did not work
They shrugged and turned away. . . .
A cycle never ending
Through all those years.

—the "unclean" woman

If you read Leviticus 15 earlier, you probably did so with mixed emotions. Why would a God who created woman and her physical functions and cycles lock her into a box and call her unclean for something she could not avoid? Isn't that adding insult to injury?

Levitical emphasis on ceremonial cleanliness is symbolic of our need for inner spiritual cleansing: "All of us have become like one who is unclean . . ." (Isaiah 64:6). Whatever we use to hide or cover our uncleanness comes in contact with the contagion and becomes unclean as well: "All our righteousness—our best deeds of rightness and justice—are as filthy rags or a polluted garment" (64:6, Amplified).

POINT TO PONDER: Menstruation is the body's rejection of the womb's unnecessary preparation for a new embryo. The bloody mixture must leave the body so that the normal cycle may continue; retention would stagnate the womb. Even so confession of sin frees us to advance spiritually; retaining sin—keeping silent and covering it—saps our strength.

"I praise you because I am fearfully and wonderfully made" (Psalm 139:14).

SACRIFICE AND SCAPEGOAT

"This is to be a lasting ordinance for you:
Atonement is to be made once a year for all the sins
of the Israelites." (Leviticus 16:34)

Read Romans 7:14-25

The leaders of our people
Were of no help to me.
They kept their distance from
Those who would taint their touch
And then . . . I heard of Jesus!
They said He cared for all.
They said He did not shrink
From those who were unclean.
—the "unclean" woman

Ceremonial cleanliness is symbolic of holiness. Instructions are given in Leviticus for five different kinds of offerings, including peace, sin and trespass offerings, to atone for day-by-day failures and continuing sins. Strict moral codes were established, and yet Leviticus 16 tells of an annual day of atonement that was needed over and above the regular sacrifices to atone for the sins of the people of Israel.

On this special day two goats were set aside or consecrated for use. One goat was killed as a sacrifice to atone for the people's sins; the other, the "scapegoat," symbolically carried the sins of Israel into the desert wilderness to be seen no more.

True, all our own righteousness is as filthy rags, but Jesus is our peace offering, our sin offering, our trespass offering. He took all our sins upon Himself and became our Scapegoat *and* our Sacrifice for sin. "Therefore, there is now no condemnation for those who are in Christ Jesus . . ." (Romans 8:1). Jesus is our way to fellowship, our at-one-ment with God.

Thank You, Jesus, for Your sacrifice for me.

17 – Friday

JESUS AND JAIRUS

"Jesus ignored their comments and said to Jairus, 'Don't be afraid. Just trust me.' " (Mark 5:36, TLB)

Read Luke 8:41-56

But how was I to see
This man who cared for all?
I couldn't be in a crowd
Contaminating others.
I had to take the chance—
Or why continue living?
So I came out of hiding
And found Him . . . passing by.
—the "unclean" woman

Jesus was on His way to Jairus' house, and Jairus was in a hurry. His twelve-year-old daughter was at the point of death, and Jairus, leader of the local synagogue, was too desperate to care that he was risking his important position by being involved with Jesus. (Jesus had already had several run-ins with the Jewish religious leaders.)

Jairus probably knew the woman who had touched Jesus, and we can imagine his tense impatience. This undesirable woman had suffered for twelve years; surely she could wait to talk to the Master just a short time longer! (Is it coincidental that Jairus' daughter was twelve years old—one young joyful life pitted against twelve years of misery?)

But Jesus did not pit one against the other. He took time for both. Although at that moment Jairus was told that his daughter had died, Jesus simply said: "Don't be afraid; just believe." Just trust Him, Jairus!

Father, I too need to learn trust. Perhaps the reason I find it so difficult to trust is that impatience is hindering my communication with you. Search me, O God.

FAITH AND A FRINGE

"Daughter, your faith [that is, your trust and confidence in Me, springing from faith in God] has restored you to health. Go in (to) peace, and be continually healed and free from your (distressing bodily) disease." (Mark 5:34, Amplified)

Read 1 Corinthians 15:51-58

The crowd was so intense—
Each one desired His touch!
I crept up close behind Him
And reached out just in time
I'd touched His robe, His garment;
He didn't pull away!
It slipped between my fingers
But He knew I was there.
And now He walks beside me
Through all the years.

—the "unclean" woman

The timid but determined woman had come up behind Jesus and touched the fringe of His garment. The fringe, or sacred tassel, hanging from a Jewish cloak reminded the owner of his obligations to the law (Numbers 15:38-40). But Jesus canceled out the laws regarding ceremonial defilement by acknowledging the woman's touch, and He did not pull away.

POINT TO PONDER: The disciples had seen only the crowd. While jostled by the impatient people and hurried by Jairus' urgent need, Jesus sensed the presence of a quiet yet even more desperate need. His words dismissed the rejection and frustration of those twelve painful years; His words turned a "nobody" into a "somebody"—a woman of faith.

"Take heart, daughter. . . . Your faith has healed you" (Matthew 9:22). "Go in peace and be freed from your suffering" (Mark 5:34). "And the woman was healed from that moment" (Matthew 9:22).

And then Jesus calmly walked on to face and defy death itself.

Thank You, Father, for giving us the victory through Jesus! In Your presence death is a loser.

Week 18

Susanna the Support Person

If you were mentioned only once in Scripture, what would you want the Gospel writers to say about you?

When it came to Susanna, Luke (writer of the Gospel of Luke) was a man of few words:

> The Twelve were with him, and also some women who had been cured of *evil spirits and diseases:* Mary (called Magdalene) from whom seven demons had come out; Joanna the wife of Cuza, the manager of Herod's household; *Susanna;* and many others. *These women were helping to support them out of their own means."* (Luke 8:1-3, emphasis added)

Support is defined as "to carry or bear the weight of; keep from falling, slipping or sinking; hold up; to give courage, faith, or confidence to; help or comfort; to give approval to or be in favor of; uphold; to maintain or provide for with money or subsistence; to show or tend to show to be true; to bear; endure, submit to, tolerate."

Perhaps the most interesting definition is this: "to act a subordinate role in the same play (with a specified star)."

Although Luke 8:3 may have been referring to Susanna's financial support of Jesus' ministry, it's likely that Susanna also showed her support by cooking and doing laundry for Jesus and the men who followed Him. McDonald's—or McDavid's—fast food was not available. And since there were no convenient laundromats for disciples' dirty robes, the stepping stones of hillside streams may have doubled as scrub boards for Susanna.

The position of second fiddle is not always favorably recognized among the "first chairs" of the orchestra—or their fans. Servanthood takes a special kind of person.

Susanna was that kind of person.

Each time a person possessed by an evil spirit fell on his knees before Jesus . . . each time someone with leprosy was cured . . . each time a paralytic walked, did Susanna sense her own healing anew? And imagine her reactions when Susanna witnessed, within one day, the healing of a woman called "Unclean!" for twelve years—and the bringing back to life of a beloved little twelve-year-old girl.

BACKGROUND READING: Philippians 2:1-11

MY LITTLE DAUGHTER IS DYING . . .

"The leader of the local synagogue, whose name was Jairus, came and fell down before him, pleading with him to heal his little daughter. 'She is at the point of death,' he said in desperation." (Mark 5:22-23, TLB)

Read Matthew 5:4; 2 Corinthians 1:3-4

How that father loves his daughter!
And Jesus understands his love . . .
He went with him immediately
—no questions asked.

—Susanna

Was Susanna a mother? Scripture does not tell us. Perhaps Susanna sought Jesus for physical healing—or for the healing of grief, possibly in losing a child.

My friend Linda Krone says this about the loss of her twenty-year-old daughter Debbie: "Losing a child is the most difficult thing I have had to deal with in my entire life. At times the pain seems almost unbearable. In my weak moments, when my heart aches so badly, I long to be with her in heaven. But in my heart I also know that is not what God wants, and He comforts me. Heaven has become so much more real to me. 'Precious in the sight of the LORD is the death of his saints' (Psalm 116:15).

"I have experienced the death of my father and mother, to whom I was very close, and loved dearly. I feel a void in my life since their death. But," Linda goes on, "the death of a child is very different. When a mother loses a child, a part of her dies. If you were to have a heart attack, part of the heart dies, but the rest continues to live on. Part of me has died, but I will continue to go on with my life, allowing God to use me as He chooses."

Lord, I realize that other people, whatever their problems, simply made the choice to go on. On days when I lack that strength, Lord, please give me Your strength.

IF I CAN JUST TOUCH HIS CLOTHING . . .

"She had suffered much from many doctors through the years and had become poor from paying them, and was no better but, in fact, was worse." (Mark 5:26, TLB)

Read 2 Corinthians 1:5-7

I saw that woman slip in through the crowd.
I saw determination on her face.
I saw the suffering etched in lines so deep.
I saw her touch Him—
and release!

—Susanna

"If all this had happened to me five years ago, it would have destroyed me. I was proud . . . an athlete, . . . able to handle things myself. But the Lord had to put me in a place where He could say, 'Look, Ken, you are not self-sufficient! You need Me and you need what I can do to strengthen you. I happen to have chosen this way of doing it.' "

Speaking to me was Rev. Ken Schuler, at that time (1983) a pastor. A diagnosis of diabetes at age thirteen had not kept Ken from sports—or from college and seminary. In 1974 Ken went for a routine eye examination where he was told he could soon go blind. Ken also developed ulcers on his toes. Surgery cleared up both problems. In 1978 tests showed that Ken's kidneys were functioning at ten percent of normal. Months of dialysis led to putting Ken on the list for a kidney transplant. Five weeks later a kidney, almost a perfect match, became available, but it took another five weeks until the kidney began to fully function.

"It was," Ken summarized, "as if God had let us glimpse His very nature. By receiving this kidney—and the life benefits it represented—we were seeing an illustration of Calvary. There on the cross Christ died so that others might live."

On days when I've felt self-sufficient, Lord, thank You for showing me my need of You.

18 — Wednesday

"HEALING POWER HAD GONE OUT FROM HIM . . ."

"She thought to herself, 'If I can just touch his clothing, I will be healed.' And sure enough, as soon as she had touched him, the bleeding stopped! . . . Jesus realized at once that healing power had gone out from him." (Mark 5:28-30, TLB)

Read 2 Corinthians 4:7-12

"Who touched me?" asked my Master.
"Who touched You?" asked the men.
"You ask the strangest questions . . .
Who touched You?
Everyone!"

—Susanna

If you're involved in ministry, you know the feeling of "energy" being discharged. After speaking to a group of women or, conversely, after an intense one-on-one counseling session, I have often felt more physically and emotionally exhausted than after a day of hard physical labor.

When the woman touched Him—with the touch of faith—Jesus felt energy discharged. He felt power being released. But why did He ask who had touched Him? If Jesus was omniscient, all-knowing, He not only knew the woman, He also knew her life history.

POINT TO PONDER: Jesus wanted to teach an object lesson, and the woman served as His visual illustration. He wanted that scene to be forever imprinted on the minds of His disciples. Jesus asked the question—and then waited for the woman to tell the story *from her perspective,* so that everyone would be aware of the woman's personal testimony. She may have felt her life story was unimportant, but Jesus thought differently.

Thank You, Lord, for Your reassurance that my story is also important to You.

YOU TOOK A RISK OF FAITH!

"But he kept on looking around to see who it was who had done it. Then the frightened woman, trembling at the realization of what had happened to her, came and fell at his feet and told him what she had done."(Mark 5:32-33, TLB)

Read 2 Corinthians 4:13-18

I watched as Faith stepped forward,
trembling and in tears.
I watched her kneel before Him
to give Him all her fears.
Twelve years of desperation,
twelve years of pain and grief,
twelve years of no one caring,
twelve years of uselessness . . .
—Susanna

Was it the woman's initiative in touching Jesus that healed her? Or did the finger that touched His robe serve as the connector between herself and the Source of healing?

"Faith is anything that points to the Almighty God," Rev. Jim Bollback emphasized to Grace Church in Atlanta on May 11, 1997. "Faith is having my eyes fastened on Jesus. Faith is when I'm standing in my position as God's child, looking at Him."

It was Mother's Day, and we were visiting our oldest son, celebrating his twenty-eighth birthday. As I sat in the church where Rob is associate/youth pastor, my mind was filled with many memories of Rob's growing-up years. It was good to be reminded of the Source of power in our lives, to remember when Rob was touched by that power. And to remember that every day we touch God the Father through the mediation of His Son Jesus, who "always lives to intercede for [us]" (Hebrews 7:25).

Thank You, Jesus, for Your promise of constant intercession for us.

18 -- Friday

DON'T BE AFRAID; JUST TRUST ME!

"While he was still talking to her, messengers arrived from Jairus' home with the news that it was too late—his daughter was dead and there was no point in Jesus' coming now. But Jesus ignored their comments and said to Jairus, 'Don't be afriad. Just trust me.' " (Mark 5:35-36, TLB).

Read 2 Corinthians 5:1-5.

"I didn't know . . ." she stammered,
". . . didn't mean to keep You from . . ."

"Live well,
be healed,
be blessed!"
His eyes were firm and strong.
—Susanna

"What a waste!" onlookers may have said. "That useless, sick old woman distracted Jesus' attention—she took His precious time—and now that dear little girl will never have a chance at life! All that potential—wasted!"

But Jesus had no regrets. Jesus knew exactly what He was doing—and when. Jesus is not limited by the restraints of time, as we humans are. Neither is He intimidated by the power of death.

Where, O death, is your victory?
Where, O death, is your sting?
(1 Corinthians 15:55)

"Don't listen to them," Jesus said to Jairus. "Just trust Me."

Forgive me, Lord, for listening to the voices of jealousy and resentment, the voices of gloom and doom, the voices of anxiety and fear. Teach me to trust.

WHY ALL THIS WEEPING AND CONFUSION?

"When they arrived, Jesus saw that all was in great confusion, with unrestrained weeping and wailing. . . . 'Why all this weeping and commotion?' he asked. 'The child isn't dead; she is only asleep!' " (Mark 5:38-39, TLB)

Read 2 Corinthians 5:6-10

That woman's loss of twelve long years
has also been her gain —
A heart of understanding
is a heart that's known its pain.
—Susanna

In Mark 5 we see the total physical healing of a twelve-year-old girl. In stark contrast, the next chapter tells the story of Salome, a girl not much older than she. Salome's mother Herodias encouraged her—possibly trained her—to dance sensuously before her drunken stepfather-king and his leering courtiers.

Salome, although a princess, was emotionally and spiritually vulnerable. She was completely unprotected. This child, the daughter of a commoner, was protected, loved and cherished.

Parents, what awesome roles we play in the lives of our children! In simple decisions like choices of entertainment, we may also choose whether we will expose our children to evil—or point them to Jesus.

Lord, thank You for reminding me that the choices I make this weekend may have eternal consequences.

Week 19

The Widow of Nain

In the small town of Nain in Galilee, as in surrounding areas, an older widow's future—her security and her significance—depended almost totally upon her children.

Today's American widow has a smorgasbord of options from which to choose, but the widow of Nain did not. She could not interview in the job market. There were no "temps" in Nain. She could not go back to school; she probably had never been to school. Like Naomi, the widow of Nain may have been considered too old or undesirable to qualify for remarriage under the law of levirate marriage. (Under this system, the nearest kinsman in the family was required to marry the widow in order to father an heir who would carry on the name of the deceased.)

Yes, the widow of Nain dearly loved her son. And he was also her hope for her old age, her "retirement plan." Imagine her grief and total devastation when, possibly without warning, he died.

Due to the heat and the lack of embalming, funerals were usually conducted the same day as the death. And so the widow would probably have encountered Jesus on the day of her son's death.

Nain, just a little south and west of Nazareth, could be reached from the west by traveling up a steep road that was enclosed by rock tombs on either side. Perhaps the members of the hastily formed funeral procession, wailing as they went as a sign of respect and honor for the dead, were slowly wending their way toward these rock tombs. Mourners were hired by wealthy families, but undoubtedly the widow could not afford this luxury.

Jesus had come from Capernaum, north of the Sea of Galilee, where He had been amazed by the faith of a Gentile, a Roman centurion—faith that received a servant's healing even at a distance, without Jesus' direct physical touch. As Jesus walked southward, He may have carefully circled the hostile boundaries of Nazareth, grieved once again by the fact that His hometown crowd refused to receive Him even with respect, much less faith. His mind was so preoccupied with thoughts of His coming rejection, by many more than the citizens of Nazareth, that the distant wailing merged with the cries of birds and the sound of the wind went unnoticed by Him.

Perhaps, as Jesus rounded a turn, the rock tombs loomed suddenly on either side.

Perhaps Jesus had a foretaste of Golgotha—and a tomb carved into a rock.

Perhaps, as Jesus met the eyes of the widow of Nain, He saw the face of His own mother, grieving inconsolably.

BACKGROUND READING: Luke 7:11-17

19 – Monday

A TOWN OF TOMBS

"Soon afterward, Jesus went to a town called Nain." (Luke 7:11)

Read Lamentations 3:1-6

My son was all I had.
I have no future now.
My first, my last, my only child,
my only living relative —
and now he's gone!
—the widow of Nain

Grieving is never easy. Feelings of loss are inevitable, even if they reflect a relationship that never lived up to expectations in the past and now never will. Although we are comforted, as Christians, by "that blessed hope"—the certainty of the resurrection—pain and emptiness still confront us when we are forced to let go of someone we love.

Death is irreversible and unalterable. It is out of our control, and we feel powerless. Fear of the future can be overwhelming, at least temporarily. It is generally understood that it takes at least two years to work through the death of someone close. In the death of a spouse, that period may be longer.

The Bible describes the grief involved in the closeness of parent-child relationships. Jacob grieved the loss of Joseph and refused to be comforted. David mourned the threatened loss of his infant son and, later, the real loss of his grown son Absalom: "O my son Absalom! My son, my son Absalom! If only I had died instead of you—O Absalom, my son, my son!" (2 Samuel 18:33).

POINT TO PONDER: The Bible also confirms God's comforting presence, in the 23rd Psalm and elsewhere, as we "walk through the valley of the shadow of death" (23:4). In Isaiah 53 we learn of a Messiah who is "a man of sorrows . . . acquainted with grief" (53:3, KJV), who takes up our griefs and carries our sorrows for us.

Thank You that because You are a "man of sorrows," You understand my grief.

A FUNERAL PROCESSION

"As [Jesus] approached the town gate, a dead person was being carried out." (Luke 7:12)

Read Lamentations 3:7-18

I hate this country, land of rocks!
A cold, unyielding tomb
will hold my precious son.
I'll never have a child to hold again,
to call my own, to care for me,
no child of his to brighten my old age.
—the widow of Nain

It has been said that the intensity of grief is determined by the intensity of love. The closer the relationship between the mourner and the object of loss, the greater the grief. If the mourner was very dependent on the deceased, grief is more intense—and more likely to drag on and on. When the survivor is left with both guilt and anger, grieving is harder.

When a child is lost, parents may feel angry, guilty, self-condemning and depressed. Feelings of incompetence because they failed to protect the child from death, even when there was nothing they could have done to prevent the death, may be overwhelming. A child's death often dangerously weakens an already shaky marriage or may result in a complete communication breakdown, particularly in the area of unshared feelings and reactions.

"Aftershock" may persist for what seems to be an incredibly long time. Feelings of sadness or depression may be triggered by happy occasions in other people's lives such as, for example, the birth of grandchildren. Other people sharing their family pictures remind the mourner that never again will his or her own family be complete and whole again.

Help me, Lord, to be sensitive to the grief of others.

AN ONLY SON

". . . the only son of his mother, and she was a widow." (Luke 7:12)

Read Lamentations 3:19-24

When we first lost his father
my son just clung to me
fearing I would leave as well.
I held him tightly
told him I would never leave.
But now
there is no one to hold me
in my hour of grief.
—the widow of Nain

C.S. Lewis, in *A Grief Observed,* said that symptoms of grief come in waves, and rarely are they all present at the same time. It is important to realize that grief affects not only how a person feels, but also how he or she thinks. Feelings of anxiety, anger and depression are common; so also are errors in judgment, disorganization of routines and the realization that even activities formerly performed automatically now may require great energy and concentrated effort.

Just when the grieving person feels least able to cope, he or she must make huge decisions. The mourner feels devastated or at least deluged by unavoidable pressures—doctor and hospital bills, insurance claims, funeral expenses, meetings with lawyers to change wills, informing the provider of pensions or IRS, the need to change names on legal documents, bank accounts—which are constant reminders of the painful feelings of loneliness. The resulting stress may wear down the body's resistance and show up in physical exhaustion, headaches, indigestion or loss of appetite, shortness of breath, inability to sleep.

We just heard the beautiful story of a local Mennonite grandmother who, when calling her husband for lunch, found him dead in their garden. She was able to call for help; when the paramedics came, however, they found her body collapsed upon the body of her husband. Attempts to revive her were futile; she had gone to meet her beloved.

Help me to be sensitive, Lord, to the needs of those who are grieving.

19 – Thursday

A CROWD—WHEN JUST A PRESENCE IS NEEDED

"And a large crowd from the town was with her." (Luke 7:12)

Read Lamentations 3:25-51

I know they mean well
by their wailing.
I know they weep to share my grief
but what I need just now is
quiet.
I long to leave this place of loss.
—the widow of Nain

"Being there" for someone who is grieving may take a variety of forms. Make yourself available without becoming a nuisance or being pushy, but do not wait to be called to sense a need. Offer assistance in areas outside the griever's areas of expertise—e.g., with car repair, etc.

"Being there" for the mourner requires great sensitivity to his or her changing moods and emotions. Be willing to listen when the person wants to talk, but also be willing to back off if the mourner needs some "space" or wants to talk about something seemingly illogical or unrelated, like stories from early childhood. (Some comfort may be derived from discussing "safe" areas.) Be aware, however, that a death may trigger the disclosure of long-kept family secrets.

When decisions are absolutely necessary, offer yourself as a sounding board to help the grieving person talk through the decisions. Don't tell him or her what to do; ask helpful questions without adding pressure. Gently try to discourage major decision-making, such as the sale of a house or a move to another state, at least for a few months. Offer aid in researching, or find an expert who can help with legal problems or real estate information so that impulsive decisions are avoided.

Give me wisdom, Lord, and help me not to be pushy.

19 – Friday

UNDERSTANDING GRIEF

"When the Lord saw her, his heart went out to her and he said, 'Don't cry.' " (Luke 7:13)

Read Lamentations 5:1-22

Who is this Stranger coming now?
He stops and looks at me . . .
then smiles, so gently.
He seems to understand my grief.
But no! He's stopping the procession.
I beg of You, oh Man of understanding eyes,
do not prolong this agony.
—the widow of Nain

Jesus Christ understood the grief of this widow. In the Bible, Jesus demonstrated the importance of grieving. Early in His ministry, in the Sermon on the Mount, He encouraged "those who mourn" because, He said, "they will be comforted" (Matthew 5:4). Jesus withdrew by Himself, probably to grieve, when told that John the Baptist had been executed.

Later, Jesus was deeply moved when His friend Lazarus died. Jesus allowed Martha to vent her emotions in honest, perhaps angry confrontation—Jesus had not come when Martha expected Him. Even though He knew that resurrection power would be released in Lazarus, Jesus wept with Mary and the mourners. In the Garden of Gethsemane, Jesus was "deeply grieved." Counselors would call this anticipatory grief. As the foreknowledge of the cross and the need for acceptance of His Father's will foreshadowed that night of prayer in the Garden, Jesus' grief became so intense that He sweat "great drops of blood" (Luke 22:44, KJV).

Help me, Jesus, to weep with others, to feel the grief of others as You did.

DEATH HAS BEEN SWALLOWED UP IN VICTORY!

"Then he went up and touched the coffin, and those carrying it stood still. He said, 'Young man, I say to you, get up!'"
(Luke 7:14)

Read 1 Corinthians 15:50-58

"Don't cry!" the Man said
gently
lovingly.
Before I could respond,
explain the greatness of my grief
He touched my son.
He spoke:
"Young man, get up!"
And in a holy mystery
my son sat up—and spoke to me.
And then, of course,
there was no need for me to say a word.
—the widow of Nain

Just as Jesus demonstrated the importance of grieving, He also changed the meaning of grieving. When death ends a relationship—forever—there is no hope for the future. But the Christian does not believe that. "The fact is that Christ has been raised from the dead. He has become the first of a great harvest of those who will be raised to life again. . . . When Christ comes back, all his people will be raised" (1 Corinthians 15:20, 23, NLT).

We can comfort and encourage each other with these words because, for the Christian, death is simply a beginning—the beginning of life eternal. As long as the devil is allowed to have the power of death, physical death will still be present in our world, but because of the crucifixion and resurrection, Christ has defeated death. And He has promised that one who believes in Christ will never die.

Thank You, Lord, for enabling us to look forward confidently to the reality of the resurrection and the rapture of reunion with our saved loved ones.

Week 20

The Crippled Woman

Eighteen years—that's a long time! The woman we are going to study had, according to Luke 13:11, been crippled by "a spirit of infirmity" (KJV) for eighteen years.

What is it like to be crippled for eighteen years of your life? I wondered as I circled the track several times one morning years ago at my nearby alma mater. (I have a chronic problem with high blood pressure, and I was following doctor's orders to exercise more consistently.) As I ran, I thought again of Joni Eareckson Tada, who in *Joni's Song* expresses her desire to do all the things I take for granted or dislike doing at times—things like scrubbing floors, making beds, even combing my own hair. And as I slowed down to a tired walk, I asked my heavenly Coach what He wanted to say to me through the story of the crippled woman.

The phrase "eighteen years" kept ringing through my mind, and I suddenly laughed aloud. Fortunately, no one was around to wonder what this strange woman was up to. I had just recognized the fact that my marriage was also eighteen years old.

Was the Lord telling me something?

Should I be laughing? I had criticized my husband that very morning because he hadn't remembered (in an off guard moment) how many years we had been married. We had eloped eighteen years earlier, keeping our marriage a secret for some time because of family problems, but often I had blamed my husband for subsequent problems. Was my critical spirit "a spirit of infirmity"?

Just the night before I had misinterpreted my husband's persistent urging to accompany him to a banquet, mistaking his concern that I "get out a little" with a selfish concern for *his* public image. Was my lack of love "a spirit of infirmity"?

I tend to back up my criticisms with "proof positive" from past incidents. (Did you hear about the man who said that every time his wife became angry, she also became historical?) Is my inability to forgive and forget "a spirit of infirmity"?

"Yes!" my Coach was saying. "You too have been crippled for eighteen years, but you can be freed, so that you can 'run and not grow weary' and 'walk and not be faint' " (Isaiah 40:31).

Review:

> Therefore I do not run uncertainly. . . . But [like a boxer] I buffet my body—handle it roughly, discipline it by hardships—and subdue it, for fear that after proclaiming to others the Gospel and things pertaining to it, I myself should become unfit—not stand the test and be unapproved—and rejected [as a counterfeit]. (1 Corinthians 9:26-27, Amplified)

BACKGROUND READING: Luke 13:11-17

BONDAGE OF SPIRIT

"So Jesus said to those Jews who had believed in Him, If you abide in My Word—hold fast to My teachings and live in accordance with them—you are truly My disciples. And you will know the truth, and the truth will set you free."
(John 8:31-32, Amplified)

Read Luke 13:10-17

I've asked the leaders of the synagogue
If God could heal my crooked back and spine,
But they've no time for me or for my pain.
I'm not descended from a worthy line.
They only care for those who fill their purses,
The wealthy who can pay the proper fee.
When Jesus speaks, compassion's in His voice.
He cares for common people just like me.
—the crippled woman

The leader or ruler of the synagogue had given permission for Jesus to speak on that life-changing day; perhaps he had even asked Jesus to speak. The ruler probably regarded Jesus as a good teacher, and he may have suggested that Jesus stress the importance of belief in the glorious kingdom of God that lay ahead some day.

POINT TO PONDER: Jesus had not come merely to speak about a future kingdom; He had come to give to men and women, crippled in many ways, the Spirit of liberty and new life. How? By releasing them from the cruel bondage of spirit to which they had been subject.

This particular lady was bent almost double and could not straighten herself. Every area of life was affected by her disability: her freedom of movement, her vision, her attitude toward other people and toward life in general.

Yes, Father, I too have been crippled by satanic forces in my life. Even the church has not been a healing influence at some times that I needed help so desperately. I need Your freeing touch on my body, soul and spirit.

20 – Tuesday

SPIRITUAL DISABILITIES

"So do not worry or be anxious about tomorrow, for tomorrow will have worries and anxieties of its own. Sufficient for each day is its own trouble." (Matthew 6:34, Amplified)

Read Matthew 6:25-34

He said we cannot change the length of life
By worrying about the number of our days;
We cannot add two inches to our height
By stretching in a million different ways.
"Seek first the kingdom, and the other things
Will then be added in their proper place!"
I've come to show obedience to His words
But, most of all, to look into His face.

—the crippled woman

The crippled woman's disability affected her freedom of movement, her vision and her attitudes. Do we realize how much our spiritual disabilities and infirmities affect us?

An unforgiving spirit can coat the roadway of our lives with a blanket of freezing rain. Tense and uptight, unable to move out of the icy clutches of resentment and bitterness, we may freeze to death or suffer the aftermath of frostbite.

Worry is fog pressing against our windshields, obscuring our vision and making progress difficult. Goals are wiped out by the fear of what could happen if . . . creativity is lost in the constant flurry of anxiety.

Guilt pollutes and poisons the atmosphere of our relationships with others. *If I found it impossible to resist temptation, how could he or she not succumb?* we ask and point the finger of blame away from ourselves.

Jesus, You forgave the very ones who killed You. You knew what lay ahead but faced it calmly, trusting Your Father. You resisted every temptation . . . and yet You understand me.

20 — Wednesday

LEADERS AND THE LAW

"And He said to them, The Son of man is Lord even over the Sabbath." (Luke 6:5, Amplified)

Read Luke 6:1-11

I've listened to their teaching all my life,
But none of them has ever taught me how
To understand God's love the way He does,
For all their emphasis on Moses and the Law.
God even knows the number of my hairs
(Though mine are thinning out)—He told us so.
God knows my needs just as He feeds the birds
And He'll provide and care for me, I know.
—the crippled woman

I remember a child-care product that came out in the '70s. Similar in appearance to a dog leash, it was intended as a restraint for a hyperactive child. Imagine that this restraint included several optional additions for different parts of the child's body. What began as a safety precaution could soon become a restricting and cruel bondage.

So it was with the Jewish system of law. God had given the Sabbath as a day of much-needed rest, but human nature had built a box around the Word and then superimposed so many additional trappings that finally the original intent could not be seen. The Pharisees, by condemning Jesus for healing on the Sabbath, were saying that God's love could not be manifested on His special day.

Have I been guilty of using God's words to suit my own purposes?

I think of the many times, Father, when I have opened up Your Word for selfish motives, just to find an easy answer to my own demanding questions. Teach me to take Your words in context, to dig, to explore, to reach out for all *of what You want to tell me.*

20 — *Thursday*

SKETCHES OF THE FUTURE

"I consider that our present sufferings are not worth comparing with the glory that will be revealed in us." (Romans 8:18)

Read Romans 8:18-27

He talked about a wedding feast to come
To which I'll be invited—what a day!
And though I often can't see in a crowd,
I know there will be nothing in my way
When that day comes! My back will then be straight
And I'll be dancing with the girls again,
The dances of our people Israel. . . .
I'll never know another hour of pain!
—the crippled woman

Joni Eareckson Tada, who sits out the dance of life in a wheelchair, has unknowingly rescued me from many hours as a self-pitying wallflower. How can I feel sorry for myself because my husband's away and I have to go to one more event alone when she's praising the Lord with her voice—and a pen held in her mouth?

Joni's searching inquiries in her first book, *Joni*, are sensitively pursued—and often answered—in her second book, *A Step Further*. Her limitations here in her temporary surroundings have made her much more cognizant of the unlimited opportunities ahead:

> The good things here are merely images of the better things we will know in heaven. It's like the artwork I produce. . . . I imitate with a gray pencil what God has painted with an infinite array of colors. My drawings, bounded by the edges of a sketch pad, can never fully portray God's boundless nature. . . . And just as my artwork pleasantly but imperfectly reflects the nature I see, so this earth that we know is only a preliminary sketch of the glory that will one day be revealed. Reality—the final painting—lies in heaven.[1]

Forgive me, Father, for getting so caught up in—really, tied down to—what appears to be reality but is just a veneer, when Your future plans for me involve "the real thing."

20 — Friday

EAGER EXPECTATION

"The creation waits in eager expectation for the sons of God to be revealed. . . . We know that the whole creation has been groaning as in the pains of childbirth right up to the present time." (Romans 8:19, 22)

Read Romans 8:18-30

And so He gives me hope to carry on
And I can live with pain until that day
(Although sometimes I feel it's killing me)—
The insults too. "Old Crooked One," they say,
But now a wedding feast for me awaits—
For me, who never was a bride?
My Lord Himself is my beloved Groom
And I will dress in white and walk with pride!
—the crippled woman

Joni says:

Suffering gets us ready for heaven. How does it get us ready? *It makes us want to go there.* . . . It moves our eyes from this world, which God knows could never satisfy us anyway, and sets them on the life to come.[2]

But suffering does more than make us want to go to heaven. It prepares us to meet God when we get there.

Just think for a moment. Suppose you had never in your life known any physical pain. How could you at all appreciate the scarred hands with which Christ will greet you? What if no one had ever hurt you deeply? How could you adequately express your gratefulness when you approach the throne of the Man of sorrows who was acquainted with grief (Isaiah 53:3)? . . .

Don't you see—when we meet Him face to face, our suffering will have given us at least a *tiny* taste of what He went through to purchase our redemption?[3]

Thank You, Father, for this insight into the meaning of suffering and how it fits into Your plan for my life.

20 — Saturday

WORTHWHILE WHEELCHAIRS

"Not only so, but we ourselves, who have the firstfruits of the Spirit, groan inwardly as we wait eagerly for our adoption as sons, the redemption of our bodies." (Romans 8:23)

Read Romans 8:31-38

He's calling me—He's really calling me!
He wants me to come to Him—I must go!
The leader's angry! I can see his face.
He fears the Master, and he hated Him so!
I know they want to catch Him in a trap;
They are so careful what they do on the Sabbath day.
Whatever happens next, He is in charge!
He is my Master, and I will obey.

—the crippled woman

> And suffering does one more thing. If in our trials we are faithful, they win for us rich rewards in heaven. "For our light and momentary troubles are achieving for us an eternal glory that far outweighs them all" (2 Corinthians 4:17). It's not merely that heaven will be a wonderful place in spite of all our sufferings while here on earth. Actually, it will be that way because of them. My wheelchair, unpleasant as it may be, is what God uses to change my attitudes and make me more faithful to Him. The more faithful I am to Him, the more rewards will be stored up for me in heaven. And so our earthly sufferings don't just aid us today; they will serve us in eternity.[4]

I've quoted Joni Eareckson Tada extensively in this chapter because I do not feel qualified to speak about human suffering in the way she can. Yet, in other ways . . . my eyes filled with tears as I read the beautiful description of her loving parents and fun-filled childhood. Hurts buried under years of life surfaced once again.

We all suffer, don't we? Each in our own way . . . but Jesus is waiting to release us from our particular "spirit of infirmity," just as He did that crippled woman so long ago.

Thank You, Father, Abba, for my adoption.

Week 21

The Adulterous Woman

It was the week of the Feast of Tabernacles, a noisy carnival of events whose spiritual meaning was often buried under the dusty feet of thousands of visitors to the Holy City and the smelly aftermath of their bleating sacrifices!

Jesus had spent the night on the Mount of Olives, probably among the noisy hodgepodge of pilgrims and animals, perhaps sleeping in the Garden of Gethsemane. Early that October morning, despairing of any further sleep, He may have risen from His uncomfortable niche and wept and prayed over His beloved city.

As He stood on the mount that overlooks Jerusalem, He not only saw the entire city, but was aware of all that was happening, including the very places where adultery was taking place under the cover of darkness.

Jesus was not surprised, then, when the Jewish leaders brought the woman caught in adultery to Him after He had walked from the Mount of Olives to the temple. He knew what had happened before they told Him, just as He knows each incident of my life and yours.

I see the woman as rebellious, young and beautiful, almost arrogant in her scorn of the hypocrites who were accusing her. She knew them and what they were—perhaps some of them had even bartered for her body—yet they were ranking "her" sin of adultery with the supreme crime of atheism: "You thought no one saw you, but Jehovah sees even in the night!" They failed to recognize the "beams of timber" (see

Matthew 7:3, Amplified) blocking their own vision as they watched for the specks of sawdust in others' eyes.

The story of Christ's meeting with this young woman reminds me of the way in which an Eastern shepherd deals with his flock's "black sheep" who will not obey him.

"He broke my leg!" said the lamb
In frustrated anger and pain.
"He broke my leg in the mountains
So I wouldn't run away again.

"Doesn't he realize I'm young?
Doesn't he know my needs?
Couldn't he teach me his lessons
In the meadows and the reeds?"

"Come," said the wise, good shepherd,
"Come, and I'll carry you till
My love has mended your bruises
Yet broken your stubborn will."

The greatest lessons are taught us
When we thoroughly fail the test.
Christ finds us, lost in the mountains,
And carries us close to his breast.

BACKGROUND READING: John 8:1-11

DAYDREAMS INTO NIGHTMARES

"Have mercy on me, O God, according to your unfailing love; according to your great compassion blot out my transgressions." (Psalm 51:1)

Read 2 Samuel 11:1-27

How I hated as they dragged me
Through the alleys and the streets,
Hated those who pulled me from him,
Pushed me roughly to my feet,
Hated him for disappearing.
Why didn't he protect me? Why?
He had promised, always promised
That he'd never let me die.

—the woman taken in adultery

Caught red-handed! Would she be stoned? Hanged? Strangled? A woman was considered to be the major offender in an act of adultery; if married, she would defile the family line by giving her husband a child that was not his. (Infidelity in a husband, however, was excusable because it had no ill effects upon the family, unless he seduced a married or betrothed woman.)

Have you ever felt "used," as this woman must have? You thought your "lover" genuinely cared about you, but all he really wanted was to gratify his own ego. You were amazed at how quickly a "beautiful relationship" turned cold.

The Old Testament story of Bathsheba graphically illustrates the way in which pleasant, "innocent" daydreams can turn into nightmares of passion and violence. Thoughts flit through our minds . . . we allow them to find a home . . . they turn into patterns of thinking . . . patterns of thinking develop into actions that, at one point, we would never have considered. King David was sightseeing when he should have been committed to his responsibilities, and adultery and murder were the results.

Thank You for reminding me, Father, that I too am involved in a war against evil, just as David should have been. Help me to identify the enemy, to be aware of his power so that I am not caught unawares.

USED AND ABUSED

"Wash away all my iniquity and cleanse me from my sin."
(Psalm 51:2)

Read 2 Samuel 12:1-23

But as I called his name aloud
Again and then again,
I suddenly realized the truth!
Like all the other men,
He didn't really care for me
He had never really cared.
Our bodies were the only love
That we had ever shared.

—the woman taken in adultery

What did this woman have to look forward to? A woman suspected of adultery was subjected to the ordeal of bitter water, described in Numbers 5:11-31. A gruesome mixture was prepared—the chief ingredient was dust from the well-traveled (by man and animal) temple floor—which she was forced to drink. If the woman became sick or suffered any swelling or side effects she was considered guilty.

If actually caught in the act of adultery, however, the woman was literally dragged to a public place and killed by stoning. Sounds unbelievably cruel, doesn't it?

We recoil from this "uncivilized" way of life, but aren't the modern, "civilized" results of adultery still cruel? Don't the families caught in the crossfire of divorce suffer just as deep emotional wounds as this woman and others like her would have? What chance do the children of divorce have for an emotionally healthy future?

Father, help me to recognize adultery for what it is . . . not a break from routine, but a broken relationship . . . not an affair, but totally unfair to the children involved . . . not fun, but sin.

21 — Wednesday

THE WAGES OF SIN

"Surely you desire truth in the inner parts; you teach me wisdom in the inmost place." (Psalm 51:6)

Read 2 Samuel 13:1-20

I guess I should have realized it
So many months before,
That satisfying his own lust
Was his goal—nothing more.
No one cares that I'm a person;
He just used me for his fun.
Men are all the same, I know it!
And I hate them, every one!

—the adulterous woman

We mentioned earlier that a man's extramarital affairs were often overlooked unless he became involved with a married or betrothed woman. Since this woman's lover was allowed to go scot-free, perhaps she was unmarried, not promised to anyone, or perhaps her betrothed (or her husband) was accusing her.

Totally alone, in a completely condemning atmosphere! Hands were already reaching out to pick up stones. The young woman must have wondered how many would tear her flesh before the welcome shroud of unconsciousness would surround her.

I too have experienced the aloneness of guilt . . . the rebellion that preceded it . . . and the terrible blackness of spirit following sin's excitement. Today's scriptural reading in Second Samuel points out the aftereffects of the passing pleasures of sin. David's family was watching the palace drama: "If it's OK for Dad, it's OK for me!" And David's son, Amnon, unlike his father, had no lasting concern at all for the woman he used. What we allow in moderation, our children may excuse in excess.

Thank You, Father, for showing me the dangers of playing around with sin.

21 — *Thursday*

THE NEED FOR INNER HEALING

"Make me to hear joy and gladness and be satisfied; let the bones which You have broken rejoice." (Psalm 51:8, Amplified)

Read 2 Samuel 13:21-39

And who is this man Jesus,
Where they're taking me just now?
Is He another judge
Who will use His manly power
To scorn me even further
In His pompousness and pride?
Would the earth could open to me
So that I could run and hide!

—the adulterous woman

What was this woman's background? A harsh, abusive father or husband? No father at all? She may have been married at one time and cast off or widowed. If so, prostitution was one of the few means of support available at that time.

POINT TO PONDER: The quality of relationships with the male members of her own family strongly influences, if not determines, the attitudes a woman will have toward other men in her life. This can also be true of her relationship with God, her heavenly Father. If her own father was loving and accepting, she will find it much easier to accept God's forgiveness of her past than the girl who grew up without acceptance or love.

Some women spend their entire lives going from one relationship to another, searching for what they never received as a child, bouncing from one hurt to the next. The slightest offense may throw them into a state of regression. David's daughter Tamar spent her life in desolation after being raped by her brother Amnon. And the snowball kept rolling, accumulating size and momentum, as it sped through the valley following David's earlier failure before God and man.

Please continue to remind me, Father, of the "fringe benefits" of sin. And thank You that I am "accepted in the beloved" (Ephesians 1:6, KJV).

21 — *Friday*

NEEDED: ATONEMENT

"Hide Your face from my sins, and blot out all my guilt and iniquities." (Psalm 51:9, Amplified)

Read Leviticus 16:5-26

Oh, their hands are rough upon me
But I see lust in their eyes,
And the ones who want to stone me
Their own double life deny.
Hypocrites! I can see through them!
And I do not care to live. . . .
Love betrayed is bitter water
And my life is like a sieve.

—the adulterous woman

The month of October (Tishri), during which time this event took place, marked the beginning of the Jewish New Year, days of splendid ceremonies and solemn processions. A young bull, a ram, seven unblemished lambs and a goat were offered to the Lord in the temple as signs of repentance for the sins of all.

The Feast of the New Year was followed by Yom Kippur, the Day of Atonement, a day full of mystery to Old Testament believers. All work ceased, everyone fasted (under penalty of death), and each person was expected to spend the day in self-examination and awareness of one's individual sins. The sixteenth chapter of Leviticus describes the way in which the high priest made atonement for himself, his household and all Israel by means of animal sacrifices on this holy day.

The woman caught in adultery had probably commemorated the Day of Atonement along with everyone else—after all, it was a national holiday. Perhaps she prayed the traditional prayer: "My God, Thy people have committed many sins . . . grant forgiveness for all faults in Thy mercy, on this day of atonement." But isn't it easy to repeat words without absorbing their meaning?

I thank You, Father, for the way in which You sent Your Son to make atonement for my sins. Help me to examine myself and to find any traces of spiritual adultery.

LOVE IS NOT THROWING STONES

"Create in me a clean heart, O God; and renew a right, persevering and steadfast spirit within me."
(Psalm 51:10, Amplified)

Reread Psalm 51

But this Man who sits before me
Has no anger in His eyes.
He is writing—is it my name?
And I watch Him slowly rise
As He says: "The one among you
Who has never sinned may throw
The first stone at this young woman."
And they all begin to go.

—the adulterous woman

The day of Atonement was followed by the Feast of Tabernacles, jubilantly celebrated by temporarily moving into little huts or booths made of branches, wherever olive groves or vineyards could be found in the area. Wine must have flowed freely, with spirits high. The dark days of introspection and penitence were over, and what had been "given up for Lent" could now be freely enjoyed. What a natural setting for an "affair"!

Was Jesus condoning, overlooking, winking at this woman's sin? Certainly not! His act of writing on the ground simply ignored the Pharisees and showed that He was not interacting with the local judicial system, at the same time pointing out their need to see the meaning behind what was written in the Law.

Jesus was saying that the one-flesh relationship of marriage required faithfulness from both women and men. Adultery not only involved hurt in the family, but injury to the soul.

Thank You, Father, for baring my heart and reminding me that it "is deceitful above all things" (Jeremiah 17:9). Please search my heart, examine my mind, purify my life. Thank You for giving me a second chance, just as You did the woman taken in adultery, but continue to remind me of Your words to her: "Go, and sin no more" (John 8:11, KJV).

Week 22

The Mother of the Blind Man

My husband's youngest brother is severely retarded, incapable of intelligible communication of any kind. The years after my father-in-law's death were difficult ones for my mother-in-law, as it was impossible for her to go anywhere (when Jeffrey was not in school) without a "baby-sitter"—and Jeffrey was no longer a cuddly baby.

During this time in our lives God gave our family a surprise bonus; I became unexpectedly pregnant with our third son. Since my mother-in-law lives next door to us, I saw Jeffrey regularly, however, and I became aware of a rash of concerns and fears regarding my unborn child, many of them probably related to my proximity to Jeffrey. Due to problems with an IUD, a doctor advised me to terminate the pregnancy while it was still "too early to matter" (his feelings, not mine).

That pregnancy was a real "sorting-out time" for me—separating my beliefs from the ones I had simply absorbed or adopted as my own, realizing that life had no pat answers. At the same time, a recent period of chastisement had both painfully cleansed my life of the past and reassured me of God's love. Now He was asking me to trust Him for the future.

"All things work together for good. . . ."
How often I've quoted those words from Romans 8:28
to someone facing a personal problem . . .
A family crisis . . . a business failure.

But when my own body shows signs of falling apart,
My husband's business is on the verge of bankruptcy,
And my mother is facing her second cancer surgery,
There are times when
Someone who has not experienced my pain
Glibly quoting Romans 8:28 in my ear—
Quite honestly,
Can make me angry.

After years of prescribing pat answers,
Through my own crises, I'm realizing that
Sometimes
It's better to hold the "appropriate words"
And cry instead with the one who hurts.
Bear her burdens with her,
Give her time to grieve,
And prove I care and share her loss.

Only then will she believe God cares
And perhaps someday—
When she's ready—
Quote Romans 8:28 on her own.

BACKGROUND READING: John 9:1-38

22 — *Monday*

BLIND SINCE BIRTH

" 'Neither this man nor his parents sinned,' said Jesus, 'but this happened so that the work of God might be displayed in his life.' " (John 9:3)

Read 2 Corinthians 6:1-10

All these years we too have suffered,
Wondering if it was our sin
That condemned our son to running
In a race he could not win.
Since he could not see, he reached out,
Tried to touch each voice he heard,
But the children all ran from him—
Left alone in his small world.

—the mother of the blind man

How do we see people with problems? Perhaps I should ask: *Do* we see people with problems? Or do we react to pain and misery with a "Somebody really ought to do something"? Do we merely step around problem situations, wishing they hadn't ruined the aesthetic beauty of the day?

People reacted in various ways to the blind man in the ninth chapter of John. Most passersby simply saw a beggar, if they saw him at all. (After all, he had been blind since birth, and therefore he had probably sat by the road begging for years.) The Pharisees viewed him as a theological issue, something they could use in their campaign against Jesus. The disciples saw him only as a sinner, and even his parents seemed to consider him a problem.

POINT TO PONDER: How do I see people with problems? Do I see them, do I intercede for them, do I reach out in a tangible way to let them know I care? Or do I simply use them in an argument with God to say to myself and others, "He can't really care," when in reality *I* don't!

There is a situation I have been ignoring, Father. You know what it is; please show me what You want me to do about it.

PURPOSES OF HEALING

"Three times I pleaded with the Lord to take it away from me. But he said to me, 'My grace is sufficient for you, for my power is made perfect in weakness.' " (2 Corinthians 12:8-9)

Read 2 Corinthians 12:1-10

Destined for a life of begging—
My dear son, my child, my own!
And was it my sin that caused it?
Or what had my husband done?
Many people pointed fingers,
Many gave advice—but none
Cared enough to weep, pray with me
Or to spend time with my son.

—the mother of the blind man

Dr. Keith Bailey, in a comprehensive treatment of healing in his book *The Children's Bread,* makes some interesting points:

> The healing of a Christian does not occur for the primary purpose of publicly certifying the power of God. A believer's healing may have a public effect, but this is incidental to the spiritual benefit the healing effects in the believer's inner life. *The purpose of God is to bring each of us into conformity with the image of His Son, the Lord Jesus Christ.* The physical healing of a Christian must be considered in this frame of reference. Often silent and unnoticed, the touch of God brings miraculous restoration to the Christian's body. The believer experiences a divine schooling while suffering physical illness.
>
> Healing comes only when the divine process is complete. Significant issues in one's life are uncovered and dealt with. Sickness in the believer can be the chastening of the Lord to bring about spiritual growth.[1]

Check my tongue, Father, when I begin to sound like a spiritual know-it-all. When I enjoy good health, let me never assume for a moment that my life is more pleasing to You than that of my sick or handicapped sister.

PURPOSES OF SUFFERING

"Who sinned, this man or his parents, that he was born blind?" (John 9:2)

Read Romans 8:15-30

I withdrew from public gatherings,
Closed my eyes to what was said,
But my son would not be sheltered
Or confined to home or bed.
Though he could not learn through seeing,
Life became an open book.
He was listening, always listening,
Undisturbed by angry looks.

—the mother of the blind man

In Jesus' day, medical practices were more superstition than science. Parents, by implication, were often blamed for the suffering of their children.

As mentioned earlier, suffering can be corrective; I classify a three-week bout with chicken pox when I was twenty-nine as a "spanking" from the Lord that I sorely needed. Suffering is also constructive; my husband was in bed with a bad back at the same time, and the Lord turned our marriage around during that "yellow-light-slow-down" period. I was ugly, he was miserable and we were both too weak to do anything but talk to each other for a whole week. And how we needed to talk!

God sometimes heals thought patterns and attitudes without healing bodies in the process. The way in which Joni Eareckson Tada has worked through her paralysis has been a means of bringing encouragement and help to many other handicapped people. Have I attempted to impart that same feeling of value to people in my life, like my legally blind friend whose husband walked away from her and their children? By standing by silently, am I not by my apathy projecting an it's-not-my-problem-you-deserved-it-somehow attitude?

May each experience I encounter, in my own life and in the lives of others, bring glory to You as I look to You for wisdom and guidance.

GOD HAS NO SECOND-CLASS CITIZENS

"As a mother comforts her child, so will I comfort you; . . . your heart will rejoice." (Isaiah 66:13-14)

Read 2 Corinthians 11:24-29

His intelligence surprised me—
So aware of everything!
He would know each neighbor's footstep,
Recognize each voice's ring.
But in spite of all his talent,
There was no one who could give
Reading skills to eyes unseeing.
He had just one way to live.

—the mother of the blind man

The heart-warming autobiography of the deaf and blind Robert J. Smithdas should be read by all who take good vision for granted. The terrifying feeling of helplessness experienced by the blind, described so vividly by Smithdas, must have been even greater in Jesus' day, when such "second-class citizens" were consigned to a life of begging. Dependent on others to lead them to a public place, they spent day after wretched day crying out for alms, vying with others to see who could attract the most attention.

The blind man could not see Jesus and he could not seek him out. He was also too poor to hire someone to find Jesus. It thrills me to know that, realizing the man's helplessness, Jesus came to him.

A baby's helplessness as we discussed earlier, does not frustrate its mother; it simply endears the child to the mother. A loving mother delights in meeting the needs of a helpless child, and our heavenly Father delights in meeting our needs. He also uses us to meet the needs of others . . . if we are willing.

I feel inadequate, Father, in the face of so many needs. Show me one small way to begin—perhaps reading to a blind person or providing transportation. Turn my apathy of inadequacy into love in action.

GOD WORKS IN MYSTERIOUS WAYS

"For I consider that the sufferings of this present time (this present life) are not worth being compared with the glory that is about to be revealed to us and in us and for us, and conferred on us!" (Romans 8:18, Amplified)

Read 2 Kings 5:1-14

One day he came home, excited!
A new Voice he'd heard that day,
A Voice that rang out with assurance:
"I am the Life, the Truth, the Way!
If you thirst, you may find water,
Not the water from Siloam,
But eternal, living water,
Water from My heavenly home."

—the mother of the blind man

Water from the Pool of Siloam was considered to have special healing properties. It was carried to the temple in a golden pitcher and used as a special offering during the Feast of Tabernacles.

Jesus sent the blind man to wash in this miraculous water—yes, but first Jesus did a strange thing, something that reminds me of the story of Naaman in the Old Testament (2 Kings 5). Naaman, the Syrian commander-in-chief, expected a dramatic healing from leprosy after he made the long trip to the home of the prophet Elisha; instead, he was told to dip in Jordan's muddy shallows seven humiliating times.

Jesus, in His encounter with the blind man, used a very commonplace agent in healing, but one that might seem offensive to us today. He spat on the ground, mixed His spittle with the clay and applied the mixture to the blind man's eyes. (Apparently this was a commonplace medicinal practice, since there was a law against such "work" on the Sabbath). *Then* Jesus sent the man to the Pool of Siloam.

Thank You, Father, for pointing out that I will not always find Your ways pleasant or inviting, for telling me that I need to leave behind my prissiness and prejudice.

22 — *Saturday*

NO FEAR IN LOVE

" 'We know he is our son,' the parents answered, 'and we know he was born blind. But how he can see now, or who opened his eyes, we don't know. Ask him. He is of age; he will speak for himself.' " (John 9:20-21)

Read Romans 8:31-39

As I listened, I feared greatly
For the safety of this Man.
I had heard the Jews would kill Him
Once they had Him in their hands.
I feared, too, for my son's safety;
In a riot he couldn't run.
So I warned him, yet I wondered,
Could this Prophet help my son?

—the mother of the blind man

Jesus did help their son, but the most surprising part of this story is the parents' attitude toward their son's healing. It seems as though fear of excommunication from Jewish life had so paralyzed them that they lost the capability for natural parental affection and, certainly, the desire to praise God.

Had all those years of public censure destroyed all traces of feeling? Or were they simply too afraid to admit their feelings? Rather than follow the Master who offered abundant life, they chose to stay within a society that provided only a small pittance, if that.

POINT TO PONDER: There is an old saying: "The good can be the enemy of the best." How often have we settled for the good, or, as in this case, for what was being portrayed (by the Pharisees) as good, when Jesus Christ was holding out to us His very best?

Help me, Father, to recognize any fears that are paralyzing my life. Help me to give them completely to You, so that my hands are empty to receive what You want to give so generously to me.

Week 23

The Widow in the Temple

The widow who gave her all is very real to me; I find that I have a clear picture of her in my mind. She was not beautiful, but she carried herself with the dignity of a queen. The day that Jesus observed her, she walked straight and tall through the crowds in the Women's Court of the temple, unashamed of the patches on her threadbare clothes, unmindful of the stones caught in the holes in her worn sandals. The always-in-a-hurry rich men pushed past her, elbowing her at times; undisturbed, she continued to make her way toward the large urns where the offerings were deposited. Hers was a sacrificial offering, but she was at peace—at peace with herself, with the world and with her God. She had given her all.

I can visualize this regal lady so well because of a similar lady in a scene etched upon the canvas of my mind. On December 27, 1983, my husband, my youngest son and I watched and listened as my mother answered a series of questions kindly and carefully posed to her by the administrator of our church nursing home which, on her doctor's recommendation, she was about to enter.

Question: "Do you own any real estate?"

Answer (smiling): "No, I do not."

Question: "Do you have any money in the bank?"

Answer: "No."

Question: "Do you have any CDs, stocks or bonds?"

Answer: "No."

Question: "Do you have any investments?"

My mother, still smiling, was about to repeat the same answer when I interrupted: "Yes! I am one, and here beside me is another growing investment . . . and there are many more!"

Poor? By the world's standards, practically penniless! By heaven's standards? Rich above measure!

BACKGROUND READING: Mark 12:41-44

23 — *Monday*

THE SACRIFICIAL GIFT— A GRATEFUL SPIRIT

"Why are you cast down, O my inner self? . . . Hope you in God and wait expectantly for Him, for I shall yet praise Him."
(Psalm 42:5, Amplified)

Read Hebrews 13:5-16

There is so little I can bring,
The smallest kind of offering,
And yet I know He understands—
It is the thought that He commends;
My wish to serve Him as I can,
To radiate His love to man.
Although my gift is very small,
He knows I'm giving Him my all.
—the widow in the temple

Over the years our ministry has been blessed by people who contribute on a regular basis. One lady in particular stands out in my mind; although she is a senior citizen on a very limited income, she contributes $2 *every* month.

Laurin's letters are as regular as her contributions. Although crippled by arthritis, she has written many times about her greatest pleasure, the children's Bible club she held in her backyard for many years. Through this children's club, parents and other adults have also come to know Laurin's Lord.

This present-day widow's contributions are just as precious to us as are larger amounts. We feel unworthy of her gift, because it is given sacrificially. As Jesus commented, "I tell you the truth, this poor widow has put more into the treasury than all the others" (Mark 12:43).

By comparison, Father, I have often given so little. Teach me to give as You gave.

23 – Tuesday

GIVING OF YOURSELF

"And if, as my representatives, you give even a cup of cold water to a little child, you will surely be rewarded."
(Matthew 10:42, TLB)

Read Mark 10:13-16

There is so little I can say
And no one listens anyway
Except perhaps the children hear.
And when I whisper in their ear
And tell them of the One who cares
And with us all His bounty shares,
Their eyes shine so, for they believe
And hold out small hands to receive.

—the widow in the temple

We have several friends to whom children are drawn as to a magnet, not by offers of candy or gum, not by a hyperactive personality, but by a steady, calm, loving interest.

One of these people is a single lady, Bev Helwig, who served as secretary to our ministry for many years. Over the years our children have dubbed her "Nanny" (shortened to "Nan" as they grew older), and she is one of the best-loved members of our family.

Not just our family, however; Bev has become "family" to many other people. Why? She is one of those people you instinctively trust. You sense almost immediately that here is a person who gives of herself, over and over and over again. We salute you, Bev!

Thank You, Lord, for the people in my life who have helped me get to where I am today.

LITTLE MINDS DREAM BIG!

"Train up a child in the way he should go [and in keeping with his individual gift or bent], and when he is old he will not depart from it." (Proverbs 22:6, Amplified)

Read 1 Samuel 3:1-19

There is so little I can do.
My work is endless and yet new!
With each new day there's more to clean
And yet the dust is always seen.
My life is full of mundane things,
But as I clean, my voice can sing
And someone listening, as he goes,
May have his heart washed white as snow.
—the widow in the temple

Another dear friend, Sally Walker, has the special gift of storytelling. I will never forget the time I took her with me to a track and field competition in which our first grader was involved. I began talking to another mother and lost track of Sally for several minutes. When I spotted her again, she was sitting on the ground with a half-circle of youngsters gathered around her, hanging on her every word as she told the story of "The Three Bears" in her own inimitable way.

The secret of Sally's success is that she is able to dream like a child, yet think like an adult. We adults sometimes forget how to dream. *Well, I'm a realist!* you may protest.

But Jesus commended the faith of a child and tells us to encourage that faith. Sally makes sure her stories are faith-building as well as entertaining. Each one contains the message of salvation, and she has led many little ones to the One to whom they truly belong.

Thank You, Jesus, for not brushing the children aside when You were here on earth. Remind me not to get so caught up in "grown-up business" that I neglect the little hearts so open to Your Word.

A QUIET SPIRIT

"Love your neighbor as yourself." (Matthew 19:19)

Read Galatians 5:13-26

There is so little I can change.
I'm sure I never will arrange
  To take a trip around the world
  Or see the nations' flags unfurled.
Perhaps I'll help my neighbor, though,
  To strike back at an unseen foe,
To calm her fears before they grow,
  To see the beauty in a rose.

—the widow in the temple

Years ago a bright-eyed lady at Chapel Pointe in Carlisle captured my attention. Her brother, Myron Bromley, was a missionary in Irian Jaya, Indonesia, but Florence Bromley was confined to a wheelchair. At one time she had traveled and spoken in many churches; but she found it necessary to sell her home and depend on strangers to take care of her. Bone cancer made a fractured pelvis almost impossible to heal.

But no complaints ever greeted me in the times I visited her. Instead, she asked me about my family and remembered the name and age of each of our sons. With bright, inquisitive eyes fixed on them, she asked questions of each one, even recalling their answers from the last visit.

"Fix your thoughts on what is true and good and right. Think about things that are pure and lovely, and dwell on the fine, good things in others. Think about all you can praise God for and be glad about" (Philippians 4:8, TLB).

Thank You, Lord, for people like Florence Bromley, who prove that age need not be senility, and pain need not be all-encompassing.

23 – *Friday*

A REVERENT SPIRIT

"Teach the older women to be reverent in the way they live, not to be slanderers or addicted to much wine, but to teach what is good." (Titus 2:3)

Read Titus 2:1-8

There is so little I can be.
These eyes are much too tired to see
The fine print by the candlelight . . .
But I have taught my son to write.
And though I'll never make them proud
By speaking to a cheering crowd,
My children call me truly blessed.
Of all rewards, that is the best.

—the widow in the temple

I will always remember our church's "Aunt Elsie." She was not an orator or author, but junior church had its own unique personality because of her influence.

Aunt Elsie has a way of inspiring kids to memorize Scripture—and enjoy it. Participation in contests was spurred on by prizes ranging from Bible markers to "real" Bibles. And then there were those promises of outings, fishing trips. . . .

Elsie's ministry was not limited to children in our church. Often a discreet phone call would inform her of a quiet need. Elsie always seemed to be the one who would round up the women of the church for important projects or special prayer times together. Her spacious but lived-in home was available when women needed a place to meet. When Elsie left our church to become part of an extension church, it seemed things were never quite the same.

But now Elsie's son, as he teaches, captivates the attention of each member of the children's church.

Thank You, Lord, for the quiet, faithful ones who serve You so well.

A SERVANT'S SPIRIT

"Work hard and cheerfully at all you do, just as though you were working for the Lord and not merely for your masters, remembering that it is the Lord Christ who is going to pay you, giving you your full portion of all he owns. He is the one you are really working for." (Colossians 3:23-24, TLB)

Read Matthew 20:25-28; 18:19-20

There is so little I can give
Except . . . I pray my life is lived
As a "sweet sacrifice of praise."
To Him my hands and heart are raised.
I do not envy those who bring
Their gold and silver offerings.
My heart is where my treasure lies—
Not on this earth, but in the skies.

—the widow in the temple

As I write, I am thinking of a dear friend who may be surprised to know that her greatest testimony to me has been her willingness to clean shower houses. Each summer the Jacobs Brothers, the evangelistic association in which our family is involved, runs a camp meeting and four-week-long children's camp. One of the most difficult jobs is getting and keeping the bathrooms clean, as you well know if you have ever served as a "flush fairy." Without being paid or asked to do it, this dear lady scrubs toilets and showers year after year in the July heat. Her major concern is not her aching legs or blistered hands, but that those stalls never seem to get clean enough.

That's not the only time of year we hear from Grace Garland. Many a time during the year our office receives little notes from her, sharing "gems of wisdom" from Sunday school teachers, her pastor or radio preachers. Once she got up at 1 a.m. to type me a letter telling me what Chuck Swindoll had just said on his radio broadcast. And Grace always assures us of her regular prayer support. I'm sure that's part of the reason we are still able to do the ministry to which God has called us.

Thank You, Lord, for Your gift of Grace . . . and for the many others like her who work behind the scenes.

Week 24

Martha of Bethany

We of the Christian community have gotten ourselves into trouble because we have let the world push us into its hospitality mold. We call having company "entertaining," and that is what too many of us do. We have company to display our abilities (culinary or otherwise), to build up our egos (bigger and better than the Joneses) and to pay our social debts (we have to have them because they had us). In this framework, entertaining can become a pain in the neck at best, and for many it becomes a form of sheer torture.[1]

Well said, Vivian Anderson Hall!

May I suggest that when we keep the commandment to be witnesses, we share with others what we know about God's love; and when we keep the commandment to be hospitable, we express God's love by sharing what we have. God never asks His children to do the impossible, but He tells us to be hospitable. Therefore, we who have accepted God's love have the ability to share what we have with the people God sends into our lives at the time He chooses to send them. And that is obeying the hospitality commandment.

The skills that make this obedience to the hospitality commandment easier are skills that can be learned. I was fortunate to learn many of the skills in my childhood. But I have adult Christian friends who minister effectively in the area of hospitality, yet they had very little opportunity to practice hospitality in their parental homes. It is never too late to learn how to keep God's commandment to be "given to hospitality" or to become more effective as we keep this commandment.

If you do not have the "gift of hospitality," do not worry about it—just begin to share what you have with those God sends into your life at the time that He sends them. When you do this, sooner or later someone will say to you, "Oh, but it's easy for you to have company. You have the gift of hospitality!"[2]

Now we begin a visit with Mary and Martha, the two sisters from the little town of Bethany, suburb of Jerusalem. Certainly Martha had the "gift of hospitality"—or did she? After reading the preceding excerpts from Vivian Anderson Hall's book *Be My Guest*, would you call Martha's efforts "hospitality" or "entertaining"? Think of how you would describe your own reactions to the words "Company's comin'!"

BACKGROUND READING: Please take time to read Luke 10:38-42 carefully . . . and prayerfully.

24 – Monday

BOTHERSOME BURDENS

"Come to Me, all you who labor and are heavy-laden and over burdened. . . ." (Matthew 11:28, Amplified)

Read Ephesians 4:28-32

Sure, I'd like to sit down
And relax a little while—
But when there's so much work to do,
I can't sit there and smile!
Mary's satisfied to listen
And just look into His face,
But I fall asleep each time
I try to slow down from this pace.
—Martha

Most of us know what it is to labor, to be heavily laden and overburdened with pressing weights. We also realize that there are times in our lives when even a light load feels unbearable because it is the proverbial "last straw" that seems to break our backs.

It seems that Martha was alone, single or widowed, and she probably carried a heavy burden with her all the time. Perhaps she saw each servant as one more person for whom she was responsible, instead of as a helping hand to lighten the load. Her sister Mary, who could have been her closest friend, became a thorn in the flesh.

POINT TO PONDER: "Irritation is a signal I need to change." Those words pierced my consciousness at some point—when or where I'm not sure. I reacted negatively at first to the statement, but on second thought . . . on second thought . . .

Father, is there something in my life that needs to change? Is my schedule too hectic for the sake of my family? Do I have enough time for my relationship with You?

24 — Tuesday

SARCASTIC SISTER

"My yoke is . . . not . . . hard . . . but . . . pleasant. . . ."
(Matthew 11:30, Amplified)

Read Exodus 15:20-21; Numbers 12:1-16;
Deuteronomy 24:8-9

After all, who'd do the work
If I didn't keep on going?
Lazarus throws his things around
And Mary's never doing
What I think she should be
And the servants must be told.
Can I help it if I worry, fret
And sometimes even scold?
—Martha

The yoke mentioned in the preceding verse has several meanings, one of which was particularly suited to the many farmers who listened to Jesus' words. A yoke was a wooden frame or bar with loops at either end that were fitted around the necks of a pair of oxen. This harnessed them together and facilitated (as well as forced) their working together.

Your family members are also yoked together—for life—and they are often not people you would have chosen to be linked to! Family relationships often become frustrating simply because irritations have built up over so many years. The problem is that you may find you can never get away from family members. You will see them at holiday activities, at funerals, at weddings, perhaps for the rest of your life!

Yes, Martha was irritated with her sister, just as you may find that being with someone in your family creates tension in you. (Have you ever stopped to consider that perhaps you have the same effect on that family member?) And yet you may really love that person—and other people tell you she is simply the greatest!

Thank You, Father, for being the Lord of the impossible. Thank You that there is no lock for which You do not have the key.

24 — Wednesday

GET IN TUNE!

"My yoke is . . . not . . . sharp . . . but . . . gracious. . . ."
(Matthew 11:30, Amplified)

Read Psalm 96

Well, I guess I scold quite often
When I'm feeling tired and blue.
It just seems that there is always
So much more than I can do!
Why do I get so frustrated
While my sister seems so calm?
Yet I know that she feels guilty
And she never means me harm.
—Martha

Another meaning of the word "yoke" is an arch (as a "yoke of spears") under which the conquered were forced to pass in ancient times; hence, a yoke can mean any mark or symbol of bondage or servitude. How difficult it is to serve our "trying family member"!

POINT TO PONDER: Instruments do not make sweet music unless they are in tune with one another. No matter how great their commitment to one another, people cannot communicate with one another unless they are sensitive to one another's needs; people too must "tune up." And many times we rush into the presence of Almighty God, signal an emergency request in our noisy "hoarse code" (we talk to everyone else first) and rush out again . . . without ever taking time to become attuned to His presence.

We are Jesus' love slaves. His yoke is gracious; He does not force us to do His will. We are given the choice, but so often the "tyranny of the urgent" takes hold, and we neglect the things we know are most important for the demands that scream the loudest.

Forgive me, Father, for rushing through Your gates without thanksgiving, for noisily entering Your courts with complaints instead of praise. Teach me to sit at Your feet.

WHAT'S MY MOTIVATION?

"My yoke is . . . not harsh . . . but comfortable. . . ."
(Matthew 11:30, Amplified)

Read Isaiah 30:15-29

I too want to serve the Master
And I serve as best I can
But I guess I overdo it when
He comes here with His men.
I wouldn't need so many flowers
I could serve a simpler meal . . .
But I want it all just perfect!
Does He know the way I feel?
—Martha

Are you a perfectionist? I think Martha was. Everything had to be "just right." Jesus' coming to Bethany should have been a time of great rejoicing, yet for Martha it was preceded by tension, pressure, the big push to get every corner sparkling clean, every flower picture-perfect, every dish cooked to perfection.

So how did Martha handle the resulting tension? How do we handle the tension in our lives? Often not very well at all. Perhaps it would be easier to prevent it.

POINT TO PONDER: Let's analyze our lifestyles. How much of our rushing around is actually necessary? How much of what we do is consciously or subconsciously motivated by an effort to impress others? Is "making a good impression" what Christ would have us do, or is it simply a carnal desire? What are my true motivations?

Thank You for reminding me, Father, that strength is to be found in quietness, in time spent at Your feet. Please nudge me from time to time when I forget that hospitality is sharing and serving, not keeping count or showing off.

ENCUMBERED AND CAPTIVE

"My yoke is wholesome (useful, good)—not . . . pressing."
(Matthew 11:30, Amplified)

Read Psalm 39

You see, I want to please Him
As I know my sister does
But my best is never good enough.
I guess that is because
I'm not happy with myself,
I'm so tired of rushing 'round.
I've never learned the way of life
I know my sister's found.
—Martha

The King James Version tells us that Martha was "cumbered about much serving . . ." (Luke 10:40). The original meaning of the word "cumber" is "to draw away or distract." Martha was occupied with things that were good in themselves, but she was overoccupied to the point that it distracted her mind and spirit and drew her away from her Lord. The Living Bible simply says that Martha was "the jittery type."

The Martha in me started feeling very jittery one morning some years ago as I looked around and saw everything that needed to be done. Our family had just returned from a rainy camping weekend, preceded by a Saturday wedding. Two brand-new pairs of white slacks had stain combinations of trumpet-valve oil, grape juice, grease, fruit salad and mud. In addition, of course, there was the regular wash. The house needed a thorough cleaning since my husband had been tearing apart (and *slowly* putting back together) the bathroom for the past four weeks—a necessary measure before the tub fell into the basement. To add the last straw, my vacuum cleaner died noisily in a farewell cloud of dust, and I was left with my mother's antique cleaning device.

And our office needed help and a book deadline was looming. Yes, Martha, I felt jittery too—and you didn't have three kids!

Lord, I feel very much encumbered . . . but Your yoke is not pressing, You say? Have I created this yoke that presses down so harshly on my neck?

24 — *Saturday*

SHARING OR SHOWING OFF?

"Lord, don't you care that my sister has left me to do the work by myself? Tell her to help me!"
"Martha, Martha . . . you are worried and upset about many things, but only one thing is needed." (Luke 10:40-42)

Read Psalm 91

His words may sound like a rebuke
But His voice told me He cared
And that He appreciated
All the food I had prepared
And the other work I'd done—
He knew it was for Him.
But He wants me just to rest with Him
As the lights are growing dim.
—Martha

"It's just not fair!" Martha burst into the dining area where the disciples were resting, catching one more glimpse of her sister Mary, who was oblivious to everything but Jesus' voice. Perhaps Martha had rejected Mary's ideas for a much simpler meal that could have been prepared earlier in the day, enabling all of them to enjoy the evening together.

Did it happen that way? Or was that a rerun of you or me as we "tensed up" after a hectic day of preparing for guests—guests who simply wanted to spend time with us and enjoy our companionship?

POINT TO PONDER: Entertainment is showing off . . . hospitality is sharing. Entertainment is keeping count . . . hospitality is serving. Entertainment is the tenseness of perfectionism . . . hospitality is living and loving and laughing and learning.

Help me to remember, Jesus, that You are the most important Guest of all.

Week 25

Mary of Bethany

Jesus was a Jew, "born of a woman, born under law" (Galatians 4:4). He was nurtured in a Jewish home, attended the synagogue on the Sabbath and worshiped at the temple. His teachings draw heavily on the Jewish Scriptures. And so in these ways He maintained continuity with His past.

But whatever else may be said of Jesus, He was not conventional. Shortly after the beginning of His earthly ministry, He was bodily evicted from His home synagogue. Even Jesus' family did not understand Him and was not fully supportive during His lifetime. Even His closest friends, the Twelve, lagged behind, at times openly opposing Him. And His ministry ended in crucifixion by the Romans—and His own people.

In many ways, Jesus crossed the orthodox, well-established lines of behavior. His followers struggled, caught in a tug-of-war between the pull of their Lord's example and the push of the world in which they lived.

It may not be so obvious to us that the familiar story of the two sisters illustrates Jesus' unconventional, freeing behavior. Why *shouldn't* Jesus encourage Mary to sit at His feet, listening attentively to His words? Today's woman asks: Why *shouldn't* a woman be included in a theological discussion with males?

> Jewish women were not permitted to touch the Scriptures; and they were not taught the Torah itself, al-

though they were instructed in accordance with it for the proper regulation of their lives. A rabbi did not instruct a woman in the Torah. Not only did Mary choose the good part, but Jesus related to her in a teacher-disciple relationship. He admitted her into "the study" and commended her for the choice.

A Torah-oriented role for women was not unprecedented in Israel . . . but the drift had been away from it. First, women were excluded from the altar-oriented priestly ministry, then the exclusion encroached upon Word-oriented ministry for women. Jesus reopened the Word-ministry. Mary was at least one of his students in theology.

The story vindicates Mary's rights to be her own person. It vindicates her right to be Mary and not Martha. It vindicates a woman's right to opt for the study and not be compelled to be in the kitchen.

Luke's story of Jesus in the home of Martha and Mary puts him solidly on the side of the recognition of the full personhood of woman, with the right to options for her own life. In "socializing" with both sisters and in defending Mary's right to a role then commonly denied a Jewish woman, Jesus was following his far-reaching principle of human liberation.[1]

BACKGROUND READING: Psalm 139

SEPARATION OF THE SEXES

"Take my yoke upon you and learn from me." (Matthew 11:29)

Read Judges 4:4-14

The Rabbi says the Torah
Is only for the men.
They've said that it is better
To destroy or burn it than
To teach it to a woman!
But I know He wouldn't agree. . . .
He has time for men and *women.*
He has time for even me.

—Mary

In Old Testament times women played a part in the religious life of Israel. Moses' older sister Miriam—the first cheerleader!—led the people in praise; her advice was probably highly respected by Moses. (After all, she had saved his life!) In this section you will find a background reading about Deborah, one of Israel's judges. Another reading, about Huldah the prophetess, points out the value in asking a woman's counsel when her words come from the Lord. Even the king of Judah accepted a warning of impending disaster from Huldah without question. (Much more information about Old Testament women is included in my first book, *They Were Women Too.*)

In the period between the Old and New Testaments, however, women's religious privileges were curtailed. Why? At least partially because of Israel's increasingly closer ties with the surrounding heathen nations.

In their intriguing and informative book *Woman in the World of Jesus,* Evelyn and Frank Stagg mention the presence of "sacred prostitutes" in the fertility cults so popular in Canaan. Baal, mentioned over and over in the Old Testament, was the god of rain, storm and fertility, and prostitution was involved in his worship. Gradually woman began to be seen more and more as the embodiment of temptation; the simplest solution to the problem was to keep the sexes separated.

Thank You, Jesus, for commending Mary for daring to go against tradition and to sit at Your feet.

25 — Tuesday

INADEQUACY STRIKES AGAIN

"Find rest . . . blessed quiet—for your souls."
(Matthew 11:29, Amplified)

Read 2 Kings 22:8-20; 2 Chronicles 34:14-29

For years I've watched my sister
As she hustles to and fro,
But no matter how I try,
I will never be a pro
At the endless list of duties
She performs with skill and ease.
And her work will never end
And her labors never cease.

—Mary

Perhaps you're one of those people who seem to do everything well, or perhaps you're one who sometimes stands back and watches the person with the "Midas touch" as everything under her fingers turns to gold. Mary, probably Martha's younger sister (possibly the house belonged to Martha), may have felt very inadequate beside her efficient sister.

What to do when you're tempted to say, "I just can't do that!" or "I could never learn to do that!": Use your feelings of inadequacy to draw you closer to the One who said brokenly, "If it is possible, may this cup be taken from me. Yet not as I will, but as you will" (Matthew 26:39).

I am *not* advising taking on more than you can handle. Many children have been terribly cheated of what they really needed in life—love and time—because their well-meaning parents spread themselves too thin. But if God is asking you to be a Huldah (2 Kings 22:14), don't let Him down by lamenting, "Why did He ask me to do that? I can't!" Have you prayed about it? Have you taken the chance of failing—and tried?

If at first I don't succeed, Father, help me to put my pride aside and try again—after I've spent time at Your feet.

25 — Wednesday

MARYS AND MARTHAS

"Find rest . . . recreation . . . for your souls."
(Matthew 11:29, Amplified)

Read Psalm 84

Oh, I've tried to be just like her
But there's something deep inside
That draws me to a quiet place
Where I can sit beside
A rippling stream, unfolding flower
And think on things He's said.
If I don't stop to think and pray
My heart grows cold and dead.
—Mary

All of us have days when we long to put our work aside and simply enjoy the beauties of God's great outdoors, but a Mary wants more than that. She desires to hear a still, small voice echoed in the call of a bird. She wants to feel His touch in the caress of the summer breeze. She looks for God in everything about her.

Marthas often don't understand the Marys' deep yearnings. They are unsympathetic to Mary's need for privacy, quiet times alone. Martha sees Mary as impractical, a disorganized visionary who never gets anything really important accomplished. And Marys tend to feel smugly spiritual, privately putting down their efficient counterparts as "somewhat shallow."

POINT TO PONDER: What does God want of us? At one time I saw two separate classes, the Marys and the Marthas, and "never the twain shall meet." But wait a minute! God created both Mary and Martha, and He loves them both! Maybe Mary needs to serve a little more so that Martha has more time to sit at Jesus' feet; maybe that will help Martha to sense her need to do so.

Help me, Father, to recognize the supernatural in the midst of the mundane.

YOUR SPECIAL GIFT

"You will find rest for your souls." (Matthew 11:29)

Read Psalm 143

And yet I feel so guilty
As my sister's work goes on.
My mother always told me,
"Women's work is never done!"
I want to be responsible,
I want to do my part
But I know that I must follow
The leadings of my heart.

—Mary

Yes, Marys need to learn to serve. Those who sit at Jesus' feet should be the first to sense His desires, and Jesus always reached out to others. But there are different ways of reaching out. Martha next door may be a pro at taking hot casseroles to someone who is sick, and the Martha up the street may be able to put together the cheeriest little centerpiece to grace the table of a senior citizen, but maybe your desserts always seem to flop and your centerpieces always resemble the Leaning Tower of Pisa. What then?

I have a dear friend who has a "card ministry." She spends many hours on Saturdays finding just the perfect card for someone in the hospital, someone convalescing at home, someone experiencing her first Mother's Day as a mother, someone moving into a new home—I could go on and on! That's Bev's ministry, and I guarantee the Lord has one handpicked for you. Ask Him about it, and then watch for opportunities to use your gift.

When you feel the thrill of serving someone else by using your special gift—whether it's cleaning their house, writing a poem or offering yourself as chauffeur—you'll be hooked! But remember, for service to be effective, it must be preceded by time with the most creative Person of all, the Creator of all that is beautiful and good.

Thank You, Father, for my gift. Free me to use it freely and well, so that it will glorify You.

25 — Friday

A WOMAN OF WORTH

"Find rest . . . refreshment . . . for your souls."
(Matthew 11:29, Amplified)

Read Psalm 27:4-14

I know that He is coming soon
But Martha needs me now.
I yearn to see the Master
And hear His words of power.
The Master! He's exhausted
From walking in this heat.
He'll need some water, towels
To soothe His tired feet.

—Mary

In *Woman Liberated,* Lois Gunden Clemens points out Christ's freeing relationship with women:

> While Judaism excluded woman from the study of the Torah, Christ opened to women and men alike the way to the knowledge of God. His call to salvation recorded in Matthew 11:28-30 was for all who were weary and heavily burdened. This certainly was a welcome invitation to the women of His day. In placing personal salvation within the sphere of the individual, He showed no distinction between man and woman. . . . He commended Mary of Bethany for sitting at His feet to hear His word, an act unheard of for a woman in that time. . . . Jesus saw woman's worth as residing in her own person, rather than in her relation to man.[2]

As Paul puts it in his letter to the Galatians, "There is neither Jew nor Greek, slave nor free, male nor female, for you are all one in Christ Jesus" (3:28).

Thank You, Jesus, for caring enough about Mary to liberate her from the social traditions of her day. Help me not to be tied up in knots about similar contemporary issues.

25 — *Saturday*

A NEW CREATION

"Find rest . . . ease . . . for your souls."
(Matthew 11:29, Amplified)

Read Psalm 103

He understands my deepest needs,
He looks into my heart!
He even said I'd chosen,
In His words, "that good part!"
The rabbi may deny us
The study of the Word,
The Master is the living Word.
My Master and my Lord.

—Mary

I believe that when Jesus put His stamp of approval on Mary's life, Mary was released from whatever self-doubt she may have lived with up to that point. If there had been years of comparing herself unfavorably with her capable sister, the comparison ended that day, never to haunt her again.

Are you ready to stop living under the clouds of insecurity, waiting for them to burst again and again? Are you ready to step out from under them and proclaim, "I can! I can do anything Christ asks me to do because He will give me strength and wisdom! I am a *new* creation; the old is gone, and this is the first day of the rest of my life!"

Remember, Jesus' yoke fits perfectly because it has been uniquely designed with only one person in mind. Unlike "designer jeans," it adjusts as I grow.

Thank You, Father, for Your perfect plan for imperfect me!

Week 26

Martha Misunderstands

Do you remember Mary, who poured the costly perfume on Jesus' feet and wiped them with her hair? Well, her brother Lazarus, who lived in Bethany with Mary and her sister Martha, was sick. So the two sisters sent a message to Jesus, telling him, "Sir, your good friend is very, very sick."

But when Jesus heard about it he said, "The purpose of this illness is not death, but for the glory of God. I, the Son of God, will receive glory from this situation."

Although Jesus was very fond of Martha, Mary and Lazarus, he stayed where he was for the next two days and made no move to go to them. Finally, after the two days he said to his disciples, "Let's go to Judea. . . . Lazarus is dead. And for your sake, I am glad I wasn't there, for this will give you another opportunity to believe in me. Come, let's go to him." . . .

When they arrived at Bethany, they were told that Lazarus had already been in his tomb for four days. (John 11:1-7, 14-17, TLB)

It is easy for us to look back from a Monday-morning quarterback perspective and say, "Why didn't the disciples understand what Jesus was going to do? Why didn't Martha believe in His resurrection power?" But what if you or I had been there that day in Bethany? Would we have understood? Probably, almost surely, not!

I can visualize Martha's state of mind by this time; disappointed in the Master, disillusioned with His lack of power and concern, despondent with grief and the burden of work and funeral responsibilities. I can imagine her feelings quite easily because I have had days like that. Haven't you?

I have a special poem that I call my "Selfish Song." I allow myself to sing it on days when I'm exhausted.

What do you do when there's no more of you?
Where do you go when you don't know what to do?
Your head is swimming—seems you don't know your name
And you don't want to play one more silly little game.
Go away, people! I don't wanna smile
I just want to be at the end of the mile,
Away from this busy life that I lead,
Away from fulfilling another person's need.
Where do you go when you don't know what to do?
What do you do when there's no more of you?

BACKGROUND READING: John 11:1-30

26 – Monday

PURPOSE: PATIENCE

"Consider it pure joy . . . whenever you face trials of many kinds. . . ." (James 1:2)

Read Psalm 43

Where were You when we needed You?
  How could You let us down?
We waited for Your coming
  Despite reproving frowns.
He waited for You too, my Lord,
  Although he could not speak
When all his strength had disappeared
  And fever reached its peak.
—Martha

"You'll never learn patience until you grow up and have children of your own!" As my mother's words rang in my ears, I muttered to myself, "What does she mean? I'm already patient!"

My mother's words still ring in my ears. When I became the mother of teenagers, her words took on a whole new meaning. As our older sons constantly stretched my horizons, our youngest son took my hand and pulled me back to a child's world. Three different sets of school activities—three different baseball teams one year—made scheduling and transportation a constant hassle, not to mention Dad's ever-changing itinerary. When did Mom have time to be a person?

But all these daily priority decisions that often put Mom's preferences on the back burner do have a way of developing Mom's patience—just as *her* mom predicted. And, although many days I still feel light-years away from the kind of person I really want to be, I realize at least a slow growth in character.

But wait a minute—we're supposed to be talking about Martha! It seems Martha had a problem with patience, and now, as she hurried out to confront Jesus, her impatience was compounded by hurt misunderstanding.

As I see purpose in trials, Father, I can thank You for them. Help me to thank You, by an act of the will, even when I see no purpose.

26 – Tuesday

HER FRIEND FAILED HER

"The testing of your faith develops perseverance." (James 1:3)

Read Psalm 69:13-17; 70:1-5

He wouldn't have died if You had come,
Come when we sent for You.
We gave You time to get here, Lord,
An extra day or two.
We know this area's dangerous,
But how Your heart must bleed!
Why didn't You come and save His life?
O Lord, You knew our need!
—Martha

Martha's Friend, her powerful Friend, had failed Lazarus and let her down. Why hadn't He come when she had called? Why hadn't things gone as she had hoped and prayed they would? Where had Jesus been when she needed Him?

I understand Martha's feelings. I remember the day I found out my mother had cancer and needed immediate surgery. I remember sitting out in my front yard that night, feeling like I wanted to throw rocks at the silent sky. *Why her, Lord, after all she's already been through? What possible reason can You have for this?* Like Martha, my impatience of spirit was complicated by hurt and anger at the "unfairness" of it all.

God didn't immediately answer the questions I hurled at Him that night, but neither did He strike me down with a bolt of lightning. Instead He gave me strength (and good weather throughout the month of December) to take my mother for twenty-five radiation treatments. As my youngest son and I took "Pukah" (the boys' nickname for their grandma) to Harrisburg each morning during that Christmas season, I realized God's greatest gift of all—His love—was alive and well in my mother's heart. No anger, no resentment, no bitterness tinged the joy of the season for her, and as she radiated her heavenly Father's love to the others in the hospital waiting room, my spirit was also touched and healed.

Thank You again, Father, for the trials.

26 – *Wednesday*

HEAD KNOWLEDGE OR HEART KNOWLEDGE

"Perseverance must finish its work so that you may be mature and complete, not lacking anything." (James 1:4)

Read Romans 4:16-25

But yet I know that even now
Whatever You may ask
Of God, our God in Heaven,
Is but an easy task.
I do believe Your power
Is greater than we know.
You could have healed our brother,
Your love and power showed.
—Martha

Martha had faith in Jesus' power, but her faith was limited by what she understood. She believed (head knowledge) that Jesus could heal, even that He had resurrection power, but her heart did not confirm Jesus' power to raise her brother from the grave. In one breath she stated that God would give Jesus anything He asked; with the next breath she limited God's resurrection power to a future time, the resurrection at the last day.

POINT TO PONDER: Head knowledge is very different from heart knowledge. The excitable servant girl Rhoda joined in prayer for the Apostle Peter's release from prison (Acts 12:12-17) but then left Peter—the answer to prayer—still knocking for entry at the door while she ran to spread the good news of his release. Rather a cold welcome! Have you ever prayed about a seemingly hopeless situation, then been surprised and even unbelieving when the answer to your prayer came?

Why does this happen? Because we try to fit God into our timetable, our schedules of living. Like little children, we want our demands fulfilled *now*! But God's thoughts are not our thoughts; His ways are not our ways (Isaiah 55:8). We must learn to set our watches by His time.

Thank You for telling me about Martha and Rhoda, who are so much like me. Teach me to wait.

26 – *Thursday*

MARY AND THE MOURNERS

"If any of you lacks wisdom, he should ask God, who gives generously to all without finding fault, and it will be given to him." (James 1:5)

Read Romans 10:5-17

You are the Resurrection!
  You're Life personified!
I understand that, Lord,
  And I am satisfied.
Lazarus will rise again
  On Resurrection Day.
I'll go and call my sister
  To meet You on the way.
—Martha

Martha had heard Jesus teach many times. Probably, since Jesus' gentle rebuke to her in her home, she had put aside her work and listened more carefully. She knew Jesus' identity; she knew Him as the Christ, the Son of God. Now that she had aired her feelings and had satisfied herself that Jesus was aware of the situation, she was content to go back home and to tell Mary, still among the mourners, that the Master had arrived and was asking for her.

Isn't it interesting that Mary was still among the mourners? Martha had grown tired of the traditional weeping and wailing that went on for days in a vivid demonstration of grief, but Mary seemed to sit stupefied, paralyzed by the intensity of their loss. Martha had probably found out from the servants that Jesus was on His way, but Mary was not able to slip back into the normal patterns of life. She sat among the mourners until she heard that Jesus was coming.

And just as He understood Martha's angry impatience, Jesus understood Mary's paralysis of grief.

Thank You, Jesus, that just as You understood these totally different personalities, You also understand me . . . and *my annoying family member.*

26 – Friday

THE PAUSE THAT BLESSES

"We know that the one who raised the Lord Jesus from the dead will also raise us with Jesus and present us with you in his presence." (2 Corinthians 4:14)

Read 2 Corinthians 4:13-18

I didn't understand until
The stone was rolled away—
That huge, cold block between
Our night and glorious day.
I wanted to believe the Lord
And leave my doubts behind
But a boulder, too, had split my heart.
A stone had blocked my mind.
—Martha

Martha had called Mary, and then with her usual quickness of movement had returned to the tomb to satisfy her natural curiosity and find out what was happening. (Don't you just love Martha?) Probably she got there just a little ahead of Mary and watched as Mary approached with her train of mourners.

Or perhaps Martha stopped in the kitchen first to supervise lunch preparations and approached just in time to see Jesus' eyes fill with tears as He saw the entrance to the tomb where His friend Lazarus lay. Perhaps she was impressed with a new realization of Jesus' humanity, although just minutes earlier she had called Him the Son of God. This God-man who so obviously loved her brother—what was He going to do?

The weeping and nose-blowing came to a sudden stop as Martha and the mourners realized that something was about to happen.

Thank You, Jesus, for not being bound by my limitations of doubt.

LIMITING THE LORD

"Jesus said to her, Did I not tell you and promise you that if you would believe and rely on Me, you should see the glory of God?" (John 11:40, Amplified)

Read Mark 9:14-32

But when He said, "Remove the stone!"
I realized Jesus' plan—
Yet even then I couldn't trust
This Friend who was God-man.
"The smell, my Lord—four days entombed!
You can't do this, my Lord!"
But Jesus' words cut through my doubt
As with a two-edged sword.
—Martha

Martha's protest was probably almost involuntary, a protest born out of shock at this defiance of conventionality. Remove a dead, smelly body from a tomb? Perhaps she imagined Jesus would have to pray over her brother's mummified body while everyone watched . . . and whispered . . . and held their noses.

Just as we take our family members and their abilities for granted, so Martha limited the Christ she loved by her familiarity with Him. She had still not made a complete break with her old nature, and quick-thinking, quick-acting, quick-tongued Martha had to receive one more gentle rebuke.

"Did I not tell you that if you believed, you would see the glory of God?"

Lord, "I do believe; help me overcome my unbelief!" (Mark 9:24).

Week 27

Mary . . . at His Feet Again

Mary was immobilized by the paralysis of grief. Those of us who have not experienced its pangs in a close, personal situation find it easy to sympathize during the week of a funeral, but more difficult to empathize during the following weeks and months. Grief heals within different lengths of time for different people, but it's important to recognize that, at bare minimum, grief takes six months to a year to begin to heal.

In crisis situations we could say that our minds and bodies go on "automatic pilot," while our emotions do one of two things, depending on how easily we express or repress our emotions. A family we know lost their mother in a tragic explosion in their home. One child screamed for fifteen minutes when the news was broken to her; another child retreated into silence.

Martha probably threw herself into almost frantic activity immediately after Lazarus' death. Conversely, Mary's "automatic pilot" dictated a frozen numbness, oblivious to all that was happening around her.

Let us be very sensitive to the mourner, the one who grieves. Let us not criticize a Martha for her seeming insensitivity or a Mary for her temporary stupor. Each person deals with grief in his or her own way.

The following poem is dedicated to my brother and sister-in-law, John and Shirley Jacobs, whose four-year-old Matthew was hit and killed on a busy street corner after a Wednesday night prayer service.

Take time to grieve, dear brother.
Our heavenly Father understands.
His great heart yearned in anguish too
When His Son died.

Take time to grieve, dear brother.
God does not frown upon our tears.
He does not ask us to suppress
Emotions lying deep within.

The love we feel, He planted there.
The grief we feel, He knows.
And so, dear brother,
Take time to grieve.

But then rejoice, dear brother,
As sunshine follows storm.
We have that blessed hope;
We know we'll meet again.

BACKGROUND READING: John 11:31-46

27 – Monday

THE PARALYSIS OF GRIEF

"Weeping may endure for a night, but joy comes in the morning." (Psalm 30:5, Amplified)

Read Psalm 30

At one time I was frightened
To face the outside world;
I couldn't confront the fiery darts
That Satan at me hurled.
But sitting at the Master's feet
And looking in His face
Has given me a whole new life,
My doubts and fears erased,
Yet Lazarus' death was such a blow—
I couldn't face the pain
I sat among the mourners,
Tried to smile again in vain.

—Mary

Have you ever had a "mountaintop experience"? Perhaps you attended a weekend retreat where hearts were touched and lives changed through the purifying power of the Word. You felt uplifted, refreshed, transformed! Then you came home, and your mountaintop turned into a mountain of laundry, your "holy ground" became dirty floors and your spirit wilted along with your unwatered plants.

Mary may have felt transformed and liberated by Jesus' love, but I think she probably shared Martha's lack of understanding in the face of Jesus' seeming unconcern for Lazarus' sickness. After all, didn't He love Lazarus too?

I remember sharing a day with a close friend, the day that had brought the news of her husband's sudden death. Ava did not cry or scream hysterically; like Mary, she sat numbed and paralyzed by the cruel blow. No matter how strong our faith in Christ's power, grief is momentarily overwhelming. Grief takes time to work through—take time to grieve.

Thank You, Father, for the mountaintops . . . and thank You as well for the refining valleys that teach us compassion, so that we learn to comfort others as You have comforted us (2 Corinthians 1:4).

27 — Tuesday

THE PRESSURE OF GRIEF

"We take captive every thought to make it obedient to Christ."
(2 Corinthians 10:5)

Read John 21:15-19

When Martha told me He was
On His way to Bethany,
I knew the question I must ask;
I knew He'd answer me.
There was no question in my mind
Of whether I should meet
The Master; He was here at last!
I fell down at His feet.

—Mary

"Our thoughts are our conversation with God." I felt almost stunned the first time I heard—*really* heard!—that statement. Not the words I carefully formulate into a proper prayer meeting supplication, not the emergency signal I flash skyward, but each one of the thoughts I carelessly entertain comprises my daily dialogue with Almighty God!

At 6:30 in the morning on a Memorial Day Monday I walked along the pier at Sandy Cove Bible Conference in Maryland and was amazed at the strange collection of items that had been washed up on that shore: a broken ladder, rusty cans, a toy rubber spoon with a faded smiley face, a tampon case, three dead (smelly) fish and a mammoth tree stump. A phrase from Scripture, memorized years earlier, came to my mind: "lest . . . I myself should be a castaway" (1 Corinthians 9:27, KJV).

What was God saying to me that quiet, misty morning? That He can change the flow of the unpredictable thought currents that sometimes trickle across, sometimes dramatically flood my mind. Only He can filter out the pollution with His Word until the flow becomes refreshing and invigorating. And as He once waited for Peter beside the Sea of Galilee, He waits to walk along the lonely shorelines with us and ask that same question: "Do you truly love me more than these?" (John 21:15).

Father, take captive every thought. Bring my thought patterns and attitudes under Your control . . . and then my actions will please You.

27 — Wednesday

THE PANGS OF GRIEF

"Jesus wept." (John 11:35)

Read Hebrews 4:14-5:10

"If You had been here, Master,
Lazarus wouldn't have died!"
I raised my eyes to meet His . . .
And He gently, softly cried
As if to say, "It's all right—
I understand your grief."
He asked me where the body lay;
His words were tear-filled, brief.
—Mary

Mary was at His feet again, but this time she was weeping, and, in response, "Jesus wept." Two short words, but what a world of meaning they hold! Recognized as the shortest verse in the Bible, those two words tell us more than pages of narrative. "He was deeply moved in spirit and troubled" (John 11:33).

POINT TO PONDER: Jesus experienced the terrible pangs of grief just as we do. "For we do not have a high priest who is unable to sympathize with our weaknesses, but we have one who has been tempted in every way, just as we are—yet was without sin" (Hebrews 4:15). "The Word became flesh and made his dwelling among us" (John 1:14) so that He could experience our griefs and our joys, our humiliations and our mountaintop experiences.

"Let us then approach the throne of grace with confidence, so that we may receive mercy and find grace to help us in our time of need" (Hebrews 4:16). Mary had approached. It did not matter to her that a crowd had gathered, that the mourners had followed her. She was conscious only of the presence of Jesus.

Thank You, Father, for allowing even me to approach the throne with confidence, because I am a daughter of the King.

27 – Thursday

THE PROMISE IN GRIEF

"I am the resurrection and the life. He who believes in me will live, even though he dies. . . ." (John 11:25)

Read Psalm 118

He challenged death that day—and won!
Defeated death at last!
Defeated him at his own game,
Defied his icy blast.
In warm sunshine Lazarus came forth,
In death's strange uniform,
The breath of life breathed into him
By One who calmed a storm.
—Mary

The Grim Reaper, the "nevermore" separator of friends and family, the heretofore unbeatable foe of mankind—death—had been overcome. Did Mary stop to think about the implications of what had happened? I'm sure she realized only that her dearly loved brother had been restored to her.

Can you imagine the dramatic impact of that mummified body emerging from the dark cave of death? Can you imagine the gasps from the crowd of spectators? Can you imagine Mary's reaction?

Profound philosophical and theological statements may mean little or nothing to us until we experience their reality in our lives. Mary may have heard Jesus say, "I am the resurrection and the life" many times, but now those words had a whole new meaning for her.

"He who believes in me will live, even though he dies. . . ." What do those words mean to *me*?

Help me, Jesus, to hear Your words as though I had never heard them before.

THE PURPOSE IN GRIEF

"Whoever lives and believes in me will never die.
Do you believe this?" (John 11:26)

Read 1 Corinthians 15:50-58

And when my brother lived again,
I gained new strength as well.
It didn't matter that the Jews
Were plotting how they'd kill
The One who held life in His hands—
He had no fear of them!
Why should I fear? He'd promised us
He'd surely rise again!

—Mary

Fear can be faced squarely if we can keep in mind that even the greatest disasters have underlying benefits. A loved one's death can draw a family closer together than ever before; even bankruptcy can serve as an unparalleled teacher of good financial judgment in the future.

The question is: Are we able to learn from our problems, our trials, our crisis situations? Mary had faced the ultimate tragedy—death—and now she could say, "Where, O death, is your victory? Where, O death, is your sting?" (1 Corinthians 15:55).

Yes, Mary had faced the ultimate tragedy, but not alone. She had watched the Master turn it into triumph. Jesus Christ is willing and able to do the same for each of us. He can take that trial, that unforgivable failure, and use it to enrich your life and enable you to help others who have also failed.

Thank You, Father, for removing the sting.

OUR POSSESSION IN GRIEF

"I tell you the truth, wherever this gospel is preached throughout the world, what she has done will also be told, in memory of her." (Matthew 26:13)

Read Mark 14:3-9; Matthew 26:6-13

I didn't fully understand
But I desired to give
Some token of my love to Him
Who'd caused us all to live.
Some didn't understand my heart,
Were quick to say "She should . . ."
I gave the best I had to Him;
I gave Him all I could.

—Mary

Perhaps the bottle of ointment with which Mary so tenderly anointed Jesus was left over from the embalming spices purchased for Lazarus' funeral. How meaningful to think that even the accessories of death served the One who was the Resurrection and the Life! Judas criticized Mary's action, but betrayed Jesus a short time later for thirty pieces of silver—an amount only a fraction of the price of Mary's ointment.

Mary's broken alabaster vase would fill the world with its fragrance down through the ages. Mary spilled out its contents, giving all of her most valuable possession (the equivalent of a workman's yearly salary) in an act of complete abandonment. In a similar gesture, God spilled out the life of His Son, His most valued possession. Am I prepared to spill out my life for Him?

Oswald Chambers points out that it is only what God is able to pour *through* us that really counts, not what we gain in the process. God does not collect beautifully rounded grapes; He squeezes the sweetness from us to provide refreshment for others.[1] Can our vases be spilled, our grapes be squeezed? Or are we sitting high on a shelf, away from the unwelcome pressures of life?

Father, I give You even my most precious, valued, beautiful possessions and gifts to be spilled out, to be used as You see fit.

Section 4:

Other Daughters . . .

Week 28

Salome, Daughter of Herodias

How was Salome, the daughter of Herodias, affected by her mother's lifestyle?

In Richard Strauss' opera *Salome*, the daughter of Herodias is pictured as a young temptress who performs the traditional Dance of the Veils. As Herod and his court looked on with bulging eyes, Salome flung caution to the winds along with her veils. She pleased her uncle-father with her dance so completely that he promised her *anything*! And what did he expect in return?

Incest may have been the result of Salome's sensuous dance before her uncle-father. We can be sure that from that time on, his lustful eyes remembered the removal of each veil from her young, lissome body.

The power-hungry Herodian family boasted an unbelievable number of incestuous intermarriages. Salome's natural father was the son of Herod the Great (as was also her stepfather); her mother was the granddaughter of Herod the Great; and Salome later married her father's (and stepfather's) half-brother, who was also her great-uncle.

What does this say to us? We cannot change the facts of Salome's life, but we can be alert to the needs of present-day Salomes all around us, girls whose lives are being scarred and possibly ruined by the totally selfish desires of the very people who should protect them.

The National Center on Child Abuse and Neglect has estimated that at least 100,000 cases of sexual abuse occur within American families each year. Other authorities consider 250,000 to be a conservative estimate. One researcher concluded that incest implicates at least five percent of the population and perhaps up to fifteen percent.[1]

Dr. Ruth Weeks, of the division of child and adolescent psychiatry at the University of Virginia Medical Center, noted that many adults involved in incest are considered pillars of the community and include judges, ministers, university professors, doctors, teachers, skilled workers, white-collar workers, farmers and unskilled laborers.

In comparison with other problems, little is said about the problem of incest. Yet

> the preponderance of evidence is that an incestuous relationship is damaging. . . . The consequences may be short-term, with the incest causing stresses that can be handled and resolved within a relatively short time, or the incestuous relationship may leave scars that last a lifetime.[2]

In Israel, we have often heard bright-eyed little Jewish boys and girls calling "Abba, Abba!" The word actually means "Daddy" and is used by children involved in a close relationship with a loving parent. This is the same word Jesus used in speaking to God, His heavenly Father, and in Romans 8:15 we are assured that we too have the right to use this same word of address in prayer.

BACKGROUND READING: Matthew 14:1-12; Hebrews 2:11-15

28 – Monday

FLASHBACKS

"For I know my transgressions,
and my sin is always before me." (Psalm 51:3)

Read Psalm 51:1-12

Take it away! I cannot bear
To see those eyes that cannot see!
They haunt my days, my nights, my dreams.
Those searching eyes stare back at me—
In search of what I do not know—
A mirror image of my own
I cannot work or sleep or play;
No rest or peace my mind has known.
—Salome

Those who have lived or fought in war-torn countries can testify to the far-reaching effects of violence and death on their lives. Vivid memories come to life in unexpected flashbacks and nightmares, and everyday events serve as reminders of a past that will not be put to rest.

Can you imagine the horror of the scene in which the grisly head of John the Baptist was displayed for all to see? And can you imagine the guilt young Salome experienced as a result of her part in the bloody panorama—guilt that may have been intensified by her stepfather's follow-up to her dance of seduction?

POINT TO PONDER: What about today's victims of incest? Because of feelings of guilt, anger against her abuser and hesitancy to make close friends for fear of their finding out her secret, the girl in an incestuous family often finds it difficult to relate to any man in a fulfilling way. She feels that all men will exploit her or use her, and she is unsure of her own reactions to them. She interprets any sign of affection as a sexual advance.

Abba, Father, You know all about me. You know my past . . . but You have made me a new creation. . . . "The old has gone, the new has come!" (2 Corinthians 5:17). Thank You for that assurance.

28 – Tuesday

CONFUSED EMOTIONS

"Cleanse me with hyssop, and I will be clean; wash me, and I will be whiter than snow. . . . Do not cast me from your presence or take your Holy Spirit from me." (Psalm 51:7, 11)

Read Psalm 54

Could I know why my mother asked
I dance for Herod? 'Twas her wish!
I shrank from facing his eyes too,
Avoided his fond father's kiss.
I hated him with all my heart
And yet enjoyed the lust he showed,
Felt flattered by his compliments,
Wanted to show my womanhood.
—Salome

A girl involved in an incestuous relationship often experiences severe problems in adjusting to a marriage relationship later in life. The woman who has been involved in brother-sister incest may wonder why she overprotects her daughters and overreacts to her sons, feeling anger and resentment toward them for unexplainable reasons.

Families, like other organizations, function well only when there are clear lines of authority and clear role expectations. In incestuous families, there is neither; there is blurring of generational lines.

When a daughter has sex with her father, she often gains a special power over him, and she can wield that power like a club. The child in the incestuous family assumes power over the parents, and sometimes over the whole family. At the same time, the child is still a child. Role confusion exists for everyone.[3]

Abba, Father, thank You for understanding and accepting me—no holds barred.

28 – Wednesday

SECRET GUILT

"Where can I go from your Spirit? Where can I flee from your presence? . . . For you created my inmost being; you knit me together in my mother's womb." (Psalm 139:7, 13)

Read Psalm 139

But as I danced that dance for him,
Discarded each one of my veils,
The sensuous movements I had learned
Belied my fears. I could not fail!
I knew she watched and urged me on,
The traitor mother I'd adored
Until she snared my uncle's love
For what his power could afford.
—Salome

Why didn't Salome rebel against her mother's orders? Blair and Rita Justice write:

> A girl caught up in an incestuous family may welcome the attentions of the parent. Even if she feels there is something wrong with what they are doing, the sexual activity may be the only source of love and attention available to her. So she may be reluctant to turn her father away. She also may feel the strong sense of responsibility . . . to take care of her father and mother by taking over her mother's role in the family.
>
> . . . To the child an incestuous relationship with a parent seems preferable to no relationship at all. . . . They struggle, sometimes all their lives, to get that nurturing and a feeling of belonging and being cared for. [4]

POINT TO PONDER: Perhaps the most tragic result is that the victim of incest feels isolated. She thinks she is the only person in the world to whom this has happened and so it must be her fault. Her false guilt may keep her story a lifelong secret.

Abba, Father, help me to be aware of the needs all around me and to be sensitive to Your direction in each differing situation. Thank You that I belong to You.

28 – Thursday

BITTERNESS BEGINS

"Even my close friend, whom I trusted, he who shared my bread, has lifted up his heel against me." (Psalm 41:9)

Read Psalm 91

Why leave my father? Was it love
That drew her to another man?
Did she know how to love? Or did
She use us all to suit her plans?
Could she have twisted my young mind,
Enjoyed the way she wrecked my soul,
If she had loved me—really loved?
Her gods were power and control.
—Salome

Would Herodias have listened if Salome had tried to confide in her? Did Salome ever try?

A girl caught in an incestuous relationship may try to confide the truth in someone (her mother, for example), only to find that her painful confession is met with reproach, blame, punishment or complete disbelief. The offending male may deny that he ever touched the girl, and his word may be taken against hers. In this kind of situation, the girl's initial distrust of the male may develop into a full-grown bitterness toward her family and men in general. She sees herself as unwanted, untrusted, unprotected, unloved.

Sadly enough, the girl may reach out to someone who resembles her abuser in some way (age or otherwise). She may seek endlessly for a father figure to give her the nurture and sense of belonging she needs so desperately, spending her life going from one man to another in search of the security she was denied as a child.

Thank You, Abba, Father, for being my Refuge and my Fortress. Thank You that I can trust You even if everyone else fails me.

28 – Friday

AFTEREFFECTS

"Then, after desire has conceived, it gives birth to sin; and sin, when it is full-grown, gives birth to death" (James 1:15)

Read Psalm 103:1-13

And so my lissome body moved
As she sat, calculating, cold.
And as I bared my body there
Her plans unfolded and took hold.
She forced me—I could not rebel!
She said she knew the best for me.
O God, would I had fled that place
Before her plans had come to be!

—Salome

Perhaps the most pervasive long-term consequences of incest are the effects it may have on the daughter's self-image. These effects stem from years of being weighted down with feelings of both anger and guilt. As a small child, the daughter may not have known the incestuous behavior was wrong and, therefore, she did not put up resistance. Once she realizes society condemns it, she starts blaming herself for having participated. At the same time, the daughter is often angry at her parents for having exploited instead of protected her and angry at herself for having been unable to do anything to stop the incestuous behavior. . . . In short, the woman often sees herself as worthless and may become seriously depressed.[5]

POINT TO PONDER: The "death" mentioned in James 1:15 does not necessarily refer to physical death. In an effort to blot out their pain and loneliness, women turn to different types of self-destructive behavior, such as drug abuse or prostitution. The Chicago Vice Commission found in a survey that 51 out of 103 prostitutes reported having their first sexual experience with their own fathers.[6]

Help me, Abba, Father, not to allow the pain and guilt of earthly relationships to enter into and interfere with my relationship with You.

28 – Saturday

THE ALTERNATIVE

"He is like a father to us, tender and sympathetic to those who reverence him." (Psalm 103:13, TLB)

Read Psalm 103:14-22

Take it away! I cannot bear
To see that grisly head again!
I see it when I first awake,
I see it in the evening when
I try to get just one night's rest.
There is no rest for such as I!
That dance of death cut off my life.
I should have been the one to die.
—Salome

What happened to Salome after that fateful dance in the court of Herod? Was she considered fair game by other men who had watched her entertain her uncle-father? She later married another great-uncle. Was the marriage an effort to run away from the court of Herod Antipas?

Remember the two basic inputs needed for a sense of personal worth—significance and security? Obviously a woman who has been sexually abused as a child needs to be unconditionally loved, accepted and cared for.

"Who shall separate us from the love of Christ? . . . For I am convinced that . . . neither the present nor the future [or the *past*!] . . . will be able to separate us from the love of God that is in Christ Jesus our Lord" (Romans 8:35, 38-39).

God has seen me at my worst and still loved me to the point of giving His life for Me! That's security!

Thank You, Father, for removing my sins as far as the East is from the West. Thank You for Your love, as great as the height of the heavens above the earth.

Week 29

The Woman at the Well

The story of the Samaritan woman at the well, told only in the Gospel of John, centers on one woman's need. Before we meet her, however, we need some historical background on Samaria.

In the Old Testament book of Deuteronomy, under Moses' leadership, the Israelites were in sight of their goal, but Moses died before they actually crossed the Jordan River and entered the Promised Land. God had given clear directions to Moses, directions that outlined the "dos and don'ts" of life in Canaan. Obedience would result in blessing and their own protection, but disobedience would be followed by punishment.

Just west of the Jordan River, two mountains—Mt. Ebal and Mt. Gerizim—stand like twins, Ebal slightly more than 3,000 feet high, Gerizim slightly less. To make sure the people understood the game rules, Israel's new leader, Joshua, separated the twelve tribes into two groups. Using the perfect natural acoustics, Joshua directed six tribes to stand on Mt. Gerizim and call out God's blessing, while the other six stood on Mt. Ebal to proclaim God's curse if His commandments were ignored or broken (Deuteronomy 11:26-32; Joshua 8:30-35).

From that time on, naturally enough, Mt. Gerizim was known as the "mount of blessing." Mt. Ebal was the "mount of cursing."

The year 721 BC was a year of great change. The Assyrians,

under King Sargon, conquered Israel and deported thousands of Israelites, repopulating the area between Mt. Gerizim and Mt. Ebal with captured "foreigners" who eventually intermarried with the remaining Israelites. This mixed race came to be known as Samaritans, and they were despised by the "pure" Jews.

The Samaritans, however, contended that their heritage was genuine and that Mt. Gerizim was just as sacred as Mt. Moriah (in Jerusalem). These opposing beliefs developed into hostility and hatred between the Jews and their Samaritan neighbors.

So when Jesus visited Samaria, he walked into a hotbed of hostility and prejudice. Did He carry a sword? Did He stage a debate between Himself and the head religious honcho? Did He mount a soapbox beside the gathering place, the well? No. He simply reached out to one hurting individual. He ignored what others had told Him and relied only on His intimate knowledge of the nature of His heavenly Father—Abba, Father.

Abba, Father! Abba means trust, security, commitment, love—everything the woman at the well needed.

BACKGROUND READING: John 4:1-32

LOVING THE UNLOVELY

"Oholah is Samaria. . . . She lusted after her lovers, the Assyrians. . . . She gave herself as a prostitute." (Ezekiel 23:4-5, 7)

Read Luke 17:11-19

They always told me I was born
In the shadow of the mountain
And for many years I thought
It was Gerizim they meant:
Gerizim, the mount of blessing,
Gerizim, the worship place,
Gerizim, home of our temple,
Mecca of the Samaritan race.

—the woman at the well

After a tempestuous visit to Jerusalem (John 2), where He had thrown the money changers out of the temple for the first time, Jesus was on His way back to Galilee. He must have been tired emotionally as well as physically. Most Jews would not have dreamed of walking through Samaritan territory; instead, they completely avoided the whole area by crossing the Jordan in a roundabout route. Jesus must have been tired, but He was not seeking a shortcut. When John says that Jesus *had* to go through Samaria, it was because the tremendous need for His love forced Him in that direction.

The little town of Sychar, where Jacob's Well can still be seen by tourists today, lies in the valley between Mt. Gerizim and Mt. Ebal. As you picture Jesus resting in the shadow of the mountains, reflecting on what has happened in Jerusalem, realizing what lay ahead for Him, notice that He did not withdraw into His own emotions. Instead, He reached out to the person who, according to the standards of His day, was most undesirable.

Jesus loved the unlovely. Who is lowest on *your* list?

Father, You know the person I'm thinking of. Please radiate Your love through me.

29 – Tuesday

REACHING OUT FOR LOVE

"You, therefore, have no excuse, you who pass judgment on someone else, for at whatever point you judge the other, you are condemning yourself, because you who pass judgment do the same things." (Romans 2:1)

Read Romans 2:1-11

Then one day I heard them talking
When the time for marriage came:
"She is cursed as is the mountain!"
Ebal was the mountain's name!
Not the blessing, but the cursing—
Fate had chosen one for me,
And I would live in its shadow.
It was always meant to be.

—the woman at the well

Pagan religions were very fatalistic: one's fate was determined before or at one's birth, and nothing could change it. The Samaritans had been greatly influenced by the Assyrian beliefs, and the woman at the well may have felt that there was no possibility of change in her life.

As with many other women mentioned in this book, much of the poetry concerning their backgrounds is conjecture (see Preface). The Bible does not provide many case histories, and so you are free to form your own ideas, just as I have done. I imagine that this Samaritan woman had a very confused childhood and adolescence. She may have carried her resulting insecurity from adolescence into one marriage after another—a total of five. When Jesus met her, she was living with still another man, a lover. (I use that word reluctantly.)

POINT TO PONDER: The victim of insecurity constantly reaches out for the reassurance of being loved. Sexual promiscuity is basically a search for closeness, for a depth in relationship that, failing with one partner, continues the search unendingly.

Thank You, Father, for being able—and willing—to change lives!

MY BODY: THE HOLY SPIRIT'S HOME

"When you . . . pass judgment . . . and yet do the same things, do you think you will escape God's judgment? Or do you show contempt for the riches of his kindness, tolerance and patience, not realizing that God's kindness leads you toward repentance?" (Romans 2:3-4).

Read Proverbs 5:1-20

Cursed I was—just ask the women!
How they hated me! Each one
Fearing she would lose her husband
Or perhaps one of her sons.
Cursed I was—so why should I care
If the men liked what they saw?
And so men became my pastime
Though my soul was rough and raw.

—the woman at the well

"Have your next affair with us!" the billboard proclaimed blatantly to any and every passerby. Semantics allowed a variety of meanings, but my mind immediately pictured a luxurious room featuring a king-size bed, with two people running away from back-home responsibilities. The sign did not mention the cost in dollars and cents; neither did it comment on the other kinds of expenses involved in affairs.

Admit it or not, each time a woman gives her body, she gives a part of herself. It was true of the Samaritan woman, and it is true today.

> That is why I say to run from sex sin. No other sin affects the body as this one does. When you sin this sin it is against your own body. Haven't you yet learned that your body is the home of the Holy Spirit God gave you, and that he lives within you? Your own body does not belong to you. For God has bought you with a great price. So use every part of your body to give glory back to God, because he owns it. (1 Corinthians 6:18-20, TLB)

Teach me to glorify You, Father, with every part of my body.

29 – Thursday

UNDERSTOOD BY A STRANGER

"There was a time when some of you were just like that but now your sins are washed away, and you are set apart for God, and he has accepted you because of what the Lord Jesus Christ and the Spirit of our God have done for you."
(1 Corinthians 6:11, TLB)

Read Proverbs 6:20-35

Yes, the day that I met Jesus
I'd avoided everyone,
Gone for water when the women
Stayed out of the noonday sun.
When I saw the Man who sat there,
I just looked the other way.
He was Jewish, and we didn't
Care to mix in any way.

—the woman at the well

The long walk to the well was a daily chore for each of the women of Samaria. For most of them it was a social time, anticipated as a chance to catch up on town gossip and news. Many of the women probably took care of this chore early in the morning. Possibly this woman had entertained a new lover the night before and had slept late.

Whatever the reason, as her bracelets jangled on that long walk to the well, the woman's thoughts were jangling as well. She was preoccupied. She made no flirtatious moves to attract Jesus' attention when she reached the well. A Jew would ignore her anyway.

But He spoke to her. To her amazement, He asked her for a drink. Not to be outdone, she mentioned her surprise, speaking as freely to Him as she would have to any Samaritan man. The ensuing conversation is delightful in its unprecedented frankness, for even good Jewish women were frowned upon if found conversing with men who were not family members. (In those days a Jewish man could divorce his wife for spinning in the street. Her place was in her home, unless it was necessary for her to work in the fields.)

Thank You, Jesus, for Your acceptance and understanding of women.

29 – Friday

A DIFFERENT KIND OF WATER

"Jesus answered her, All who drink of this water will be thirsty again. But whoever takes a drink of the water that I will give him shall never, no never, be thirsty any more. But the water that I will give him shall become a spring of water welling up (flowing, bubbling) continually within him unto (into, for) eternal life." (John 4:13-14, Amplified)

Read Proverbs 7:6-27

So I thought . . . until He asked me,
Kindly: "Could I have a drink?"
As I listened to this stranger,
I found life's once-missing link
He said He had living water
And I would not thirst again
If I drank from His own well
That had not been dug by men.

—the woman at the well

Jesus put the woman's natural inquisitiveness, "How can you ask me for a drink?" to good use by changing the topic of conversation. Not accustomed to speaking in the abstract, the woman asked questions in terms of ropes and buckets. Jesus answered in terms of the eternal, but the woman was still grappling with a tangible problem—the daily chore she so despised, the long, lonely walk to the well.

But Jesus knew how to make the transition in the woman's mind. He manifested His complete knowledge of her past and present. She woke up abruptly from her spiritual stupor and tried to evade Jesus' searching gaze into the cobwebby corners of her existence. Like Eve with her fig-leaf cover-up, the woman attempted to divert Jesus' attention to another area, the old Jewish-Samaritan argument: Where was the proper place to worship, Mt. Moriah (Jerusalem) or Mt. Gerizim? Again Jesus saw through the subterfuge: "It's not *where* we worship that counts, but *how* we worship—is our worship spiritual and real? Do we have the Holy Spirit's help?" (John 4:22-23, TLB).

Help me, Jesus, to worship You in a real way, *not in mere form or ritual.*

29 – *Saturday*

"ACCEPTED IN THE BELOVED"

"Many of the Samaritans from that town believed in him because of the woman's testimony, 'He told me everything I ever did.' " (John 4:39)

"We must have his help to worship as we should." (John 4:24, TLB)

Read Psalm 139

Even though He knew my status,
He did not look down on me
When I asked of the Messiah:
"I who speak to you am He."
Life had changed, and would keep changing!
I no longer felt the curse
I, the harlot of Samaria
I had found Messiah first!

—the woman at the well

Actually, Jesus found her—the completion of a long, loving search that had begun the day she was born. Jesus was there through all her unfruitful yearnings and rejections . . . waiting, just as He waited at Jacob's Well for her coming that day.

POINT TO PONDER: Just as Jesus transferred the emphasis from His physical need for water to the woman's spiritual dryness, again He changed the course of her questioning. He explained that since God is Spirit, we must worship Him in spirit (with our whole heart) and in truth (in keeping with His revealed Word). By revealing her sinful condition, He made her aware of her guilt and spiritual need and was now offering her the solution.

The disciples, who had walked into Sychar to buy food, now came onto the scene and were amazed to see the Master conversing with a Samaritan woman. Probably sensing their confusion and unable to contain her own feelings, the woman headed for town, leaving her waterpot at the well to signify her intention of returning.

I never cease to be amazed, Jesus, that You know everything about me, and still love me. Please help me to share that understanding with someone today.

Week 30

The Syro-Phoenician (Canaanite) Woman

"Leave them; they are blind guides. If a blind man leads a blind man, both will fall into a pit." (Matthew 15:14)

Strong words that Jesus used! About whom was He talking? Non-Jewish leaders from neighboring countries? Surprisingly, no. Jesus was referring to the Pharisees, the Jewish religious leaders.

Jesus had had enough of repetitive ritual that ignored realistic needs. He turned away from the Pharisees' private investigation delegation and walked the fifty miles to an area that was off-limits to the Pharisees—Tyre and Sidon.

The disciples must have muttered to each other as Jesus strode ahead of them, "Why are we going to those terrible places? Have they not been cursed by God? What is He thinking of? Why is He taking us there?"

True, God had given the prophet Ezekiel terrible words to say against the Phoenician seaports of Tyre and Sidon:

> Therefore the Lord God says: I stand against you, Tyre, and I will bring nations against you like ocean waves. They will destroy the walls of Tyre and tear down her towers. I will scrape away her soil and make her a bare rock! Her island shall become uninhabited, a place for fishermen to spread their nets, for I have spoken it, says the Lord God. Tyre shall become the prey of many nations. (Ezekiel 26:3-5, TLB)

> I am your enemy, O Sidon. . . . I will send an epidemic of disease and an army to destroy; the wounded shall be slain in your streets. . . . Then you will know I am the Lord. (28:22-23, TLB)

This prophecy had been spoken in 588 BC and partially fulfilled a short time later by the invasion of King Nebuchadnezzar of Babylon. In 332 BC Alexander the Great used the remains of the city of Tyre as a foundation for a road from the mainland to the island, literally creating a "bare rock" from the rubble of Tyre. Sidon was also completely destroyed.

Why had God been so angry at Tyre and her sister-city, Sidon? Ezekiel answers that question: "Through your widespread trade you were filled with violence, and you sinned. . . . Your heart became proud on account of your beauty, and you corrupted your wisdom" (28:16-17).

Tyre and Sidon had not only been the trade capitals of the ancient world because of their coastline location, they had also been the worship centers for Baal and Ashtoreth (or Astarte), a worship in which prostitution was a central focus. These pagan deities demanded the ultimate in sacrifice—human lives, young and tender lives.

When I first reviewed the story of Jesus' meeting with the Greek woman (born in Syrian Phoenicia), I evaluated Jesus' effort to remain unknown as a desire for a vacation, a rest from His constant harassment by the Pharisees. But even though Jesus had human emotions and human reactions, He also was all-knowing. He knew the woman would approach Him and that there would be no rest. He also knew why the woman's daughter was being oppressed by demon possession—and, as usual, He had a lesson for His prejudiced disciples.

BACKGROUND READING: Matthew 15:1-28

30 — Monday

CUTTHROATS IN TOPHET

"And they have built high altars to Baal in the Valley of Hinnom. There they have burnt their children as sacrifices to Molech." (Jeremiah 32:35, TLB)

Read Jeremiah 19:1-15

How can He hear one such as I?
His race and mine have always been
Such enemies! I am not fit
To sit at a table with this Man—
And yet I have no other hope.
My daughter grows much worse each day.
I may be turned away, it's true,
But there is left no other way.

—the Syro-Phoenician woman

The Old Testament is full of warnings against the worship of Baal, and archaeologists have unearthed some of the reasons for God's hatred of this cult. An old burial ground in Carthage, a Phoenician settlement in Africa, has yielded thousands of clay pots containing the remains of babies and young children who had been sacrificed to Baal.[1]

By approximately 990 BC these practices were brought into Jerusalem itself by some of Solomon's wives—Moabites, Ammonites, Edomites, Hittites and Sidonians—700 in all. In the Valley of Hinnom, which could be seen from the citadel of Jerusalem, King Solomon erected altars for the god Molech, whose horrid rites were revived from time to time in the same vicinity by later kings. In 742 BC and later, Kings Ahaz and Manasseh made their children "pass through the fire" (1 Kings 11:7; 2 Kings 16:3; 2 Chronicles 28:3, 33:6). Jeremiah mentions it about 590 BC.

The fiendish custom of infant sacrifice to the fire-gods seems to have been kept up in Tophet, the "holy place" in the Valley of Hinnom. An infant intended for sacrifice had its throat cut by a priest and was then placed in the embrace of a bronze statue, whose white-hot arms may have been mechanically operated to drop the dead child into a furnace or grate.

Help me, Father, to take a stand against the age-old sins of child abuse and child murder.

BATTLE WITH BAAL

"For no matter how much they used, there was always plenty left in the containers, just as the Lord had promised through Elijah!" (1 Kings 17:16, TLB)

Read 1 Kings 17:1-24

Yes, I have heard He spoke of one
Whose race was just the same as mine,
The widow that Elijah saved,
Supplying food in desperate times
Elijah saved her son as well
(He would have died for lack of food)
Because she was obedient
And knew the word of God was good.
—the Syro-Phoenician woman

The Old Testament prophet Elijah fought a never-ending war against Baal worship and the immoral practices it entailed, but it is important to notice that before his greatest battle, the Mount Carmel marathon, he spent three years in Zarephath (now Sarepta), a little Phoenician village near Sidon. Why? Because God gave him definite directions to go there.

Once there, Elijah, like Jesus, met a poor widow who was willing to obey the God of Israel and to share her last morsels with Elijah, even though she also had a son to feed. God blessed and multiplied her food supply so that it lasted through the time of famine, and later raised her son from death to further demonstrate His power and concern for this poor widow.

POINT TO PONDER: What was God saying through all this? The widow asked Elijah a searching question: "O man of God, . . . what have you done to me? Have you come here to punish my sins by killing my son?" (1 Kings 17:18, TLB). God had already made it clear that He hated the sin that was being practiced by the Phoenicians. Now He was saying that He still hated the sin, but He loved the sinner. When Jesus looked at this Phoenician woman, He saw simply a woman in need, and His love reached out to her immediately.

Thank You, Jesus—Your love sees no difference in nationality, in color, in background, in wealth or health or lack of it.

30 — *Wednesday*

DEMONS AND DEATH

"Have mercy on me, O Lord, Son of David! My daughter is miserably and distressingly and cruelly possessed by a demon!" (Matthew 15:22, Amplified)

Read John 17:14-21

Elijah stayed there in her home.
Uncaring of the words of man.
He saved her son a second time,
Raised him from death to live again.
I know the Master knows of this.
He's come to us to show His love,
And I must seek Him out this day,
For help comes only from above.

—the Syro-Phoenician woman

The fact that the Phoenician woman addressed Jesus as "Son of David" indicates that she had some knowledge of Jewish history and theology. Since Elijah had spent three years in her area centuries earlier, she may have been familiar with his visit to Zarephath; perhaps it was the story of God's kindness to the widow (through Elijah) that gave her the courage to seek Jesus out. If the God of Israel had saved the life of the widow's son, then He could also save her daughter from a fate worse than death.

If you have ever nursed a sick child through an illness, you know how physically and emotionally drained *you* (the mother or nurse) feel by the time the child has regained health. You're ready to go to bed for a week.

Imagine watching your child in deep emotional trauma while you stand by helplessly. Perhaps you have had that experience. I have not shared your grief, but I can tell you that a Father God watched His only beloved Son experience the worst emotional trauma possible . . . and still loved the persecutors.

Thank You, Father, for being the God of the impossible.

HELPLESSNESS IS NOT HOPELESSNESS

"While we were yet in weakness—powerless to help ourselves—at the fitting time Christ died for (in behalf of) the ungodly." (Romans 5:6, Amplified)

Read Mark 7:24-30

Have mercy on me, O my Lord!
Yes, Son of David, hear my plea!
My daughter's life hangs by a thread,
Her soul no longer can be free.
A demon troubles her by day
And fills her night with dreams of hell.
Oh, help me, Lord, I beg of You!
There is no other I can tell.

—the Syro-Phoenician woman

The mother's helplessness was obvious in her agonized plea.

Do you feel that your prayers, your conversations with God, must be worded properly and profoundly for Him to hear and answer? If you are a mother, think back to the time when your tiny baby's cry sounded an alert. The reason may have been hunger, cold, fear, heat or a messy diaper (or none of these). You did not stop to cross-examine the baby as to the cause of the problem. As the mother, you simply investigated all the possibilities and tried to fulfill the need, with perhaps a hug and a kiss thrown in for good measure.

POINT TO PONDER: Our heavenly Father said to Paul, "My grace—My favor and loving-kindness and mercy—are enough for you, [that is, sufficient against any danger and to enable you to bear the trouble manfully]; for My strength and power are made perfect—fulfilled and completed and show themselves most effective—in [your] weakness" (2 Corinthians 12:9, Amplified).

Prayer, then, may begin by simply telling God in what areas we feel completely helpless. Perhaps you are dealing with a guilt that simply will not quit—abuse, adultery, abortion. . . . The list could go on and on.

Abba, Father, here I am with this seemingly hopeless problem. Thank You for not being like humans, who say they forgive but cannot forget. Thank You for the atoning power of Your blood which covers every *sin.*

30 – Friday

A BOTHERSOME BEGGAR WOMAN

"Now it is an extraordinary thing for one to give his life even for an upright man, though perhaps for a noble and lovable and generous benefactor someone might even dare to die. But God shows and clearly proves His [own] love for us by the fact that while we were still sinners Christ, the Messiah, the Anointed One, died for us." (Romans 5:7-8, Amplified)

Read Mark 7:1-23

I'm not a child of Abraham;
  I don't expect the children's bread!
I would be happy for a crumb
  After the children have been fed.
I am content just where I am,
  I seek no higher rank or role.
I only seek Your mercy, Lord.
  Your healing is my only goal.

—the Syro-Phoenician woman

In spite of the woman's obvious need, Jesus gave her no reply. The disciples, thinking He was ignoring her, urged their Master to send her away so that she would no longer bother them. After all, she was only a Phoenician woman. To them she was a nobody.

After an interesting conversation with her, however, oblivious to the disciples' glares, Jesus regarded the woman and rebuked the uncompassionate disciples at the same time: "Woman, you have great faith! Your request is granted" (Matthew 15:28).

In prayer, helplessness must be accompanied by persistent faith—faith that keeps asking when there is no reply, faith when the odds are against us, faith that keeps believing because we know He wants what is best for us.

Thank You, Father, for this example of a "nobody" who was important to You.

30 – Saturday

YESTERDAY'S GODS IN CONTEMPORARY GARB

"For if while we were enemies we were reconciled to God through the death of His Son, it is much more [certain], now that we are reconciled, that we shall be saved [daily delivered from sin's dominion] through His [resurrection] life." (Romans 5:10, Amplified)

Read Mark 5:1-20

He said my faith was very great;
I simply knew His power could heal!
I know my daughter waits for me,
That she will join me in a meal.
That demon power has disappeared,
Those eyes that once were strange and wild
Will now be beautiful and clear
As when she was a little child.

—the Syro-Phoenician woman

By coming to Jesus for help the woman was not only risking the disciples' scornful put-down, she was also taking a chance on being ostracized from her own community. Baal worship and worship of the God of Israel could not coexist.

I feel sure that the woman whose daughter was healed through God's mighty power did not return to the worship of a child-sacrificing god housed in a fire-bellied bronze statue.

POINT TO PONDER: What about the god named Irresponsible Pleasure who seems to dominate the contemporary scene? We, as well as our children, are assured that we can experiment with sex as a positive, pleasurable experience without fear of punishment, and that there is nothing sinful or unethical about simply disposing of any unwanted by-products. Disposable containers . . . disposable relationships . . . disposable life. The sacrifices are the same. The god has simply changed his name.

Father . . . perhaps some situations are not as hopeless as they seem, or perhaps I should say I am not as helpless as I feel. Help me to exercise my faith in Your power by putting feet to my prayers where there are things I can do, protest letters I can write, appointments I can make. Break through my apathy.

Section 5:

Preparing My Heart for Outreach: "You will be My witnesses in Jerusalem . . ."

Week 31

Mary Says Good-bye . . . Again

"Then they returned to Jerusalem from the hill called the Mount of Olives, a Sabbath day's walk from the city. . . . They all joined together constantly in prayer,
along with the women and Mary the mother of Jesus, and with his brothers. *(Acts 1:12, 14, emphasis added)*

After the ascension, Mary must have experienced the entire gamut of emotions, from blissful euphoria to the grief of sudden loss. Jesus was "taken up before their very eyes" (Acts 1:9)—and if she had found it hard to believe her eyes, the fact was confirmed by "two men dressed in white" (Acts 1:10), reminiscent of the Resurrection angels.

Nonetheless, her Son was gone. Despite Mary's faith, the loss must have *felt* very permanent.

The story motivated me to review many memories of saying hello and good-bye to family members. My husband Bob has been on the road in evangelistic ministry ever since I met him in 1963. I thought I was experienced at saying good-bye, but I learned that lesson over and over again when our two older sons each spent four years at Toccoa Falls College in Georgia.

Then came the weekend of Rob's Georgia wedding. On Saturday of that August weekend in 1991, we said good-bye to Rob and our new daughter-in-law Gina. We would not see them again for months, possibly not until the next year. The next day we said good-bye to Ric, who would be staying in the South to begin his senior year of college. After a Sunday evening concert in Lilburn, Georgia, my husband and I left for Pennsylvania with our youngest son Dave.

Saying good-bye this time—and letting go—was one of the most emotionally wrenching things I ever had to do. On the way home, the only Scripture in which I could find comfort was the story of Hannah's long-distance relationship with her son Samuel.

Hannah had promised Samuel to the Lord before he was born, just as we had given our sons to the Lord. Although the Lord's representative turned out to be an old priest with a bad track record in raising sons, Hannah kept her promise. She gave Samuel to the Lord through entrusting him to the old priest Eli, but she did not forget him. Each year she brought Samuel a coat that she had sewed for him; I believe each stitch of that coat represented his mother's covering of prayer over his life.

God was telling me that it was time for me to learn to pray in a new way. Even if they lived in the sunny South the rest of their lives, our family members needed the protection of "prayer coats"!

You may be saying, "The author obviously doesn't know what *real* grief and loss are like. Her sons are still alive." That is true. Each one of us has our own unique areas of grief and loss. God will allow you to share *your* story, to minister to others in your own unique way, as you allow Him to heal your grieving spirit.

God *has* been there, and He *does* know all about it. And He has sent the Holy Spirit to be our Comforter.

But at times even Mary probably needed to be reminded.

BACKGROUND READING: 1 Samuel 1

31 — Monday

SIBLING RIVALRY

"When they arrived, they went upstairs to the room where they were staying. Those present were Peter, John, James and Andrew; Philip and Thomas, Bartholomew and Matthew; James son of Alphaeus and Simon the Zealot, and Judas son of James . . . along with the women and Mary the mother of Jesus, and with his brothers."
(Acts 1:13-14, emphasis added)

Read 1 Samuel 2:1-10

Why did they wait so long to see it?
Why did it take the Cross
for my sons to believe it?
He rose from the dead
before they trusted Him.
He ascended to heaven
before they put their faith in Him—
He was their Brother . . . Jesus.

—Mary, mother of Jesus—and James

For centuries, certain questions had been discussed in every place where Jewish leaders met and talked: How will Israel be liberated from pagan domination? How will the kingdom of God be realized? What is the ultimate destiny of the righteous—and the wicked? When will the chaos and the evil of history come to an end? And what will follow?

Women, particularly young women who prayed and pondered, asked another question: *The Promised One has not yet come . . . could I be the one chosen to be the mother of the Messiah?*

But, it seems, no one asked: "Will *my brother* be the Messiah, the Promised One?"

It took Jesus' death and resurrection to prove to His brothers—we do not know about His sisters—that He really was who He said He was. Their brother, the son of their mother, was also the Son of God.

Think about it . . . . Had you been in their place, would *you* have believed?

As I absorb Mary's grief into my own, Lord, teach me what I need to learn from this story.

31 — Tuesday

PETER THE LEADER

"In those days Peter stood up among the believers (a group numbering about a hundred and twenty) and said, 'Brothers, the Scripture had to be fulfilled which the Holy Spirit spoke long ago through the mouth of David concerning Judas, who served as guide for those who arrested Jesus—he was one of our number and shared in this ministry.' " (Acts 1:15-17)

Read Acts 1:12-26

If I had chosen leadership,
it wouldn't be Peter . . .
perhaps discerning John
who has become a son to me
or James his brother.
I remember when their mother asked
for leaders' spots for them . . .
Ah, well, I understand her thoughts!
I hope she has forgiven me
for borrowing her son.

—Mary, mother of Jesus—and James

Salome may have been the sister of Mary. How did she feel when Jesus said from the cross to *her* son John, "Son, behold thy mother"—and set his face toward Mary?

How did Salome feel when Jesus said to Mary, "Woman, behold thy son!" and cast a long, pleading look at John? And how did another Mary, mother of a disciple called "the Lesser," react to the fact that her son was overlooked in many ways?

POINT TO PONDER: Jealousy, an unwelcome visitor, comes unbidden. It can spring to life in the most sincere and loving heart, especially when it concerns our beloved children. But God the Father, who shared His Son with the world, understands our vulnerability to this uninvited guest. If we open our hearts to Him, He stands ready to heal the hurt.

And when our sons are "beaten out" by other mothers' sons, God can also open our hearts to those sons—the impulsive, abrasive Peters as well as the tenderhearted Johns—and their mothers as well.

Help me, Lord, to lay down the old grudges . . . at the cross.

FROM PASSOVER TO PENTECOST

"When the day of Pentecost came . . . all of them were filled with the Holy Spirit and began to speak in other tongues as the Spirit enabled them. . . . When they heard this sound, a crowd came together in bewilderment, because each one heard them speaking in his own language." (Acts 2:1, 4, 6)

Read Ephesians 2:14-22

How He keeps changing our ideas!
Parthians, Medes and Elamites,
Judeans, Asians, Libyans,
Romans, Cretans, Arabs . . .
on this great day of Pentecost
they all *have heard!*
Just fifty days past Passover
even our old enemies, the Egyptians,
He's not passed over . . .
He's included them as well
in this new day of pouring out.

—Mary, mother of Jesus—and James

During my childhood, my family attended many different churches. As a result, in later years I experienced a great deal of spiritual confusion. It was comforting to read in Oswald Chambers' biography, *Oswald Chambers: Abandoned to God,* the story of his "dark night of the soul":

> I see now that God was taking me by the light of His Holy Spirit and His Word, through every ramification of my being. The last three months of those years, things reached a climax; I was getting very desperate. I knew no one who had what I wanted; in fact, I did not know what I did want. But I knew that if what I had was all the Christianity there was, the thing was a fraud.
>
> Then Luke 11:13 got hold of me, "If you then, though you are evil, know how to give good gifts to your children, how much more will your Father in heaven give the Holy Spirit to those who ask him!"[1]

Father, help me to know Your Spirit as I come to know You more and more.

31 — Thursday

PETER THE PROPHET, PETER THE FOOL

"In the last days, God says, I will pour out my Spirit on all people. Your sons and daughters will prophesy, your young men will see visions, your old men will dream dreams. Even on my servants, both men and women, I will pour out my Spirit in those days." (Acts 2:17-18)

Read 1 Corinthians 3:18-22

After today, I recognize
not just our thoughts have changed,
our understanding of the Spirit's power—
but Peter's changed as well.
Although I wouldn't have chosen him,
I understand
my ways are not God's ways
my thoughts are not God's thoughts
and now I know
that Peter is the one
God's chosen for this hour.

—Mary, mother of Jesus—and James

How is God pouring out His Spirit in these "last days"? Chambers' biography emphasizes that feelings and ecstatic experiences are not the most important proofs of the Holy Spirit's infilling of our lives. God asks us to simply take Him at His Word and believe His promises to us as His children.

"But how could I," Chambers continued, "bad motived as I was, possibly ask for the gift of the Holy Spirit? Then it was borne in upon me that I had to claim the gift from God on the authority of Jesus Christ and testify to having done so. But the thought came—if you claim the gift of the Holy Spirit on the word of Jesus Christ and testify to it, God will make it known to those who know you best how bad you are in heart. And I was not willing to be a fool for Christ's sake. But those of you who know the experience, know very well how God brings one to the point of utter despair, and I got to the place where I did not care whether everyone knew how bad I was. I cared for nothing on earth, saving to get out of my present condition."[2]

Thank You, Lord, that Peter became content to be considered a fool for Your sake. Please teach me Your ways.

31 – *Friday*

"A SWORD SHALL PIERCE THINE OWN HEART ALSO"

"Repent and be baptized, every one of you, in the name of Jesus Christ for the forgiveness of your sins. And you will receive the gift of the Holy Spirit. The promise is for you and your children and for all who are far off—for all whom the Lord our God will call." (Acts 2:38-39)

Read Philippians 3:7-14

Peter's words bring back
the prophecy of old Simeon,
the words I've pondered for many a year
and now again:
This child is destined for
the fall and rise of many Israelites
to be a sign that will be spoken against
so that the thoughts of many hearts
will be revealed.
And a sword will pierce your own heart too.

—Mary, mother of Jesus—and James

"God brings one to the point of utter despair. . . ." Chambers emphasized this, and the apostle Peter, I'm sure, would agree. "I cared for nothing on earth, saving to get out of my present condition. And then and there I claimed the gift of the Holy Spirit in dogged committal on Luke 11:13. 'If you know how to give good gifts to your children . . . how much more . . . ?'

"I had no vision of heaven or of angels . . ." Chambers continues. "I was as dry and empty as ever, no power or realization of God, no witness of the Holy Spirit. Two days later I was asked to speak at a meeting, and forty souls came out to the front. Did I praise God? No, I was terrified and left them to the workers, and went to Mr. MacGregor and told him what had happened. He said, 'Don't you remember claiming the Holy Spirit as a gift on the word of Jesus, and that He said: "Ye shall receive power . . ."? This is the power from on high.' "[3]

Forgive me, Lord, for the desire for "power in my own hand." Your Word pierces my heart as well.

"BE . . . AND I WILL DO THROUGH YOU"

"Now a man crippled from birth was being carried to the temple gate called Beautiful. . . . Then Peter said, 'Silver or gold I do not have, but what I have I give you. In the name of Jesus Christ of Nazareth, walk.' " (Acts 3:2, 6)

Read Acts 3:11-26

I see now how my prejudice
kept me from loving as He loved.
At last I have forgiven those
who hurt my Son.
It's though I have released them too
to carry on His work
to do His miracles
perpetuate His name.

—Mary, mother of Jesus—and James

"You ask a question about the baptism of the Holy Ghost—did I get there all at once, or easily?" Chambers asks. "No, I did not. Pride and the possession of the high esteem of my many Christian friends kept me out for long enough. But immediately I was willing to sacrifice all and put myself on the Altar, which is Jesus Himself, all was begun and done.

"Holiness is not an attainment at all, it is the gift of God, and the pietistic tendency is the introspection which makes me worship my own earnestness and not take the Lord seriously at all. It is a pious fraud that suits the natural man immensely.

"*He* makes holy, *He* sanctifies, *He* does it all. All I have to do is to come as a spiritual pauper, not ashamed to beg, to let go of my right to myself and act on Romans 12:1-2. It is never 'Do, do and you'll be' with the Lord, but 'Be, be and I will do through you.' "[4]

The early Christians—Mary, Peter, Nicodemus, Paul—flung their pride and their reputations to the wind. And, through their lives, the wind of the Holy Spirit continued to blow refreshingly over Jerusalem.

What an insight, that I might worship my own earnestness! Forgive me my self-pride, my self-righteousness.

Week 32

Dorcas, a Lighthouse Keeper

As I was finishing up a revision of this book, a friend made a working vacation possible with the gracious offer to let me use her apartment at the New Jersey shore. Along with many hours spent writing in the comfortably furnished Wildwood Public Library, the week included a visit to North Wildwood's Hereford Lighthouse.

Unaware at first that the Hereford Inlet practically bordered the lighthouse's backyard, we were surprised to find the interesting old building on what appeared to be a side street in the small community of Anglesea. The light tower actually "grew" out of the house itself! But small beginnings did not limit its radiance; its light could be seen fourteen miles out to sea. What a symbol of the light God wants to "shed abroad" from our homes!

That week I was working on this chapter, the story of Dorcas, a woman who lived in the Mediterranean seacoast town of Joppa. Spiritually, a lighthouse grew out of her humble home. She is described as a "disciple . . . who was always doing good and helping the poor" (Acts 9:36).

If Dorcas lived today, perhaps she could relate to the poem I wrote after one early-morning walk on the beach.

I walked along a shore one sunrise,
a shore untouched by human hand,
each of yesterday's sand castles
crumbled to a mound of sand.

The only footprints were the seagulls'
and I thought I'd find a shell
whose perfection would exceed
all the boardwalk shops could sell.

But as I walked on perfect seashore
looking for the perfect shell
all I saw were crushed and broken
by the ocean's ebb and swell.

I'd been so absorbed in searching
for the perfect jewel rare
I had missed the perfect sunrise.
I was startled by its glare.

I looked back at broken beauty
still ignored by human hands
and as the Son's rays touched each facet
I saw diamonds in the sand.

BACKGROUND READING: Psalm 98

A PLAYGROUND—AND A CEMETERY

"He is a rugged mountain where I hide; he is my Savior, a rock where none can reach me, and a tower of safety."
(Psalm 18:2, TLB)

Read Psalm 95

To Herod's crowd the beach is a resort
a place for parties raging wildly
through the night
and Caesarea's waves
provide a playground for the rich.
But life is not a party here
in Joppa.

—Dorcas

Built on a rock that rises about 125 feet above sea level, jutting out into the Mediterranean, Joppa has always been located well for defense. Ships could enter only from the north, where inviting, sandy beaches lured visitors. But treacherous hidden reefs, 300 to 400 feet offshore, trapped the unsuspecting invader.

In honor of Jope, god of the winds, Alexander the Great changed the name of Dorcas' hometown from Yapho to Joppa. When Joppa came under Roman rule, it became a part of the territory of Herod the Great. The people of Joppa hated Herod, however, and Herod knew it. So he built his summer home, Caesarea, some forty miles to the north, and Joppa declined in importance.

In Joppa, unlike Caesarea, the sea was not seen as a playful force. Many seacoast families depended on the waters of the mighty Mediterranean for their living, but the treacherous rocks and winter storms regularly demolished the sailors' primitive wooden boats. Because it was the only natural harbor from Egypt to Mount Carmel, the bodies of fishermen and seamen often came to rest on the shores of Joppa.

I remember, Lord, that Jonah ran away from You, departing from Joppa. Make me like Dorcas, who bloomed where she was planted.

A COAT OF PRAYER

"No mere man has ever seen, heard or even imagined what wonderful things God has ready for those who love the Lord."
(1 Corinthians 2:9, TLB)

Read Psalm 93

I watch the women
as they watch the stormy sea
I watch the women as they bargain with the gods—
if only they will send their husbands back . . .
I watch the women as they find their men . . .
I watch the women as they weep.
—Dorcas

Imagine Dorcas walking the beach in the early morning hours, praying for her family and friends. . . .

Imagine her coming across a sailor's body, realizing that meant one more widow, one more fatherless family. . . .

Imagine Dorcas as she broke the news to her newly widowed friend, wrapping one of her own finely and prayerfully stitched coats around the woman to protect her from the fierce Joppa winds. . . .

Dorcas reminds me of Hannah, who each year sewed a coat for her greatly missed, beloved son Samuel.

God the Creator is the One who instills in us our creativity. One woman sews beautifully, another is a gourmet cook, another uses her artistry in decorating. Just as our Creator has given us these gifts, He desires that we give them back to Him in joyful service.

Lord, sometimes my gift seems so unimportant in comparison to those of others. Please show me how to use my gift in ways that will bring honor and glory to You.

A MOTHER'S HEART

"We know about these things because God has sent his Spirit to tell us, and his Spirit searches out and shows us all of God's deepest secrets." (1 Corinthians 2:10, TLB)

Read Acts 10:24-28

I watch the children
too young to understand finality and death.
I watch them sob
then turn to build more castles in the sand
their mothers weeping all the while.
I watch them
and my heart breaks for their pain—
the pain they face today
and then tomorrow
and again.
—Dorcas

Sometimes the woman with no biological children of her own has a mother's heart that reaches out to children desperately in need of her nurturing ability. She may find herself drawn to the most challenging—and challenged—cases.

My friend Cathy, while on a missions trip to Russia, saw an infant girl in an orphanage whose face and body had been severely burned by saline solution in an attempted abortion. Cathy was unable to take care of the child medically, but she carried the little one in her heart, upholding her in prayer. After some time, Cathy heard that the little girl had been adopted by a Christian couple who were able to provide for the child's medical expenses.

Scripture does not tell us whether Dorcas ever married or had children of her own, but we know that her love nurtured many. Isaiah 54 tells the woman who never bore a child to shout for joy, to burst into song. She will forget the shame of her youth, she will no longer remember the reproach of her widowhood.

Thank You, Lord, for filling many of the gaps in my life as I have reached out to fill the needs of others.

WHEN I GIVE TO OTHERS, LIFE IS RICH

"No one can really know what anyone else is thinking, or what he is really like, except that person himself."
(1 Corinthians 2:11, TLB)

Read Acts 11:1-18

I see the suffering from my ocean home.
I have but little
and sometimes I wonder
why my life's been spared
but when I give to others
life is rich.
I love to sew,
creating beauty
bringing smiles to eyes
that weep through lonely nights
and if a child may laugh aloud
as to her heart she holds a doll I've made
I feel it in my heart—
I've been the hand of God.
—Dorcas

Lighthouses have aided mariners for centuries, guiding ships to port and alerting them of navigational hazards.

Up until recent years, the lighthouse keeper was the key element in lighthouse operation. Though the keeping of U.S. lighthouses was originally regarded as a male activity, from 1820 to 1852 special consideration was given to the widows of lighthouse keepers. Over the years, many women were involved in the lighting of the lamp.

John Walker was the first keeper of the Robbins Reef Light in New York. When he died, his widow Kate applied for the position. She was almost denied it because she was only 4′ 10″ and weighed barely 100 pounds. However, Kate not only kept the light burning but, in addition, rescued more than fifty fishermen in distress. She also raised two sons, rowing them a mile each day to Staten Island so they could attend school!

Lord, may I always be open to the special opportunities You present in my life. Make my heart the heart of a lighthouse keeper.

LIKE EBB AND FLOW OF WIND AND WAVE

"And no one can know God's thoughts
except God's own Spirit." (1 Corinthians 2:11, TLB)

Read Acts 9:32-43

One day my life just ebbed away.
Without a warning
it was gone
like ebb and flow
of wind and wave
—or so they tell me.

Then the big fisherman—Peter—came.
He knelt and prayed.
He said, "Arise!"

I heard his voice.
It was a miracle.
I arose
and life has never been the same.

—Dorcas

For reasons known only to Him, God chose to raise Dorcas from the dead. Why Dorcas rather than someone else? Was her life more exemplary than other early Christians who lost their lives in martyrdom?

There is only one answer. "For my thoughts are not your thoughts, neither are your ways my ways" (Isaiah 55:8). Whatever God chose to do in Dorcas' life was His decision. He had created her, and she had given back her life to Him.

The first seven chapters of Acts tell how the Church was born. Chapters 8-12 describe a time of dynamic growth for the Church. Daily, the good news of salvation was changing lives, breaking down walls of prejudice between Jews and Gentiles.

Through all of this, Peter had become the central character, but now it was time for him to slip into the shadows, giving way to Paul's leadership. Through using Peter to touch the life of an unselfish, generous woman named Dorcas, God evidenced—one more time—His special love and forgiveness for a big fisherman named Peter.

God, You are amazing.

32 — Saturday

I FEEL HIS SMILE ON ME

"And God has actually given us his Spirit (not the world's spirit) to tell us about the wonderful free gifts of grace and blessing that God has given us." (1 Corinthians 2:12, TLB)

Read Jonah 4

Ah, why should I,
a humble maid of Joppa,
be touched by God
to speak His praise?
If I forget to praise Him
the sand itself will speak.
I do not know or understand
why God was pleased to intervene
but I continue
to do the only thing I know.
For when I sew
I feel His smile on me.
—Dorcas

After Herod built his winter home, Caesarea, to the north, Joppa declined in importance. Dorcas was just a humble citizen of a mediocre town. But people also said of the hometown of Jesus: "Can anything good come out of Nazareth?" (see John 1:46).

Fame and fortune are fleeting, but "to enjoy your work and to accept your lot in life—that is indeed a gift from God. The person who does that will not need to look back with sorrow on his past, for God gives him joy" (Ecclesiastes 5:19-20, TLB).

POINT TO PONDER: Dorcas and Jonah had the city of Joppa in common, but that's where the similarity ends. Jonah ran away from the Lord, but he certainly didn't have a whale of a time in doing so. Dorcas bloomed where she was planted, and God rewarded her in a unique way.

Thank You for this story of a humble woman who lit up her little world by giving her life back to You.

Week 33

Mary, the Mother of John Mark

It was about this time that King Herod arrested some who belonged to the church, intending to persecute them. He had James, the brother of John, put to death with the sword. When he saw that this pleased the Jews, he proceeded to seize Peter also. This happened during the Feast of Unleavened Bread. After arresting him, he put him in prison, handing him over to be guarded by four squads of four soldiers each. Herod intended to bring him out for public trial after the Passover.

So Peter was kept in prison, but the church was earnestly praying to God for him.

The night before Herod was to bring him to trial, Peter was sleeping between two soldiers, bound with two chains, and sentries stood guard at the entrance. Suddenly an angel of the Lord appeared and a light shone in the cell. He struck Peter on the side and woke him up. "Quick, get up!" he said, and the chains fell off Peter's wrists.

Then the angel said to him, "Put on your clothes and sandals." And Peter did so. "Wrap your cloak around you and follow me," the angel told him. Peter followed him out of the prison, but he had no idea that what the angel was doing was really happening; he thought he was seeing a vision. They passed the first and second guards and came to the iron gate leading to the city. It opened for them by itself, and they went through it.

> When they had walked the length of one street, suddenly the angel left him.
>
> Then Peter came to himself and said, *"Now I know without a doubt that the Lord sent his angel and rescued me from Herod's clutches and from everything the Jewish people were anticipating."*
>
> When this had dawned on him, *he went to the house of Mary* the mother of John, also called Mark, *where many people had gathered and were praying.* (Acts 12:1-12, emphasis added)

When Peter finally realized that God had sent His angel to deliver him from prison, he knew exactly where to go to let the "pray-ers" know that their prayers had been answered.

Where did the Jerusalem Christians go to pray? *Mary's house was where the "pray-ers" hung out.*

Does your home—your house, your apartment, your place of business—have that reputation? Or is the TV always on, turned up so loud that you can't hear people talk, much less pray? Is the activity level so frenzied that people never think of stopping to pray?

Lord, make my house a house of pray-ers.

BACKGROUND READING: Acts 4:1-22

AN IMPULSIVE YOUNG MAN

"Then [His disciples], forsaking Him, fled, all [of them]. And a young man was following Him, with nothing but a linen cloth (sheet) thrown about [his] naked [body]; and they laid hold of him, but leaving behind the linen cloth (sheet), he fled from them naked." (Mark 14:50-52, Amplified)

Read Mark 14:26-49

Oh, my dear impulsive son!
That night you ran from home to Jesus' side,
clothed only in a linen sheet
you'd pulled from bedclothes,
you heard they'd come to get Him—
and you were gone!
But when they grabbed you
you left the sheet and ran for home.

—Mary, mother of John Mark

The very short story told in Mark 14 is probably the bitter-sweet memory of a mature man looking back on a night in his youth when he acted quickly and spontaneously. Mark was his Latin or Gentile name; John, his Jewish name.

After the Last Supper, when Jesus led the disciples out of the city of Jerusalem to the Mount of Olives and the Garden of Gethsemane to pray, perhaps John Mark decided to go home. Maybe he was tired; maybe he was feeling sick; maybe he needed something. Maybe John Mark just wanted to go home to wake up Mary and ask her to pray. Can you hear him?

Perhaps at that point, feeling covered by prayer, John Mark fell asleep in his mother's home—to be awakened by the news that a mob, led by the chief priests and other Jewish leaders, was heading for the Mount of Olives. He grabbed a sheet, wrapping it around himself as he ran. The rest is history.

I ask you, as you look back over the family stories of your life—can there be any greater honor than to be asked, by those younger than yourself, to pray?

There is no greater joy, Lord, than to hear that my children walk in truth. Thank You for patience, the fruit of Your Spirit, that You are developing in me as I sit in this waiting room.

BARNABAS THE GREAT-HEARTED

"Joseph, a Levite from Cyprus, whom the apostles called Barnabas (which means Son of Encouragement), sold a field he owned and brought the money and put it at the apostles' feet." *(Acts 4:36)*

Read Acts 4:32-37; Hebrews 13:1-8

Our cousin Barnabas—
He's brought encouragement so often.
He cares for others
more than for himself.
I hope he does not give his all away.
—Mary, mother of John Mark

Originally Levites did not inherit or own land, but this regulation may not have applied at this time in Israel or in other countries like Cyprus, Barnabas' island homeland in the Mediterranean. Barnabas may have sold some Cyprian shoreland and brought the price of it to the apostles. Perhaps, if he was married, the land he sold may have been from his wife's property.

Generosity ran in the family. Mary opened her home for fellowship with other Christians. At the same time, she made sure that the atmosphere of her home was conducive not to partying, but to prayer. Opening her home meant opening her heart to the problems of those around her. And at times that can be physically and emotionally draining.

"In the Psalms," Amy Carmichael observed, "every experience of distress turns to a straight look up, and praise. . . . Surely this emphasis on praise in the Psalms is because to turn from discouraging things and look up with a song in one's heart is the only sure way of continuance. We sink down into what David calls mire, slime, deep waters, if we do not quickly look up and, turning our back on the discouraging, set our faces again toward the sunrising."[1]

Remind me, Lord, that when I am exhausted from listening to family or friends, I can set my face toward the sunrise, and think of the day when You *will wipe away every tear.*

BARNABAS, UNAFRAID TO BE A FRIEND

"When [Saul] came to Jerusalem, he tried to join the disciples, but they were all afraid of him. . . . But Barnabas took him and brought him to the apostles. He told them how Saul on his journey had seen the Lord and . . . how in Damascus he had preached fearlessly in the name of Jesus." (Acts 9:26-27)

Read Acts 11:19-30

He is the one who always helps the others.
"Son of comfort"
he is called.
But to defend this
man of death?
Can we be sure
Saul's to be trusted?

—Mary, mother of John Mark

Perhaps the first conversation between Barnabas and Saul took place in Mary's home—a "safe place" for Saul after his narrow escape from the Damascus Jews. But would Mary have felt safe? After all, the disciples in Jerusalem were very much afraid of Saul—and for good reason.

In the book *Life Mapping,* author/counselor John Trent coined the term "flash point," a dramatic turning point in one's life. Or a flash point can be as quiet and unspectacular as a child's prayer at a mother's knee, inviting Jesus to come into his heart.

Was Mary eavesdropping from another room as Saul told Barnabas about the flash point that changed his life? "As I neared Damascus on my journey to find any there who belonged to the Way, to take them as prisoners here to Jerusalem, suddenly a light from heaven flashed around me. I fell to the ground and heard a voice say to me, 'Saul, Saul, why do you persecute Me?' I asked in amazement: 'Who are you, Lord?' 'I am Jesus, whom you are persecuting.' He told me to get up and go into Damascus. I tried to obey, but when I opened my eyes, I could see nothing. Then my dear brother, Ananias, laid his hands on me. It was as though scales fell from my eyes! My sight was restored—and Barnabas, I'll never be the same."

Thank You, Jesus, for the time when I met You. Renew that encounter in my heart.

33 – Thursday

FIRST FRIEND OR SECOND FIDDLE?

"In the church at Antioch there were prophets and teachers: Barnabas, Simeon . . . Manaen . . . and Saul. While they were worshiping the Lord and fasting, the Holy Spirit said, 'Set apart for me Barnabas and Saul for the work to which I have called them.' So after they had fasted and prayed, they placed their hands on them and sent them off." (Acts 13:1-3)

Read Acts 12:19-25

And now it seems
my brother's dominated
by this new convert Paul
who once was Saul,
a hater and a killer
of us all.

—Mary, mother of John Mark

Another term Trent uses is "freeze point," most easily illustrated by the picture of a boy with his tongue frozen to a flagpole. The boy in that picture is "stuck," and he's not going to go anywhere without a lot of pain!

Mary might have become "stuck" in her attitude toward Saul, even after he was renamed the apostle Paul. After all, most of the Jerusalem Christians were totally turned off by the man's track record. How did they know this conversion to Christianity wasn't just an act, an act that would end when Spy Saul was sure of the identities of all the Christians in the city?

The problem with freeze points is that we can't enjoy the fellowship of anyone who isn't similarly stuck. We can't grow as long as our tongue is anchored. We can't progress in our Christian walk until we get loose from the flagpole. And when we stay in a freeze point for too long, it can become a "flesh point."

Lord, please check my life for freeze points. Help me to let go of the hurt so it will not become a flesh point.

33 – Friday

BLOOD IS THICKER THAN WATER

"Barnabas wanted to take John, also called Mark, with them, but Paul did not think it wise to take him, because he had deserted them in Pamphylia and had not continued with them in the work. They had such a sharp disagreement that they parted company. Barnabas took Mark and sailed for Cyprus, but Paul chose Silas and left. . . ." (Acts 15:37-40)

Read Acts 15:22-41

My son had difficulty
in seeing eye-to-eye
with that strange man
and so, when he came home
to think things through
Mark was not on the best of terms with Paul.
—Mary, mother of John Mark

It's a little disappointing to recognize that giants of the faith like Paul and Barnabas had a sharp disagreement, a "falling-out." In a way, though, maybe it's also comforting. Personality differences and family feuds—or the complications and manipulations of blood relationships—create problems in any situation, no matter how "spiritual" the people involved.

Paul and Barnabas had enough sense to part company, to cool off and to "let bygones be bygones." Later, Paul spoke warmly of Barnabas in the epistles, stating in First Corinthians 9:6 that only Barnabas worked for a living as he (Paul) did. In Galatians 2, Paul condemned "the circumcision group" whose hypocrisy was so persuasive that *"even Barnabas* was led astray" (emphasis added) for a time. Paul's respect for Barnabas is obvious, even if they had disagreed in the past. As far as we know, Paul and Barnabas disagreed in only one area. Given time, it seems that John Mark, their focus of disagreement, grew up!

Have you noticed how often time heals even heels—or your relationships with them? It's amazing what great times you can have talking to former classmates, people with whom you had little in common at the time. (Now you have age in common!)

Lord, I never thought I'd ask You to bless a certain person . . . but now You have my permission!

ALL'S WELL THAT ENDS WELL

"Get Mark and bring him with you, because he is helpful to me in my ministry." (2 Timothy 4:11)
"Ephaphrus, my fellow prisoner in Christ Jesus, sends you greetings. And so do Mark, Aristarchus, Demas and Luke, my fellow workers." (Philemon 23-24)

Read 1 Peter 5:1-13

We all changed as the years went by.
We learned to love,
accept each other,
forgive the past,
begin anew,
support each other in the work of Christ.
—Mary, mother of John Mark

Commentaries suggest that John Mark gathered the memories of the apostle Peter into the Gospel according to Mark. Scholars think Mark spent considerable time with Peter (the Scriptures do not mention Mark's father). Perhaps Peter and Mark shared the same kind of temperament—outspoken, impulsive, confrontative.

Both Peter and Paul use affectionate terms for Mark, indicating a close association with both men. When Paul wrote to the Colossians, he asked them to welcome Mark, indicating that Mark was in Rome, that Mark and Paul were cordial toward each other again and that Mark was about to leave for a tour of the churches in the East.

Several years later, Paul's second letter to Timothy suggests that Mark was away from Rome but was needed by Paul. First Peter indicates that Mark joined Peter at Rome, possibly before Paul's execution, and most early historians state that Mark was with Peter at Rome when Peter died. All ancient traditions agree that Mark died a martyr.

Thank You, Lord, for those who have filled in the gaps in my life.

Week 34

Rhoda

Few people are familiar with Mary, the mother of John Mark (commonly called Mark), writer of the second Gospel and a co-worker with Paul and Peter. Tradition has placed her home on the south end of the western hill of Mt. Zion, a well-to-do residential section of Jerusalem.

Mary was also a close relative of Barnabas, a prophet and teacher in the early Jerusalem church (Colossians 4:10). Evidently she was a mothering influence, heavily involved in the growing pains of the new body; the prayer group met in her home. This was not only evidence of her dedication, but also of Mary's quiet, fearless spirit in the face of danger.

It was to Mary's home that Peter came after his release from prison. But isn't it sad that praying Christians, supposedly in touch with their heavenly Father, can be blind and deaf to what is really happening around them? Although they were asking for his release, they could not believe it was actually Peter standing at the door.

Rhoda was a young woman who worked as a maid in John Mark's home. Since she is one of the only girls mentioned by name in the New Testament, let's spend a little time exploring her possible thoughts and reactions to those exciting days of the early Church. She's a lovable figure, easy to remember and identify with, but doesn't she seem to be an airhead?

Then again, do you remember the veritable multitude of thoughts that were flying through your gray matter when you were a teenager? Life was all ahead of you, and there was so much to think about . . . and feel . . . and wonder about. . . .

BACKGROUND READING: Acts 12:1-17

34 – Monday

A DISEASE CALLED IBS

"Don't let anyone look down on you because you are young."
(1 Timothy 4:12)

Read Acts 9:36-40

What could the Lord have in store for me?
What does He want me to do?
Will I marry a man like Peter or Paul?
Will I travel to Athens too?
Peter's wife goes along with him—
How exciting that would be!
I'd like a chance to see the world—
What does God have in store for me?
—Rhoda

Rhoda was young, full of anticipation, probably bursting with dramatic dreams of the future. Youth, with its abundance of energy and natural optimism, is the time of life God provided for dreaming, for goal setting and, at the same time, for learning the skills and abilities needed to follow through on those dreams.

The work involved in learning is essential. Anyone who is not familiar with profitable exercise of the muscles and mind will soon relapse into the disease of IBS ("I'm Bored" Syndrome).

IBS is very difficult to cure: if not treated in the early stages of the disease, it may indeed become incurable. If you are a parent, it is wise to watch for the signs of this disease early in a child's life. Symptoms include temporary deafness and dumbness, especially when the young person is exposed to certain electronic devices often found in the living or family rooms of contemporary homes. The patient may actually fall into a dead faint on the floor of these rooms and can be revived only with great effort on the part of the parent. Family awareness of the potential harm of this disease is the first step in preventive medicine.

Thank You, Father, for the tremendous potential of youth.

34 – Tuesday

A COMMITTED HEART

"Set an example for the believers in speech, in life, in love, in faith and in purity." (1 Timothy 4:12)

Read Psalm 57

John Mark's gone to Asia Minor
With Barnabas and Paul.
He seems so young to go so far
But I know he's heard the call.
What can I do to serve the Lord?
I'm only a servant girl.
My mistress tells me I can pray
But my head's in such a whirl.
—Rhoda

Taking time to pray is difficult at any age, but especially so when you're young and full of energy and life is full of exciting options. Rhoda was at a prayer meeting the night Peter knocked at the door of Mary's home, but how are you supposed to keep your mind on prayer when your body, and other bodies all around you, are sending out all kinds of interesting vibrations?

On days when my mind feels like a child's teeter-totter, my emotions are flying around a merry-go-round at high speed and my spirit has just taken a low dive and bitten the dust at the bottom of the giant slide, I need to resolve that no matter where the roller coaster of life catapults me, my love and loyalty for God will remain constant.

POINTS TO PONDER: Emotions and feelings may come and go, but I must not allow them to influence the vow I have made. Feeling must be based upon fact. "Every spirit that acknowledges that Jesus Christ has come in the flesh is from God, but every spirit that does not acknowledge Jesus is not from God" (1 John 4:2-3).

Father, please grant me the gift of discernment in this confusing world.

THE PROBLEM OF PEER PRESSURE

"The Spirit clearly says that in later times some will abandon the faith. . . . Have nothing to do with godless myths and old wives' tales; rather, train yourself to be godly."
(1 Timothy 4:1, 7-8)

Read 1 John 4:1-6

James is dead, killed by a sword!
Would I have courage to stand
Firm and true for what is right—
Or hide my head in the sand?
Yes, even Peter denied the Lord
In fear and embarrassed pride
But look at how that man has changed—
He isn't trying to hide!

—Rhoda

Rhoda may have worried, as I did, about her ability to stand for the right when under pressure; yet in my teen years I spent very little time or effort communicating my beliefs to the people around me. I was much more concerned that they would not think of me as an oddball.

Peer pressure is an extremely strong force in the adolescent years. For many young people it is all-important to look like, sound like and act like "everyone else" at school or work. Instead of arguing this need for peer approval, parents and friends of teenagers should accept it as a fact of life and encourage relationships with other Christian kids. Become involved in your church's youth activities; they can always use a coach or chaperon. If there aren't any activities, don't sit back and complain or switch churches for that reason alone—start some activities. Volunteer to help teach the teenagers' Sunday school class or help get a Bible quiz team started (a super activity in our boys' lives). Invite a group to your home for pizza or ice cream and be open to their needs. Listen instead of preaching, arguing or appearing to be on the defensive. They will read your life like an open book.

Father, open my mind and heart to the opportunities all around me.

GOD GAVE YOU A GIFT

"Devote yourself to . . . Scripture. . . .
Do not neglect your gift. . . . Be diligent in these matters;
give yourself wholly to them, so that everyone may see
your progress." (1 Timothy 4:13-15)

Read Romans 12:4-13

Peter's such a powerful preacher now.
I wonder what Herod will do.
I fear for his life—he's in prison tonight,
Perhaps dead in a day or two!
Mary keeps telling me we can pray—
I should be praying now—
But I can't quiet my mind and heart.
I just don't seem to know how!
—Rhoda

How did Rhoda feel about her position as a servant? A sure way to limit God's working in our own lives is to be envious of His gifts to others. Do you find yourself constantly murmuring, "I wish I could sing . . . or paint . . . or play the piano as well as she does"? Ask God just what gifts and abilities He has given you, and then concentrate on using them for His glory. An unrecognized talent may become obvious as you serve others.

Maybe you can't sing, but you can cook. Maybe you are scared stiff at the prospect of facing a Sunday school class, but you feel comfortable about inviting people into your home for a cup of tea and a friendly chat. Maybe you can't preach, but you can pray for the preacher.

POINT TO PONDER: Or maybe you *can* sing and teach and preach, and you need to quit praying that God will send someone and get out and *be* that someone.

Thank You, Father, for the unique gifts You have given me.

34 – Friday

THE WRONG SPIRIT

"Watch your life and doctrine closely. Persevere in them, because if you do, you will save both yourself and your hearers." (1 Timothy 4:16)

Read 1 John 3:1-10

Is that a knock I hear on the door?
Could it be the soldiers, come
To take all the Christians off to jail?
Should I answer the door or run?
There it is again! It's a quiet knock;
No one upstairs will hear.
I'll just go down and peek through the hole—
Lord, help me control my fear!
—Rhoda

In Rhoda's day Christians feared death or imprisonment by the Roman authorities. We do not live in fear of the sword, as Rhoda did, but a day may come when Christians will not be as free to worship as we are today. If your Bible were taken from you, how much of it would remain hidden in your heart?

Rote memorization of the Scriptures is valuable, but more important, Scripture can be personalized and prayed back to God. (Start with the Psalms.)

The principles of Scripture should be evident in my lifestyle. I'm sure Rhoda's neighbors were aware that she belonged to a godly household. Even in a potentially dangerous situation, the Christians gathered in Mary's house to pray. Would I have that strength of conviction? Would I have had courage to go to the door?

Father, in my own strength I feel sure I would fail, but You have promised that Your grace is sufficient, that You will not allow me to experience more than I can bear. Help me to know the reality of truth . . . today as well as tomorrow.

34 — Saturday

IT'S COLD OUT THERE!

"Stay true to what is right and God will bless you and use you to help others." (1 Timothy 4:16, TLB)

Read 1 John 3:11-24

It's Peter! He's here! He's no longer in jail!
He's here, standing outside the door!
I tell you, it's true—he's here in the flesh!
No angels, just Peter—no more!
Oh, what have I done? How could I forget him?
Forgive me, dear Peter, dear Lord.
I wanted to give them the news, but poor Peter
Is still standing outside the door!

—Rhoda

Scripture tells us that Rhoda was overjoyed when she heard Peter's voice. Joyful reactions are good, but it's important that we carefully think through each situation we encounter. Why? Because we are so easily deceived by our emotions. Thinking it through, even "praying through," may not be enough because our emotions influence our prayer life and the answers we *think* we receive from God. We need to base all our decisions and judgments on God's unchanging Word, as given to us in the Bible. And "do not be surprised . . . if the world hates you" (1 John 3:13).

POINT TO PONDER: As parents we can be so preoccupied by a child that we give her more than she knows how to graciously receive and enjoy. In any human relationship we can become so possessive in our love that we endanger the friendship. In our relationship with Christ we can become so enthusiastic about programs and promises to people that we neglect to set aside time for the One we are supposedly serving.

Rhoda left Peter outside the gate. Is Christ standing at your doorway, waiting for you to remember Him? Have you invited Him in, but then run off without actually opening the door and making Him feel welcome? How can you tell others about your relationship with Him unless you have something to tell?

It's so easy for me to understand Rhoda, Lord Jesus, because she's so much like me. Calm me down, Lord . . . please.

Week 35

Mary, Mother of James the Lesser

"Near the cross of Jesus stood his mother, his mother's sister, *Mary the wife of Clopas* [or Cleopas or Cleophas], and Mary Magdalene" (John 19:25, emphasis added).

"Some women were watching from a distance. Among them were Mary Magdalene, *Mary the mother of James the younger and of Joses,* and Salome" (Mark 15:40, emphasis added).

"Many women were there, watching from a distance. They had followed Jesus from Galilee to care for his needs. Among them were Mary Magdalene, *Mary the mother of James and Joses,* and the mother of Zebedee's sons" (Matthew 27:55-56, emphasis added).

"When they came back from the tomb, they told all these things to the Eleven and to all the others. It was Mary Magdalene, Joanna, *Mary the mother of James,* and the others with them who told this to the apostles" (Luke 24:9-10, emphasis added).

"Then they returned to Jerusalem from . . . the Mount of Olives. . . . They went upstairs to the room where they were staying. Those present were Peter, John, James and Andrew; Philip and Thomas, Bartholomew and Matthew; *James son of Alphaeus* and Simon the Zealot, and Judas [Thaddeus] son of James" (Acts 1:12-13, emphasis added).

Is it any wonder that this Mary has often been confused

with other women? She is named in various places as the wife of Cleopas (Clopas) and the wife of Alphaeus. Edith Deen's research in *All of the Women of the Bible* eases the confusion by pointing out that the names Cleopas and Alphaeus are variant forms of the same Aramaic original. And so Alphaeus/Cleopas and this Mary were parents of the apostle James the "Lesser"—or "Younger" or "Smaller"—who had a brother Joses (the Greek form of Joseph).[1]

Some scholars believe that Joses and those called the brothers and sisters of Jesus were actually cousins of Jesus and children of this Mary. They base this on John 19:25, which may be interpreted as stating that Mary the wife of Cleophas was the sister of Jesus' mother. But is it likely, other scholars ask, that two sisters in the same family would bear the same name? They identify "his mother's sister" as Salome and "Mary the wife of Cleopas" as the mother of James and Joses.

Remember the story of Cleopas, who, disillusioned by the events of Passover Week, was walking with a companion from Jerusalem to Emmaus? Cleopas was so discouraged that when Christ met them and walked with them Cleopas did not recognize Him. Not until Christ broke bread with them and then disappeared were the eyes of Cleopas and his companion opened to spiritual reality.

Was this Cleopas the father of James the Lesser? Was Mary his fellow-walker? If so, how they must have been comforted by seeing the risen Lord—together!

BACKGROUND READING: Luke 24:13-35

35 – Monday

PRAY, DON'T PUSH!

"And the Spirit of the Lord shall rest upon him, the Spirit of wisdom, understanding, counsel and might; the Spirit of knowledge and of the fear of the Lord." (Isaiah 11:2, TLB)

Read Romans 3:5-7

Why do some mothers push their sons
instead of giving them a chance
to find their own direction—
the one that God's ordained?

Remind me, Lord,
to pray instead of push,
to trust your Holy Spirit
to work in my son's life.

—Mary, mother of James the Lesser

Like all of Jesus' followers, Mary and Cleopas must have desired for Jesus to stay with them in His physical, bodily presence. As I read a little book entitled *When the Comforter Came,* I wished I could have shared it with them.

"If Jesus had continued with them in visible form," Dr. A.B. Simpson explained, "He could only have been in one place at one time and His presence would have been local and individual. He could not have spoken to one here and another on the other side of the world. But now, in His spiritual Presence, *He is omnipresent and able to give His whole attention to you, and at the same moment be in conscious fellowship with innumerable other hearts in all the world*" (emphasis added).[2]

Are we really aware of this miraculous and unlimited presence of Christ through His omnipresent Holy Spirit? The clutter and clatter of daily life is so distracting that we need to consciously "practice the presence."

Thank You, Lord, for this amazing truth, that I can pour my hopes and dreams and desires into Your attentive ear while someone else is, at the same time, pouring out his or her hopes and needs and sorrows—and You can give both of us Your focused attention!

"INEXPRESSIBLE INFLUENCES AND IMPULSES"

"Jesus said, 'Do not hold on to me, for I have not yet returned to the Father.' " (John 20:17)

Read John 14:15-21

I see the other Mary
—Mary Magdalene—
watching mothers with their sons.
Hers is a loneliness that often only deepens
as mothers become grandmothers.
And yet she has been comforted by Jesus
and now His Holy Spirit
in a special way.

—Mary, mother of James the Lesser

When Jesus appeared to Mary in the Garden after the Resurrection, He told her not to touch Him or hold on to Him. If Jesus had remained on earth, He could only have communicated with Mary—and with us—through outward touch and imperfect human language and senses. Jesus would have been an *external* Presence.

"But now He meets us in our deeper and higher nature," Dr. Simpson wrote, "by the communion of His Spirit . . . not only in actual words and thoughts but in those inarticulate and inexpressible influences and impulses which no words could ever fully convey.

"The presence of Christ and the fellowship of His life and love are 'immeasurably more than all' that words could speak or heart could think. He imparts to us His very life and feeds us with the living Bread. He breathes into us the sweetness of His peace that passes all understanding. He sheds abroad in our hearts the love of God. He rolls upon us the burden of His prayer and the fellowship of His sufferings. He even pours into our mortal frame the fullness of His resurrection life, healing . . . all our being with His life and strength. All this and infinitely more could never have been if Jesus had not gone away and then come back to us through the presence of the Comforter."[3]

Thank You, Holy Spirit, for imparting to us the very life of Jesus.

35 — *Wednesday*

SPIRITUAL BREATHING . . . SPIRITUAL SUFFOCATING

"Then Peter said, 'Ananias, how is it that Satan has so filled your heart that you have lied to the Holy Spirit and have kept for yourself some of the money you received for the land? . . . You have not lied to men but to God. . . . How could you agree to test the Spirit of the Lord?' " (Acts 5:3-4, 9)

Read Acts 4:32-5:11

Sapphira's lie,
Sapphira's death . . .
conspiracy in crime
with her late husband
(of whose death she's unaware)
testing the Spirit of the Lord
and proving once again
that the spirit of control,
emerging from the pit,
wreaks havoc in our lives.

—Mary, mother of James the Lesser

Barnabas, the "Son of Encouragement," had given a sizable gift to the church, and perhaps he had received public acknowledgment for it. Did Ananias and Sapphira desire equal attention? Barnabas had ministered to others; the guilty couple manipulated and called it ministry.

Instead of trying to control, instead of testing the Spirit of the Lord, how much sweeter life is when we breathe out—exhale—our own carnal thoughts and attitudes and breathe in—inhale—the new spiritual life from the Holy Spirit.

"And with that he breathed on them and said, 'Receive the Holy Spirit' " (John 20:22). Thank You for reminding me, Father, that I receive the infilling of the Holy Spirit by breathing in the very life of Jesus.

35 – Thursday

THE WIND OF THE SPIRIT

"After they prayed, the place where they were meeting was shaken. And they were all filled with the Holy Spirit and spoke the word of God boldly." (Acts 4:31)

Read John 3:1-21

Great fear has seized the church
since we've observed this double death
but even greater fear has fallen
on those who had not yet believed.
And more and more believers
are added to the number.

—Mary, mother of James the Lesser

As Jesus breathed into His disciples the Holy Spirit, even so, in the morning of creation, "the LORD God . . . breathed into [man's] nostrils the breath of life" (Genesis 2:7).

Later in the Old Testament, the prophet Ezekiel summoned the Holy Spirit: "Come from the four winds, O breath [or 'spirit']" (Ezekiel 37:9).

In John 3:8, Jesus also used the wind as a metaphor for the work of the Holy Spirit: "The wind blows wherever it pleases. You hear its sound, but you cannot tell where it comes from or where it is going. So it is with everyone born of the Spirit."

In Acts, the irresistible energy and power of the Holy Spirit was described as "the blowing of a violent wind . . . from heaven" (Acts 2:2).

The ways in which the Spirit works, like the wind, are mysterious in that they are usually not seen or understood by us. As Dr. Simpson said, "We cannot trace the working of His hands, but we can see and feel the purity, the peace, the joy, the love and the fruits of blessing on every hand that follows that working."[4]

Help me to be sensitive, Lord, to Your Spirit, even when it is just a gentle breeze.

LORD, RECEIVE MY SPIRIT

"While they were stoning him, Stephen prayed, 'Lord Jesus, receive my spirit.' Then he fell on his knees and cried out, 'Lord, do not hold this sin against them. . . .' And Saul was there, giving approval to his death." (Acts 7:59-8:1)

Read Acts 6:7-15; 7:54-60

Another mother's son is gone!
Another mother grieves.
So many others stood and watched
as Stephen died,
cold as the stones they threw—
especially Saul.

—Mary, mother of James the Lesser

If Stephen's face "was like the face of an angel" (Acts 6:15), imagine his mother's gaze upon him as he gave his "last will and testament," responding to false charges with a simple presentation of the facts. But his audience became furious, not repentant. His hearers responded not by heeding the message, but by killing the messenger in the one of the most cruel, humiliating ways imaginable.

Stephen's mother had probably cherished dreams of great success for him. After all, her son had done "great wonders and miraculous signs among the people" (Acts 6:8). Imagine her feelings toward Saul, who was standing there, giving approval to the stoning.

Parents may feel "orphaned"—abandoned—by the loss of a child or by a child's moving a great distance geographically. The child, it seemed, represented the future, and now the future seems full of hopeless loneliness. But Jesus promises, "I will not leave you as orphans" (John 14:18).

Back in the Old Testament God revealed Himself in the nurturing figure of motherhood: "As a mother comforts her child, so will I comfort you" (Isaiah 66:13). And this aspect of His blessed character finds its perfect manifestation in the Holy Spirit. "We have in the divine Trinity not only a Father, and a Brother and a Husband, but also One who meets all the heart's longing for motherhood."[5]

Lord Jesus, I open my heart to the nurturing of Your Holy Spirit.

THE GENTLE HEART OF THE HOLY SPIRIT

"King Herod arrested some who belonged to the church, intending to persecute them. He had James, the brother of John, put to death with the sword." (Acts 12:1-2)

Read Acts 11:1-18

How life has changed for poor Salome!
Since her son James was killed
she's but a shadow of herself.
My James may be much quieter
—and slower-moving!—
but he's alive.

—Mary, mother of James the Lesser

The sword had pierced yet another mother's heart. Salome lost her son James to the sword of Herod. Did she feel that she had also "lost" her son John to his "adopted" mother, Mary, at the cross? Did Salome experience the comforting of the Holy Spirit?

Dr. Simpson pointed out that "the Comforter as our spiritual Mother is the author of our being and gives us new and heavenly birth. We are born of the Holy Spirit, our very life comes to us through the quickening life of the Holy Ghost. As our heavenly Mother, the Comforter assumes our nurture, training, teaching, and the whole direction of our life. . . . The special feature of the Spirit's teaching and guiding is its considerate gentleness and patience. He does not force upon us truth for which we are not yet prepared but leads us gently and teaches us, as He Himself has expressed it in the Old Testament, 'precept upon precept; . . . line upon line, . . . here a little, and there a little' (Isaiah 28:10, KJV).

"The Comforter's presence in our lives enables us to comfort others as we have been comforted. Jesus' acts of tenderness and love were the manifestations of the gentle heart of the Holy Ghost. And now that Spirit that dwelt in Him has come forth from Him to dwell in us and be to us the very heart of Christ Himself."[6]

Thank You, Jesus, for Your promise that You will not leave us as orphans, that You make available to us Your very mind and heart.

Week 36

Sapphira

Young love, first love—so many songs have been written on the subject! Infatuation holds such delight in sharing with each other, such promise for a future together.

But just as there is genuine love, there is also the counterfeit item. And so it was in the early Christian Church.

The newly born church in Jerusalem had begun to grow, both outwardly, in numbers, and inwardly, in knowledge of the truth and in spiritual strength. Members of the church were not content to meet only once a week; they "broke bread" together daily, the wealthier sharing with their brothers and sisters in Christ who were not so fortunate. Proceeds from the sale of land and houses were given to the church. The harmony of this prayerful fellowship was so obvious that outsiders commented on the Christians' love for each other.

One man in particular had such a generous spirit that his name was changed from Joseph to Barnabas, meaning "the encourager." He sold some land that he owned, brought the money and laid it at the apostles' feet, a beautiful act of love!

But perhaps some were jealous of Barnabas' place of favor in the church. Barnabas loved everyone, and everyone loved Barnabas in return—except Ananias and Sapphira.

BACKGROUND READING: Acts 5:1-11

GIVING SPIRIT OR "GIMME" SPIRIT?

"Don't you realize how patient he is being with you? Or don't you care? Can't you see that he has been waiting all this time without punishing you, to give you time to turn from your sin? His kindness is meant to lead you to repentance."
(Romans 2:4, TLB)

Read 2 Corinthians 9:1-7

No one respects what we have done!
We've worked our fingers to the bone
And what we have is ours alone.
Why should we give to others?
—Sapphira

"Now this is where I draw the line," I can hear Sapphira announcing to her husband Ananias, her face, once beautiful, now wearing an angry scowl. "I don't mind giving on feast days and special occasions, as we've always done, but this is asking too much! I feel as if we're expected to give *everything* to the church."

Ananias may have agreed with his wife, but then perhaps he always agreed with Sapphira. Her name meant "beautiful," but it does not appear that she was beautiful in spirit, especially when anyone disagreed with her. She was angry now because she wanted to receive the praise that others had heaped on Barnabas for his act of sacrifice. She wanted the praise, but not the sacrifice.

POINT TO PONDER: Often we have a cheerful attitude toward giving when we can determine the amount but when God asks more of us than we feel we owe Him, when we're digging so deep it hurts, are we still cheerful givers? And was God really asking Sapphira to give all her money, or was He simply asking for all of *her*?

Lord Jesus . . . do You sense a giving spirit in me? Please show me my true motivations.

WHAT DO I LOVE?

"But no, you won't listen; and so you are saving up terrible punishment for yourselves because of your stubbornness in refusing to turn from your sin; for there is going to come a day of wrath when God will be the just Judge of all the world."
(Romans 2:5, TLB)

Read 2 Corinthians 8:1-6

We have no reason to repent—
We've no desire to make amends!
We were the first ones to attend!
Should we give in to others?
—Sapphira

The love of money is the root of all evil, and Sapphira had chewed on the root. In Hebrews 12:15 we are also cautioned about the root of bitterness that takes hold easily in our hearts. Bitterness begins with anger and resentment, and it would have been very easy for Sapphira to resent Barnabas.

Why resent a nice guy like Barnabas? If Sapphira realized that her own motivation for giving was wrong, she may have assumed that Barnabas was reacting in the same way. Or, deep down inside, she may have recognized Barnabas' sincerity and felt condemned by it. Guilt has a way of coloring our reactions to others.

It's all too easy to lose our first love for Christ, to stand back and look pious when we've lost the glow that radiates from the real thing inside our hearts. Perhaps Ananias and Sapphira had never really loved Him, because loving is giving, giving our all. And often it involves simply giving in.

Giving and giving in are so hard, Lord! Please help me.

WHAT IS MY MOTIVATION?

"He will give each one whatever his deeds deserve."
(Romans 2:6, TLB)

Read 2 Corinthians 8:7-15.

These newer people coming in
(They think their lives are free from sin!)
Are taking over! We must win—
Not lose our place to others.
—Sapphira

Perhaps Ananias and Sapphira felt threatened by Barnabas' growing leadership. Perhaps they were jealous of his popularity. In any case, their motivation for giving was wrong—perhaps not to those around them, but in the eyes of God.

The trap of doing the right thing for the wrong reason ensnares many of us. "This had better make a good impression!" we mutter to ourselves as we feel obligated to invite someone home for dinner. "She'd better appreciate this!" as we go the extra mile. *I expect to be rewarded for this, Lord!* my subconscious races ahead of the hand hovering over the offering plate.

POINT TO PONDER: As Chuck Swindoll points out, Barnabas was called the encourager because he knew the meaning of "team spirit" and exercised it in the early church. Do I have a servant spirit, a spirit that gets excited about making others successful? Or do I need to tear others down to make myself feel better?

Father, Your Word tells me that my heart is "deceitful above all things" (Jeremiah 17:9). Help me to remember that when I start feeling really "spiritual."

36 – Thursday

FULFILLING MY NEEDS

"He will give eternal life to those who patiently do the will of God, seeking for the unseen glory and honor and eternal life that he offers." (Romans 2:7, TLB)

Read 2 Corinthians 8:16-24

There must be something we can do
To show them we're important too!
We can't afford too much, it's true . . .
But we have to show the others.
—Sapphira

Dr. Lawrence Crabb writes:

> The direction in which I am motivated to follow in an effort to meet my needs depends neither on the needs nor on the motivational energy, but rather on what *I think* will meet those needs.[1]

POINT TO PONDER: Sapphira's thought patterns dictated her actions. She decided she had to have recognition in certain areas in order to meet her needs; therefore she could not be happy until she achieved that recognition. What she probably did not realize was that even when we achieve what we desire, chances are we will still be unhappy because people or circumstances do not live up to our expectations, and the cycle begins all over again.

Sapphira was not secure enough in God's love to relax and enjoy encouraging and affirming others; *she* had to be constantly affirmed and built up. But everyone was affirming Barnabas instead of Sapphira and her deserving husband, Ananias. As she thought about Barnabas and the way he had wormed himself into everyone's hearts, perhaps she resented him a little more each day.

Your Word tells me, Father, that You will meet all *my needs according to Your glorious riches in Christ Jesus (Philippians 4:19). Help me to fathom the implications of that statement.*

PANACEA FOR PAIN

"But he will terribly punish those who fight against the truth of God and walk in evil ways—God's anger will be poured out upon them." (Romans 2:8, TLB)

Read 2 Corinthians 9:8-15

We'll sell that piece of land—the one
That's on the other side of town
And then the word will spread around . . .
What we have done for others.
—Sapphira

Remember when we discussed psychologist Lawrence Crabb's statements on security and significance?

> People have one basic personal need which requires two kinds of input for its satisfaction. The most basic need is a sense of personal worth, an acceptance of oneself as a whole, real person. The two required inputs are significance (purpose, importance, adequacy for a job, meaningfulness, impact) and security (love—unconditional and consistently expressed; permanent acceptance).[2]

Sapphira could have realized that God had seen her at her worst, loved her anyhow and still had a unique plan for her within the growing body of Christ. But her thought patterns revolved around *her* needs, not fulfilling the needs of others.

Dr. S.I. McMillen writes:

> For centuries scoffers have ridiculed the advice of Jesus, to "Love your enemies." They scorned it as impractical, idealistic and absurd. Now psychiatrists have shown that this radical and life-changing attitude would prevent many of the ills man brings upon himself through resentment of his enemies. When Jesus said, "Forgive seventy times seven," He was thinking not only of our souls, but of saving our bodies from irritable bowel syndrome, coronary artery disease, high blood pressure, and many other diseases.[3]

Thank You, Father, for providing security in Your love and significance in Your service.

RESULTS OF RESENTMENT

"You, therefore, have no excuse, you who pass judgment on someone else, for at whatever point you judge the other, you are condemning yourself, because you who pass judgment do the same things." (Romans 2:1)

Read 2 Corinthians 10:12-18

We'll lay the money at their feet
And everyone will say, "How sweet
To do such an unselfish deed—
To give your all for others!"

—Sapphira

Ananias and Sapphira lived during one of the most exciting eras in history. The presence of Christ was keenly felt in the Church; many who had known Him personally were living in the area; the Church was growing by leaps and bounds because of the "fragrance" of love that seeped out through every door and window. And yet, in the midst of all this, it seems "the spirit of antichrist" was at work in the emotions of jealousy, anger, resentment and bitterness. Perhaps no one suspected Ananias and Sapphira's motivation for selling their land and giving money to the Church . . . but *they* knew. And perhaps their negative emotions had come to dominate their lives.

Dr. S.I. McMillen, in his intriguing book *None of These Diseases*, tells the story of the famous physiologist John Hunter. Dr. Hunter well knew the effect emotions have upon our physical well-being, and he made the statement: "The first scoundrel that gets me angry will kill me." Dr. McMillen narrates the story: "Some time later, at a medical conference, a speaker made assertions that incensed Hunter. As he stood up and bitterly attacked the speaker, Hunter's anger caused such a violent contraction of his coronary arteries that he fell dead."[4]

POINT TO PONDER: Did Ananias and Sapphira die for the same reason? Only God knows, but someone has said, "We are not so much punished for our sins as *by* our sins."

Lord, this is difficult. Please point out to me the emotions in my life that are not pleasing to You, and then show me what to do about them.

Section 6:

Preparing My Heart for Outreach: "You will be My witnesses . . . in all Judea and Samaria . . ."

Week 37

Mrs. Simon Peter, Missionary

Imagine being married to the man that Walter Wangerin, a master storyteller, describes in the following paragraphs:

> Simon was a blunt fellow. Physically blunt: short-fingered, broad-chested, powerfully knit and crowned with a skullbone as round as a Roman's. He wore a beard so thick and dark, the whole head looked like a war club. He could explode in talk. No ties to his tongue. He gave every impression of self-confidence.
>
> Simon was the wind that blew his brother about, in almost any company the source of a boisterous gladness, or of contention. But one sign of a vulnerable heart within him may have been the bluff cynicism with which Simon met matters of consequence and human emotion. *Ho, ho! You can't dupe me. I won't be anybody's fool.* Or perhaps he wore the suspicious exterior for protection, since he could be a man of sudden, deep and dangerous loyalties—dangerous because they were so absolute.
>
> Simon was full of young bluster, girding himself and going wherever he wanted to go![1]

Peter is one of the easiest apostles to picture. Is it because he reminds almost everyone of someone?

The big fisherman thought he was doing his best to protect his Master. When, however, he tried to talk Jesus out of going to Jerusalem to die, Jesus said, "Get thee behind me, Satan" (Matthew 16:23 KJV).

Peter loudly, proudly promised Jesus at the Last Supper that he would never forsake Him. A few hours later, however, when Jesus asked him to "watch and pray," Peter fell asleep in the garden (Matthew 26:41).

Impulsively, Peter brandished his sword, wounding a servant, when the arrest party surrounded Jesus. A short time later, however, when questioned by a servant girl, he loudly denied having anything to do with Jesus.

But as we have seen, the undependable "bigmouth" was transformed. He fearlessly preached the news of the resurrection on the streets of Jerusalem, suffering imprisonment, only to be released by an angel. From that time on he was a leader, one of the most prominent in the early Church. His later career was a busy one of traveling and preaching, and his wife traveled with him.

The tradition of Peter's martyrdom in Rome during Emperor Nero's persecution is accepted by most scholars. Another church tradition states that Peter was crucified upside down and that he and his wife died together.

BACKGROUND READING: John 21

37 – Monday

ENDING WELL

"Being confident of this, that he who began a good work in you will carry it on to completion until the day of Christ Jesus." (Philippians 1:6)

Read Luke 5:1-11

I was honored to be included
—of course, committed to the cause—
but yet, I never dreamed
that it would be so difficult
to travel with this man!
—Mrs. Simon Peter

If you've experienced car-claustrophobia—if you've ever been stuck in an auto for hours while other family members are intrigued by a radio station over which they hear game scores and you hear only annoying static—just think of the travel conditions Peter's wife must have endured!

The part of life's journey called retirement can become an annoying trip down the highway of life. The long-anticipated "sleep-in" mornings may soon become an alarm signal of goal-less days that yawn into a purposeless existence. Too much idle time spent together results in petty arguments. At least one spouse may yearn to be back in "9-to-5 Land" again—or to send the other spouse packing!

But compare this message from two "retired" missionaries, Jim and Jean Livingston, presently ministering in Inverness, Florida:

> Lord, lead us to hungry hearts, to those who came to know you at the refugee camps in Southeast Asia. Lord, use us to bring renewal to Vietnamese churches. Lord, make us living stones, helping to build the Church of the Living God among the Vietnamese people even here in the United States. We just do not have time for closure.[2]

May I trust You, Lord, to complete the good work You began in my life . . . in Your time.

FROM DENYING TO PROCLAIMING

"Then [Peter] began to call down curses on himself and he swore to them, 'I don't know the man!' " (Matthew 26:74)

Read Matthew 16:13-28

Of course, he'd changed . . .
Of course, he was a leader now . . .
But still, I used to wonder—
Was he still trying to atone
for what took place
beside the fire of Caiaphas that night?
—Mrs. Simon Peter

Had Peter been able to forgive himself? Or had that scene in the courtyard played over and over again on his mental VCR? Did he say to himself, *If only I hadn't denied the Master! If only I had more courage! If only I'd think before I talk! If only . . .*

The "if only"s hit all of us at times. Sometimes our own perfectionism can be our "fatal flaw." We keep kicking ourselves around for days—or weeks or years—after a mistake or failure.

POINT TO PONDER: Look at it this way. Sins must be confessed to God. We must ask for His forgiveness. But when we do not forgive ourselves, *aren't we minimizing divine forgiveness,* available to us only at the cost of the cross? Could we be implying that our justice is greater than God's?

Forgive me, Father. My scales of justice are certainly not more reliable than Yours.

37 — Wednesday

BURIED IN THE DEPTHS OF THE SEA

"Who is a God like you, who pardons sin . . . ? You will again have compassion on us; you will tread our sins underfoot and hurl all our iniquities into the depths of the sea." (Micah 7:18-19)

Read Matthew 17:1-24

He doesn't talk to me about it.
And if he did,
he'd say that it was in the past
and covered by the blood—
a coverage deeper than the Sea of Galilee.
But sometimes he went fishing
in his mind
and dredged the sea again.
—Mrs. Simon Peter

Perhaps you've taken your family on a vacation to the shore. Suddenly something triggers the memory of an incident from twenty to thirty years ago, one that you had totally forgotten. It grabs hold of you, and the memory devastates you. You feel like a spiritual failure. Of course, your family has no idea what's going on in your mind, and you don't want to tell them. But the day, maybe the week, feels ruined.

Satan is a pro at accusing the brethren (and also the "sistren"). He knows how to use his fiery darts to his best advantage. We must know how to resist! No matter what the temperature, put on the armor!

Begin by shielding yourself with faith. Belt truth around yourself, the truth about your life *now*. Protect your thinking with the helmet of salvation. Thank God for *His* righteousness—not yours—that iron-plates your heart and vital parts. Reply to the enemy with a swift, jabbing paraphrase of First John 1:9: "If I confess my sin, He is faithful and just and will forgive my sin and purify me from all unrighteousness." You might want to kick off your sandals as you begin to sense your Father's tip-of-your-toes-to-the-top-of-your-head peace!

Thank You, Jesus, for winning the battle at the cross! Satan is a defeated foe!

37 – Thursday

WATER WALKING

"But when he saw the wind, he was afraid and, beginning to sink, cried out, 'Lord, save me!' Immediately Jesus reached out his hand and caught him. 'You of little faith,' he said, 'why did you doubt?' " (Matthew 14:30-31)

Read Matthew 18:15-35; Galatians 2:20

Dredging drove him to despair
or to a whirlwind of activity
and then I would remind him
that when he dropped his gaze from Jesus
he began to sink.
Water-walking
cannot be done alone.

—Mrs. Simon Peter

Amy Carmichael, a missionary to India during the early 1900s, knew that little Indian girls were sometimes taken and trained as dancing girls for the Hindu temples. This, of course, meant a ruined life of evil for them, so, wherever she could, she saved children from this fate. With her as "Mother," the "Family" in Dohnavur, South India, began.

But, like all of us, this "single mom" had her times of discouragement. She clung to Galatians 2:20. But, as Miss Carmichael expresses, "just when we most earnestly desire to live like this, the weary old self seems to come to life again—the 'I' that we had trusted was crucified with Christ. It is very disappointing when this happens, and the devil watches . . . and very quietly and with great subtlety he tries to draw us into hopeless distress and despair. If he can do that, he is satisfied, for then we are occupied with ourselves, which is what he wants us to be.

"The one and only thing is to look straight off ourselves and our wretched failure, and cry to Him Who is mighty to save. He never refuses that cry; so do not fear. The moment self is recognized, look to Him. Do not be discouraged; He is not discouraged. He Who has begun a good work in us will go on to perfect it. The going on may take time; even so, He will go on till (O blessed 'till') we are perfected."[3]

I cry to You, Lord, believing in Your power, knowing that when I am weak, You are strong.

37 – Friday

"IT IS THE LORD!"

"As soon as Simon Peter heard him say, 'It is the Lord,'
he wrapped his outer garment around him . . .
and jumped into the water." (John 21:7)

Read Matthew 26:36-75

"Do you truly love Me?"
Jesus asked him.
"Yes, Lord, You know I love You,"
Peter said.
I can see those dark eyes, lamb-like,
so full of shame and hurt.
"Feed My lambs."

—Mrs. Simon Peter

Most biblical scholars accept the tradition that Peter was martyred in Rome during Emperor Nero's persecution. In the end, Peter truly obeyed His Master's words: "If anyone would come after me, he must deny himself and take up his cross daily and follow me" (Luke 9:23).

"I think often we accept the cross in theory," Amy Carmichael writes, "but when it comes to practice, we either do not recognize it for what it is, or we recognize it and try to avoid it. This we can always do, for the cross is something that can be taken up or left, just as we choose. It is *not* illness (that comes to all) or bereavement (that also is the common lot of man)."[4]

A person brought up in poverty will not miss the luxuries another takes for granted. An abandoned orphan values parental love shown to him or her in adulthood in a way that the much-loved child may never fully appreciate. An experience or lifestyle that seems a cross to one person is not necessarily a cross experience for another. Each person has his or her own cross.

Thank You, Jesus, for drinking of the cup of agony, for voluntarily taking up the cross.

37 — Saturday

ONSHORE COMMUNION

"Jesus said to them, 'Bring some of the fish you have just caught.' Simon Peter climbed aboard and dragged the net ashore. . . . Jesus came, took the bread and gave it to them, and did the same with the fish." (John 21:10-11, 13)

Read John 21:1-23

"Do you truly love Me?"
Jesus asked again.
"Yes, Lord, You know I love You."
"Care for My sheep."

"Do you love Me?"
"You know I love You."
"Feed My sheep."

—Mrs. Simon Peter

The cross is, Amy Carmichael continues,

> something *voluntarily* suffered for the sake of the Lord Jesus, some denial of self, that would not be if we were not following him; often it is something that has shame in it (this, of course, was the earliest connotation of the word), such as the misunderstanding of friends and their blame, when the principles which govern our lives appear foolishness to them.
>
> It always has at its core the denial of self and self-love in all its manifestation. Self-choices go down before the call to take up the cross and follow. They fade away and cease to be.[5]

Jesus, You know that I love You. How are You asking me to take up my cross?

Section 7:

Preparing My Heart for Outreach: "You will be My witnesses . . . to the ends of the earth!"

Week 38

Priscilla: "Corinth, Here We Come!"

On a visit to New York City last weekend, I drove by the twin towers of the Trade Center. By comparison, the ancient wonders of the world represented in the Metropolitan Museum of Art appeared dwarfed, impotent. Today the "power of Rome" lies motionless on numbered shelves or buried between the pages of dust-covered books.

Not so, however, in the time of Priscilla (a variation of the Roman name Prisca) and her husband Aquila, a Jewish couple expelled from Rome by order of the Emperor Claudius. Rome was seemingly invincible, represented by eagle-carrying legions, an imperial navy, secret police in abundance and a host of cargo carriers moving on all trade routes throughout the known world. Against the power of Rome anyone was helpless, especially the lonely members of the Jewish culture and the even lonelier followers of that controversial figure, Jesus Christ, called by Pontius Pilate the "King of the Jews" (John 19:19).

But no true Jew wanted to accept the fact that the Messiah had come and died like a common criminal. The one thing that had kept them going all these years was their certainty that their promised leader would liberate them from their enemies. Now their hopes for the future were being drastically undermined by these "Jesus freaks" who violated Jewish law by mixing with non-Jews, even accepting them into their fellowship without requiring the ancient rite of circumcision.

Formerly, Jews in Rome had been considered to be industrious and generally well-behaved, but problems between Jews and Christians must have become increasingly frequent. The Emperor Claudius, usually quite tolerant when dealing with other races and creeds, decided that this new group, who promised the imminent destruction of the Roman world by their dead (but supposedly resurrected) leader, must be ousted to avoid further conflict. The easiest way out was simply to expel all Jews from Rome.

And so we find Priscilla and Aquila on a ship headed for Corinth, one of the most famous cities of Greece. Priscilla must have wondered often about God's purpose in uprooting them.

BACKGROUND READING: Acts 18:1-28

38 — Monday

ROME WAS HOME

"I am not ashamed of the gospel, because it is the power of God for the salvation of everyone who believes: first for the Jew, then for the Gentile." (Romans 1:16)

Read Romans 1:18-32

In some ways I was glad
To leave that city, Rome—
It had become a nightmare
In the years I called it home,
God certainly will have to judge
The evil He sees there. . . .
And yet I wish we could have stayed,
His grace and mercy shared.

—Priscilla

In our visit with Claudia Procula in Chapter 3 we discussed the Romans' national pastime: pleasure seeking, which is basically a form of self-worship. The first chapter of Paul's letter to the Romans describes God's reaction to man's preoccupation with self (worshiping the created rather than the Creator).

Priscilla and Aquila must have been well aware of the results of forgetting who God is. Immorality was rampant in Rome.

Dr. Don Williams comments in *The Apostle Paul and Women in the Church*:

> The loss of identity is seen in the violation of our sexuality. No longer do men and women know how to relate properly to each other. While Paul does not condemn homosexuality as the worst sin, he does show it to be the most obvious illustration of the loss of identity. . . . Both male and female . . . express their alienation from God in the extreme form of losing their sexual identity. Both stand under the judgment of God for this, "God gave them up . . . ," and both, to be sure, are the objects of God's grace and mercy in Jesus Christ.[1]

Thank You for being our Judge, our Pardoner and our Father.

OLD WINE AND YOUNG MISTRESSES

"For in the gospel a righteousness from God is revealed, a righteousness that is by faith from first to last, just as it is written: 'The righteous will live by faith.' " (Romans 1:17)

Read 1 Corinthians 5

When all Jews were expelled from Rome,
I welcomed a new life—
Corinth must be quieter
Than all the Roman strife!
But Corinth, port of sailors,
Known for women and for wine,
Was not the peaceful countryside
I'd pictured in my mind.
—Priscilla

All roads led to Rome, and everyone wanted to go there, but if you lived in any country east of Greece, the fastest and safest route to Rome led through the Greek city of Corinth.

Greece is divided into two distinct halves, northern and southern, by a large body of water. What prevents southern Greece from being just another island off the mainland of Greece? A four-mile land bridge or isthmus, beside which the city of Corinth is located. In order to reach Rome you had to cross that little finger of land, and so almost every seafarer visited the city of Corinth at least once in his or her lifetime.

Corinth was also somewhat of a resort area for wealthy businessmen from Athens who were looking for old wine and young mistresses. Both were to be found in abundance.

Enter Priscilla and her husband Aquila, looking for peaceful surroundings in which to begin a new life. How strange and unexplainable God's leading must have seemed!

Lord, Your will for my life is sometimes hard to understand. Thank You for reminding me that others' lives have been much more difficult.

A MOUNTAINTOP EXPERIENCE?

"So Paul, standing in the center of the Areopagus [Mars Hill auditorium] said: Men of Athens, I perceive in every way—on every hand and with every turn I make—that you are most religious (very reverent to demons)." (Acts 17:22, Amplified)

Read 1 Corinthians 6:9-20

The gods of Rome were there in Corinth,
With the gods of Greece.
They all fit in together
In a tolerant kind of peace.
The temple of Aphrodite
Overshadows the whole city,
The worship of this goddess sung
In every sailor's ditty.

—Priscilla

When you stand in the ruins of Corinth, you are overwhelmed by the height of Acro-Corinthus, the "hill of Corinth," which rises like a Greek Masada from the plain to a sudden height of 1,900 feet. This giant natural fortress was Corinth's greatest defense in time of war—walls still guard the steep, rocky hill—but perhaps her greatest weakness in time of peace.

At the very top of the hill stood the famous temple of Aphrodite, the Greek goddess of love, served by a thousand priestess-prostitutes. The activity that went on within its walls must have nauseated Priscilla; worship and sexual promiscuity were inextricably intertwined.

POINT TO PONDER: The one-flesh concept of marriage had been instituted by God to reflect the spiritual union of Christ and His Bride, the Church. The temple of Aphrodite, reflecting the broken and soiled man-woman relationship, pointed its pinnacles skyward, illustrating this fact: When humankind rebels against God and breaks God's rules, they flaunt their disobedience in the face of God and eventually worship the object of their disobedience.

Father . . . have I too been guilty of idol worship?

AN UNKNOWN GOD

"For as I passed along and carefully observed your objects of worship, I came also upon an altar with this inscription, To the unknown god. Now what you are already worshipping as unknown, this I set forth to you." (Acts 17:23, Amplified)

Read Acts 17:15-34

But soon we found a place to live,
Resumed our weaving trade.
Word spread about the business;
As soon as tents were made
We found a market, made some friends . . .
And then we found out why
We'd been uprooted, sent abroad
But not allowed to die.
—Priscilla

As Priscilla and Aquila were becoming acclimated to Corinth, another Jew—a stranger to them—was traveling through Greece. The Jewish couple may have just been establishing their tentmaking business as Corinth's sister-city, Athens, made way on Mars Hill for one more visitor, Paul of Tarsus, a Roman citizen who had converted to Christianity.

Athens, the home of the greatest intellects the Mediterranean world had ever known, the place to which every wealthy Roman sent his son for a cultured education, boasted a 180-foot Acropolis flashing with the gleaming marble of the Parthenon. This splendor was protected by statues of gods and goddesses, too many to count or keep separate. In case one was missed, an altar was even built to "the unknown god." Paul seized this opportunity to disclose the identity of this unknown—the resurrected Messiah who was coming back to judge the world.

The reaction to this unknown Jew? Some laughed, as expected. Some said, "We would like to hear more." Dionysius and Damaris and others believed Paul's words, and through them "the unknown god" became understood in their hearts.

Thank You, Father, for the opportunities You give me to tell others about You. Please grant me wisdom and discernment in each uniquely different situation.

38 – Friday

ANOTHER TENTMAKER

"The God Who produced and formed the world and all things in it, being Lord of heaven and earth, does not dwell in handmade shrines." (Acts 17:24, Amplified)

Read Acts 18:1-11

We met a man who soon became
Our leader and our friend;
He taught us much about enduring
To the very end.
He feared no one, he had no doubts
He'd seen the risen One.
And when he told us of that time
His face shone like the sun.
—Priscilla

"Paul left Athens and went to Corinth" (Acts 18:1), and found . . . friends! How refreshing it must have been to find an open home and sympathetic listeners. They were even of the same trade—tentmakers. We can imagine the many long hours spent in the honest interchange that is a trademark of true fellowship.

Paul had endured so much since he had turned from the persecution of Christians to identification with the persecuted ones. He was beaten with rods three times; stoned; imprisoned; shipwrecked three times; "frequently driven to fasting by want, in cold and exposure and lack of clothing" (2 Corinthians 11:27, Amplified). Priscilla's eyes probably filled with tears as she listened to Paul tell of his journeys for Christ, and she must have wondered what lay in store for herself and Aquila. Would they ever return to Rome? And, if so, would they return as visitors—or as prisoners?

POINT TO PONDER: By comparison, what have I endured for the sake of Christ? Do I have any idea of what persecution really means?

Forgive me, Father, for complaining about so many petty problems.

38 – Saturday

MOVING ON

"And one night the Lord said to Paul in a vision,
Have no fear, but speak and do not keep silent;
for I am with you, and no man shall assault you to harm you."
(Acts 18:9-10, Amplified)

Read Acts 19:1-20

So when the conflict rose again
Between us and the Jews,
I was prepared within my heart
To face unwelcome news.
We must move on to Ephesus,
Across the sea again.
Paul has been told that he must preach
The gospel to all men!

—Priscilla

At first Paul's presentation of the gospel in Corinth seems to have been rather low key. When his friends Silas and Timothy joined him, however, he was "pressed in the spirit," and spoke more freely of the God-man whom he served.

Priscilla and Aquila watched the reaction among their Jewish friends. It was immediate and indignant. Paul "shook out his clothes in protest" of their blasphemy, leaving the synagogue for the neighboring home of the newly converted Titus Justus. Crispus, chief ruler of the synagogue, went with him, and the new church grew in size. Was Priscilla also rejected by her friends in Corinth? Perhaps only Chloe, mentioned fleetingly in First Corinthians 1:11, remained faithful.

In any case, good-byes had to be said once again as the Jewish couple made plans to accompany Paul to Ephesus. If Priscilla had felt anxious about the earlier move to Greece, this move to still another country (today's Turkey), across another sea, could have filled her heart with misgivings. However she felt, she faithfully followed the Lord's leading through Paul's direction.

Thank You, Father, for the spiritual leaders You have provided in my life. Help me to recognize Your guidance through their counsel.

Week 39

Priscilla: "Great Is Diana of the Ephesians!"

Priscilla had lived in the center of her world, Rome, and then in the center of the world of trade, Corinth. She had witnessed the worship of Rome's countless gods and goddesses, and she may have become acquainted with the priestess-prostitutes who were employed at the temple of Aphrodite.

Now she would meet women whose lives were intertwined with the worship of another powerful deity, Diana of the Ephesians. Diana was a combination of the Greek virgin huntress Artemis—Mother of Wild Things—and the ancient Egyptian Isis—Mother of the Divine Son Horus or the Great Goddess, Mother of All Things.

The embodiment of the female principle, Diana represented not only fertility, but also resurrection in the shape of new birth, the eternal return of life to the earth and, as found in a number of early carvings, the Tree of Life. In other words, Diana was all-powerful!

The temple of Diana was one of the Seven Wonders of the World. Over 400 feet long and 220 feet wide, it was surrounded by pillars 60 feet high. Paussanias, an important historian of the ancient world, called it the most beautiful work ever created by humankind.

With all this in mind, it is easy to understand why Paul's preaching of a Christ-centered gospel created instant opposition, particularly from men like Demetrius, whose way of life centered around the worship of Diana. Demetrius, the silversmith who recreated Diana so cleverly for the tourists as well as for local worshipers, could not stand by while his trade was destroyed by this Jewish troublemaker and his friends. Paul was once again headed for trouble.

And Priscilla? She obviously became an excellent teacher, with Apollos becoming a student in her home (Acts 18:26). Her life must have become an example of practical Christianity, for history tells us that a church, a catacomb and monuments of Rome were named in her honor. But none of these were in Ephesus. In Diana's city Priscilla may have been ridiculed, laughed at, persecuted. . . .

BACKGROUND READING: Acts 19:1-20

39 — Monday

GODDESS OF FERTILITY

"Great is Artemis [Diana] of the Ephesians! . . . Doesn't all the world know that the city of Ephesus is the guardian of the temple of the great Artemis and of her image, which fell from heaven?" (Acts 19:34-35)

Read Acts 19:21-41

It took my breath away . . .
That temple, towering skyward
And welcoming the sea,
Proclaims to all her greatness
Diana is their queen!
A hundred marble columns
Reflect across the waves,
Carved by earth's greatest artists
But put in place by slaves.
—Priscilla

Even after all the sights Priscilla had seen, sailing into the harbor of Ephesus must have been a once-in-a-lifetime experience. A well-lit, paved street, flanked by shops of every description, made travel into the city convenient as well as fascinating. Facing the harbor was a huge amphitheater, seating 24,000 people. Close to it was the amazing temple of Diana—the length of an oversized football field.

Priscilla was probably startled by the image of Diana, reproduced by local silversmiths as a popular souvenir for travelers as well as an object of worship. The embodiment of fertility and nurturing, Diana's chest was covered by more than twenty egg-shaped breasts. The cult centered around the worship of an oddly shaped meteorite proclaimed as an image of the goddess sent down from heaven.

Once again Priscilla was faced with a new location and new ways of thinking. How easy it would have been to retreat behind her tentmaking sign and not breathe a word of her belief in Jesus Christ, the God-man who had come into the world!

Father, I often feel like Priscilla. . . . Who would listen to me, even if I knew what to say? I know You can *speak through me—will You, please, today?*

PRIAPUS AND PROSTITUTION

"For although they knew God, they neither glorified him as God nor gave thanks to him, but their thinking became futile and their foolish hearts were darkened. Although they claimed to be wise, they became fools and exchanged the glory of the immortal God for images made to look like mortal man and birds and animals and reptiles." (Romans 1:21-23)

Read Ephesians 2:1-22

Priapus' idols everywhere,
His image planting thoughts
In minds that otherwise might yearn
To hear the real truth taught.
Even a stranger here is met
By very pointed signs:
"Pleasure awaits you just ahead . . .
Rest your body and your mind."
—Priscilla

In the fall of 1983 my husband and I visited the ancient city of Ephesus on the eastern shore of modern Turkey. Our tour of the ruins gave us vivid insights into the culture Paul, Priscilla and Aquila encountered. As a visitor to Ephesus followed Harbor Street into the city, he could hardly miss a sign, drawn in picture writing so that anyone could understand, carved into the stones of the pavement (it's still there!): "If you have an empty place in your heart, turn left. If not, go to the library!"

Across the street from the public library, on one of the main intersections of Ephesus, was the public brothel or "house of love," marked with the phallic symbol of Priapus, the god of sex. (Priapus still survives today in pornographic little souvenir statues available to the tourist.) Ephesus officially recognized prostitution and levied tax on its practitioners, the harlots of the town, who were under the protection of Diana.

How much has our world advanced since Priscilla's day? Images of Priapus have been replaced with four-color pornography on the internet. Prostitution, the oldest occupation in the world, is still in full swing—still with no retirement benefits.

Break my heart, Father, with the things that break Your heart.

THE "ARTS" OF LOVE

"Therefore God gave them over in the sinful desires of their hearts to sexual impurity for the degrading of their bodies with one another. They exchanged the truth of God for a lie, and worshiped and served created things rather than the Creator—who is forever praised." (Romans 1:24-25)

Read Ephesians 4:17-32

My heart breaks for these women.
They see themselves as free,
But they are slaves to Diana
And her false philosophy.
When I first saw her temple
Standing proud, aloof, alone,
My heart felt just as heavy
As that idol made of stone.
—Priscilla

Premarital chastity was required of "respectable" women in Ephesus, but married and unmarried men frequented the "house of love" without any greater penalty than scolding at home. Our tour guide told us that the brothel prostitutes were the lowest order of courtesans; a higher class were flute players, who provided overnight entertainment for stag parties. Even more expensive were the "companions," women of citizen class who had acquired an education by reading and attending lectures. They wore flowered robes, peroxided their hair and sometimes achieved fame by posing for sculptors and painters.

Traditions were handed down carefully from one generation of courtesans to another; some old courtesans even conducted training schools in the "arts of love."

In this culture, how foreign was the Christian concept of marriage possibly presented first to Aquila by Paul: "Aquila, you must show these men that you love your wife just as you love yourself . . . just as Christ loves the Church. For this reason you have left your father and mother, and are united to Priscilla. The two of you have become one flesh!"

Thank You, Jesus, for the way in which You personally demonstrated the commitment that is true love.

39 — Thursday

EPHESIAN NIGHTLIFE

"They are darkened in their understanding and separated from the life of God . . . due to the hardening of their hearts. Having lost all sensitivity, they have given themselves over to sensuality so as to indulge in every kind of impurity, with a continual lust for more." (Ephesians 4:18-19)

Read Ephesians 5:1-20

The many-breasted Diana
Sent down from the sky,
Symbol of love and fertility,
Says man will never die:
"Eat, drink, and be merry!
Celebrate each day!
Man and animal, rejoice!
Diana leads the way!"

—Priscilla

The great festivals in the worship of Diana often resulted in sexual orgies, regarded as "safety valves" so that monogamy could be possible during the balance of the year. Fertility was considered a sacred gift, a blessing to be procured from the goddess of all living things. Man will never die as long as he continues the race; therefore, propagation of the race was man's claim to eternal life and thus an acceptable form of worship.

It was concepts like these that Paul was fighting: "So I tell you this, and insist on it in the Lord, that you must no longer live as the Gentiles do, in the futility of their thinking" (Ephesians 4:17).

Probably it was difficult for Priscilla and Aquila to find new friends in Ephesus. Their lifestyle was so completely different from everyone else's. Paul and Aquila were probably ridiculed because they did not become involved in the Ephesian nightlife; at one point Aquila and Priscilla risked their necks to save Paul's life. More and more, however, they were learning "how wide and long and high and deep" God's love really is, and how to be "filled to . . . all the fullness of God" (3:18-19).

"Now to him who is able to do immeasurably more than all we ask or imagine, according to his power that is at work within us, to him be glory . . . throughout all generations" (3:20-21).

39 — Friday

THE GREAT LADY

"And he made known to us the mystery of his will according to his good pleasure, which he purposed in Christ, to be put into effect when the times will have reached their fulfillment—to bring all things in heaven and on earth together under one head, even Christ." (Ephesians 1:9-10)

Read Ephesians 1:3-23

Babylonians called her Ishtar,
Aphrodite to the Greeks,
To Egyptians she was Isis,
In Ephesus Diana speaks!
Artemis, Astarte, Athena,
Or Venus when in Rome—
She is the great love goddess,
She calls the world her throne!
—Priscilla

On our visit to Ephesus we were told by our Turkish guide that Mary, the mother of Jesus, was brought there by the apostle John to spend her last days on earth and that she ascended from Ephesus into heaven. Research shows, however, that this belief became popular only after the triumph of the Christian Church over the worship of Diana. Is it possible that worshipers of the Great Goddess (often called the Black Madonna), when converting to the Christian faith, simply transferred their affections to Mary, attributing to her personage the power to bestow eternal life?[1]

Certainly the Great Goddess seemed to include within her legend most of the needs and desires of the human being. She was called the Mistress of Heaven, the Mistress of the House of Life, the Mistress of Shelter, the Mistress of the Word of God. The oldest of the old, she was believed to be the one from who all life arose. In other words, she represented the whole cosmos.[2]

Thank You, Father, for stating so clearly that I need only one mediator to open the doors into the courts of heaven—Your Son, Christ Jesus (1 Timothy 2:5-6).

THE MYSTERY OF HIS WILL—THE FAMILY OF GOD

"Speaking the truth in love, we will in all things grow up into him who is the Head, that is, Christ. From him the whole body, joined and held together by every supporting ligament, grows and builds itself up in love, as each part does its work." (Ephesians 4:15-16)

Read Ephesians 5

How can I reach these women?
They think as they've been taught
That love through sexual allurement
Is the goal that must be sought . . .
And in the name of love
Diana breaks the family ties,
Proclaiming through her worship
The filthiest of lies.

—Priscilla

Christ has renewed our minds (thoughts, assumptions and attitudes) and united us into one family. Now He desires to present us to His Father as precious gifts (Jude 24-25). His gifts certainly would not be tarnished by blemishes like sex sin, greed, dirty stories, foul talk and coarse jokes (Ephesians 5:3-4, TLB).

The Ephesians were instructed to live out the meaning of their new family unity in their everyday lives, in their marriages (5:21-33) and in parent-child relationships (6:1-4).

Perhaps Ephesians 5 was a written confirmation of earlier conversations between Paul and his dear friends: "Priscilla, be sure to show respect for Aquila—honor him, prefer him, venerate and esteem him, praise him, love and admire him exceedingly" (taken from 5:33, Amplified); "As I have told you many times, Aquila, love Priscilla as you love your own body, in the same way that Christ loved the church and gave Himself up for her" (taken from 5:25-30, Amplified); "By your example, my friends, God will evidence His love through you."

Thank You, Father, for Your love that breaks down the "wall of hostility" (2:14) between the members of Your family. Please help me to make that kind of love a reality in my family as well.

Week 40

Priscilla: Getting Out of the Temple's Shadow

With Priscilla we have visited Rome, Corinth and Ephesus, the cultural and political centers of three very different geographical areas. Undoubtedly Priscilla left behind friends in each one of those areas, and I feel sure that she, as well as Paul, was brokenhearted when she heard of the terrible problems prevalent back in the little church in Corinth.

The Greek word *Korinthiazomai* had come to mean "to commit fornication." As mentioned earlier, Corinth was a seaman's paradise but a moral cesspool. The temple of Aphrodite cast its leering shadow over the entire city, plaguing every street and alley with prostitution. Divorce, drunkenness and debauchery were the norm in Corinth.

The shadow had invaded the church as well. Women were worshiping immodestly, causing problems of lust within the sanctuary. Some of the church members were visiting prostitutes. Another member was displaying his so-called "Christian freedom" by living in incest. Others were "proving their freedom" by eating meat offered to idols. Drunkenness was staining the celebration of the Lord's supper, and Christians were taking fellow Christians to court. Spiritual gifts were abused, provoking jealousy; tongues were valued for their showy ecstasy rather than prophecy for purposes of edification.

In short, both individual morality and church "body life" were on the verge of relapsing into the old sensualism. The old proverb, "Out of sight, out of mind," was proving itself to be true; since Paul had left, his wisdom and authority were being questioned.

Because we face similar problems today, it is important that we understand why the Corinthian Church was so deeply in trouble. Division was an ever-present danger because, with their leader gone, these new Christians were forgetting the word of the cross—Christ crucified—and were moving instead into an emphasis on mystical exaltation that was strangely similar to the old wine- and drug-related pagan ecstasies.

(A visit to the ruins of the ancient Greek Oracle of Delphi is an eye-opening revelation of Satan's counterfeit strategies to God's true manifestations. Pythia, a woman oracle or prophet, would utter weird, frenzied sounds that were interpreted by temple priests as the words of Apollo. Today's guides explain these "prophecies" as drug-induced hallucinations.)

As Dr. Don Williams puts it, "Paul calls the Corinthians to order in the church that will build them up rather than trip them out."[1] Rebuking them for their false emphasis, he summons them back to the cross, the resurrection of Christ, a personal morality, and love that will restore harmony and make the gospel credible to onlookers.

BACKGROUND READING: 1 Corinthians 5:1-13

40 — Monday

THE BEAUTY OF THE ONE-FLESH RELATIONSHIP

"I appeal to you . . . and beg of you in view of [all] the mercies of God, to make a decisive dedication of your bodies—presenting all your members and faculties—as a living sacrifice, holy (devoted, consecrated) and well pleasing to God, which is your reasonable (rational, intelligent) service and spiritual worship." (Romans 12:1, Amplified)

Read 1 Corinthians 6:15-20

How can one flesh be torn in two?
How can a body that is part
Of Christ be thrown away in lust?
The body's not given without the heart.
—Priscilla

To Priscilla, reports of immorality and continued traffic with temple prostitutes were shocking not only in reality but also symbolically. This abuse of "freedom in Christ" had been justified by the widespread belief that the body would be destroyed at death; therefore sexual (body) exploitation was unimportant since only the soul had an eternal destiny. Paul explained that the body is destined for resurrection and that when we become one with Christ, our total selves—soul *and* body—are united to Him and belong to Him.

Just as Aquila and Priscilla, or any husband and wife, became one flesh in marital intercourse, so their spirits and bodies joined with Christ at the moment of salvation. Therefore, Paul asked the Corinthians, how can a body that is one with Christ be joined with a prostitute or involved in incestuous union or defiled in *any* way?

POINT TO PONDER: Since my body is the temple of the Holy Spirit, it is essential that I keep the temple clean. Any pollutant must be removed as soon as I become aware of its presence. If I am married, any thought or attitude that disrupts the beauty of the one-flesh relationship must be dealt with—immediately, without giving it a chance to put down roots.

Lord Jesus, please cleanse the temple once again.

40 – Tuesday

CHRIST THE CHERISHER

"But I want you to know and realize that Christ is the head of every man, the head of a woman is her husband, and the Head of Christ is God." (1 Corinthians 11:3, Amplified)

Read Genesis 1:26-30; 2:15-25

Ephesians worship a female god
And scorn our Master and our Lord.
Yet Jesus offers liberty
Through understanding of His Word.
—Priscilla

Perhaps Priscilla acted as Paul's secretary as he wrote the letter to the Corinthians. Paul's letter to the Corinthians was delivered by another woman, Phoebe, a sister in the faith who held an official function as a "deacon" or "servant"—the same word used by Paul to describe himself, Apollos (1 Corinthians 3:5), Tychicus (Ephesians 6:21; Colossians 4:7) and Timothy (1 Timothy 4:6).

Priscilla certainly would have listened avidly as Paul discussed the meaning of headship as recorded in First Corinthians 11. (Headship is often taken to mean superiority or rule; a better definition is source or origin.[2]) As Head of the Church, His Body, Christ is its lifegiving source and its nourisher. As members of His body, we need to learn to live in dependence upon Him, strengthened and sustained by Him, just as Christ is nourished and sustained by God. In the same way the husband should exercise his leadership by cherishing and so strengthening his wife.

Paul continued by using the story of creation (Genesis 1:26-30) to point out the unity and equality of the sexes, as well as the passage in Genesis 2:18-25 to note the "vive la difference!" God allotted to each sex equal and independent value, creating both in His image; He also created the sexes for each other, to be consummated in the one-flesh union.

Thank You, Father, for the beauty of Your plan.

PAUL: A WOMAN-HATER?

"Any woman who [publicly] prays or prophesies (teaches, refutes, reproves, admonishes or comforts) when she is bareheaded dishonors her head (her husband); it is the same as [if her head were] shaved" (1 Corinthians 11:5, Amplified)

Read 1 Corinthians 11:1-16

Some think that Paul's unfair to us
But they don't understand
The problems in the Corinthian church
And elsewhere in the land.
—Priscilla

Paul has been categorized as a woman-hater—"the perfect squelch" of feminine opportunities. How, then, was he able to work with intelligent, cultured, professional women like Priscilla, Lydia (Acts 16:11-15), Phoebe (Romans 16:1-2), Mary (Romans 16:6), his "dear friend Persis," Tryphena and Tryphosa (Romans 16:12) and his "adopted mother," the mother of Ruphus (Romans 16:13)?

One of the problems in the Corinthian church is difficult for us to grasp: women were unveiling themselves while praying and prophesying during worship. The issue was not whether or not they were to speak, but the matter of modesty in the area of veiling, as Priscilla would have readily understood.

The veil in the Middle East lands symbolized a woman's honor, dignity and authority. When wearing it in public, she was regarded with respect; without the veil she was open to insult or harm. Wasn't Paul saying, then, that liberty in Christ should not involve offense to others within one's cultural setting?

Help me, Father, not to be a stumbling block to others.

"BORN OF A WOMAN . . ."

"In [the plan of] the Lord and from His point of view woman is not apart from and independent of man, nor is man aloof from and independent of woman; for as woman was made from man, even so man is also born of woman. And all [whether male or female go forth] from God (as their Author)." (1 Corinthians 11:11-12, Amplified)

Read Galatians 4:22-31

In Christ the battle between the sexes
Can finally be transcended:
Husbands express their leadership
In service. War is ended!

—Priscilla

Priscilla was obviously quite intelligent and well versed in the Scriptures, as is evident from the fact that she shared the task of teaching Apollos (a well-educated Jew) with Aquila. Each time Aquila is named by Paul, side by side we find Priscilla's name. At one place Paul even calls her "Prisca," a fond and familiar nickname.

Paul's teaching that wives should relate to husbands as Christ relates to God should in no way be seen as a put-down of womanhood; rather, it shows the intense value of the relationship. Also, instead of being ignored, untaught, segregated and silent as they had been in the synagogue, women could now participate in worship (when properly attired according to Middle Eastern custom, so as not to be vulgar or offensive). Spiritual gifts would be indiscriminately bestowed by an unprejudiced Creator who loved and cared about all He had brought into being . . . Jew and Gentile, slave and free, male and female (Galatians 3:28).

"But when the proper time had fully come, God sent His Son, born of a woman . . ." (Galatians 4:4, Amplified). As woman was taken from man in the initial act of creation so in the act of redemption God-man was born of woman. God joined the ranks of humankind in a woman's womb.

Thank You, Father, for being the God of creation and redemption—for including both in Your plan.

THE OPTION OF SINGLE-HEARTEDNESS

"My desire is to have you free from all anxiety and distressing care. The unmarried [man] is anxious about the things of the Lord, how he may please the Lord; but the married man is anxious about worldly matters, how he may please his wife. And he is drawn in diverging directions—his interests are divided, and he is distracted [from his devotion to God]. And the unmarried woman or girl is concerned and anxious about the matters of the Lord, how to be wholly separated and set apart in body and spirit; but the married woman has her cares [centered] in earthly affairs, how she may please her husband. . . ." (1 Corinthians 7:32-34, Amplified)

Read 1 Corinthians 7:1-16

God has a special plan for some,
Unknown in pagan worship here.
He gives a special chance to serve
To those who hold His love most dear.
—Priscilla

Notice how Paul speaks to both men and women in this passage, as he does in his discussion on conjugal rights (1 Corinthians 7:1-5). He is concerned that both sexes consider undivided devotion to Christ. Marriage can be a distraction and even a hindrance; single-heartedness is an acceptable and wholesome option.

Perhaps Priscilla interjected a question about widows at this point: Is a widow free to remarry? Paul's answer is yes, provided that her second husband is a Christian, but he urges the widow to consider the option of celibacy so that she can become a greater blessing to those around her. (Anna was certainly a good example of this.)

Was Paul opposed to marriage? Judging by the time he spent discussing its divine parallels, obviously not. The goal for *all,* married or single, must be "undistracted and undivided devotion to the Lord" (1 Corinthians 7:35, Amplified).

Thank You, Father, for the unique place each one has in Your family.

AN AUDIENCE OF ONE

"I am saying this to help you, not to try to keep you from marrying. I want you to do whatever will help you to serve the Lord best, with as few other things as possible to distract your attention from him." (1 Corinthians 7:35, TLB)

Read 1 Corinthians 7:17-40

An audience of only One,
More important than a million . . .
The question foremost in my mind:
"What to His *heart is thrilling?"*
—Priscilla

"Sure, it's Valentine's Day and I'd like to have someone give me flowers. Who wouldn't?" says fifty-one-year-old Sharon. "But my life is full. I was a missionary for ten years. I went to seminary. I work. I own a home. I'm involved with some singles here at church. I really have a ministry to them. I'm comfortable with what God has given me so far, but many of them are not."

In order to find peace, single persons—those divorced or widowed and those never married—need to seek God's guidance about marriage or remarriage.

One of life's paradoxes is the gift we give ourselves through sacrificial giving to others. Basic instinct urges us to grab the best for ourselves. Only as we learn to give with no thought of receiving something in return will we find the priceless fulfillment we seek.

Our God-created longing for relationship can be partially satisfied through giving to others—not by giving away our physical body, but by offering our acceptance, encouragement and support.[3]

Jesus, You are my most important listener, my audience of One.

Week 41

Lydia

At a point in the missionary journeys, young Mark dropped out. Perhaps he was exhausted, perhaps he missed his family, perhaps he had a girlfriend back home. Whatever the reason, Paul found it difficult to accept. His attitude toward Mark caused at least temporary alienation between himself and Barnabas (Mark's cousin or uncle) as well. Paul took Silas and continued on his missionary journeys to encourage and strengthen the believers in the faith.

The sixteenth chapter of Acts is quite eventful. In the city of Lystra, Paul met Timothy, the son of a devout Jewish mother and a Greek father. Friends in the area acted as character references for the young man, and Paul quickly decided to recruit him. Perhaps Paul missed the youthful enthusiasm Mark had added to the missionary journeys.

Paul felt it necessary, however, to circumcise Timothy before he became a part of the team. Why? So that the Jews in the area who knew Timothy's father was Greek wouldn't be offended. Was this legalism on Paul's part? An attempt to please people?

What an initiation to a missions trip for young Timothy! But apparently he was submissive to Paul's authority.

"Go west, young man, go west!" Paul, Silas and Timothy continued to go from town to town, presenting the simple guidelines which the Jerusalem apostles and leaders had established. Their plans to travel west, however, into the province of Asia (Turkey) were blocked by the Holy Spirit.

Through a dream in which a man begged them to come to Macedonia "and help us," God led them to northern Greece.

Although in Paul's vision he saw a man inviting them to Macedonia, the first convert to Christianity in the West (Europe) was a woman—Lydia, the seller of purple.

So in Acts 16 Paul met Timothy, who was to become his "son in the faith"; the Macedonian dream-man; and Lydia, who was to become a very influential believer in the city of Philippi. And Acts 16 holds another meeting, a strange encounter with another European woman—a woman whom historians have called "the Pythoness." But that's another chapter!

BACKGROUND READING: Acts 15:1-21

41 — Monday

THE MACEDONIANS, AN UNREACHED PEOPLE

"Dear friends, do not believe every spirit, but test the spirits to see whether they are from God. . . . This is how you can recognize the Spirit of God: Every spirit that acknowledges that Jesus Christ has come in the flesh is from God, but every spirit that does not acknowledge Jesus is not from God. This is the spirit of the antichrist." (1 John 4:1-3)

Read Acts 17:16-32

My heart is open to the God the Jewish people serve.
And yet some days, somehow,
I know that there is more . . .
a restlessness there is that stirs within my soul
to know of something more. . . .
—Lydia

If Lydia lived today, the *Fortune 500* list of top-ranking businesses would probably include Lydia's Fabrics, based in the city of Philippi in the area of Macedonia. Originally, however, Lydia lived in Thyatira in Asia, now called Turkey, in an area called the "Lydian Market." One of the market's most popular products was their famous purple fabric. Purple was the most expensive of dyes, a mark of wealth or royalty ranked in value with gold. It adorned emperors and temples and was also used for tribute and international trade.

The purple stain came from the murex, a shellfish found only along the northeastern section of the Mediterranean coast. The lifeblood of this little snail gained its vivid color when the shellfish lost its life and its contents were exposed to the open air.

Lydia's hometown, Thyatira, is also mentioned in Revelation 2:20 as the home of Jezebel, who may have been the wife of one of the elders of the early Christian Church in that city. Jezebel called herself a prophetess, but she was immoral and idolatrous. Conversely, Lydia, who had no knowledge of Jesus, was known as a worshiper of the one true God of the Jews—a worshiper with an open heart.

Lord, I too desire to be a worshiper with an open heart. Please remove any prejudices or beliefs that might hinder my worship of You.

A MOVER AND A SHAKER

"Keep a close watch on all you do and think. Stay true to what is right and God will bless you and use you to help others."
(1 Timothy 4:16, TLB)

Read Acts 16:1-10

The sea creature that provides my living
must die before it gives to me its color.
The murex' life is sacrificed
to give my cloth its purple stain.
There is a meaning here somehow
but something's missing—
a piece of life's big puzzle
that I do not know.
—Lydia

Why had Lydia moved from Turkey to Greece? Why leave her native country, perhaps aging family members, behind her? Why choose Philippi, a Macedonian city, for the new home of Lydia's Fabrics? Although Philippi was surrounded on all sides by mountains, it was located on the Egnation Highway, a well-traveled route that was the only link between Rome and Asia, and the Philippians were known for trying to outdo Rome in dress and manners.

Lydia had done her homework, and she would have known that professional organizations called guilds, for both physicians and dyers, were located in Philippi. (Tradition says that Dr. Luke, the Gospel writer and the author of Acts, was born in Philippi.)

Lydia's research probably showed that she would have many opportunities to sell her famous purple, the ancient color of kings, to legions of Roman soldiers and mercenaries, who would spread by word of mouth the beauty and durability of her fabrics. Although her trek across the Aegean Sea may have involved great personal sacrifice, relocating to Philippi was a smart business move. But business was not enough to fill Lydia's life. She was a seeker after truth.

Lord, remind me to buckle on the Belt of Truth each morning. I know that deception, avoidance and denial are not in Your plan for me.

A SEEKER AFTER TRUTH

"Then we will no longer be infants, tossed back and forth by the waves, and blown here and there by every wind of teaching and by the cunning and craftiness of men in their deceitful scheming. Instead, speaking the truth in love, we will in all things grow up into him who is the Head, that is, Christ." (Ephesians 4:14-15)

Read Acts 16:11-15

I hate to think my purple cloth
is used in pagan sacrifice.
I hate to think of Roman soldiers,
wearing robes of purple,
persecuting Jewish friends.
I hate the worship of the dyers' guilds,
the bowing before patron gods.
But yet . . . it's part of business.

—Lydia

Lydia, a seeker after truth, met regularly with a small group of women on the bank of the Ganga (Gangites) River. Together they worshiped the one true God of the Jews.

Imagine Lydia sitting on that riverbank, thinking longingly of her friends and family, separated from her by the Aegean Sea. Perhaps she would never see them again. She clung to her faith for comfort—and yet it seemed something was missing.

For the sake of her business, Lydia probably belonged to the local dyers' guild. Guilds often involved immorality . . . worship of the trade's patron god . . . feasts using sacrifices that had been offered to idols. Lydia may have seen these compromises as necessary to success.

But as she sat on the riverbank one Sabbath, perhaps Lydia's concept of success began to change. Two strangers, Paul and Silas, took the time to present the story of Jesus to a small group of women. "The Lord opened her heart to respond to Paul's message" (Acts 16:14). And Lydia put truth into practice in her life.

Lord, I want to be not only a seeker of truth, but also a speaker of truth.

A BUSINESSWOMAN WHO'S NOT ALL BUSINESS

"When she and the members of her household were baptized, she invited us to her home. 'If you consider me a believer in the Lord,' she said, 'come and stay at my house.' And she persuaded us." (Acts 16:15)

Read Romans 1:14-20

There's so much more I need to know . . .
There's so much more I need to ask . . .
The name of Jesus is so new
and yet I feel I've always known Him.
I want to spread this news to others
but will Paul trust me
as a true believer
when I know so little?

—Lydia

As the first known convert to Christianity in the West, Lydia hosted the first church in Europe in her home. Her business contacts may have introduced Paul to the "movers and shakers" of the Macedonian area. Relocating to Philippi had been a smart business move; now it became obvious that Lydia's move was a small part of God's giant plan for evangelizing the Gentile world.

A Latin inscription found in Philippi mentions a "dyeing trade" that was very much alive! Economically, the trade was highly important to the city. As far as we know, Lydia's conversion didn't change her occupation, but it dramatically changed her loyalty. From that point on, I believe Lydia primarily used her persuasive abilities not to sell, but to tell!

And perhaps Lydia used the little Mediterranean shellfish as a symbol of the One who died, who gave His life for the people of Philippi. "You see," she may have explained to her customers, "when the murex dies, the purple dye brings beauty to people's lives. Jesus the Christ gave His life on a crimson-stained cross to bring beauty of spirit . . . and to give us everlasting life."

Thank You, Lord, for the pictures in nature You have created to illustrate Your Truth.

LYDIA, A WOMAN WHO KNEW THE MARKET —AND HER NEED FOR MENTORING!

"And when she was baptized along with her household, she earnestly entreated us, saying, If in your opinion I am one really convinced [that Jesus is the Messiah and the Author of salvation], and that I will be faithful to the Lord, come to my house and stay. And she induced us [to do it]."
(Acts 16:15, Amplified)

Read Acts 14:21-23

I've found it, yes, I've found it!
The truth for which I've searched
all through my life!
To think that He knew all along
that I would move to Philippi . . .
To think that He knew all along
that I would hear this glorious news . . .
To think that He would touch my heart
and change my life!

—Lydia

Lydia was a businesswoman, and therefore she was realistic. She had learned from experience that many businesses did not survive because the owners or managers were not capable of "hanging in there" through the bad days.

Lydia also was aware that there was a lot she did not know about this new way of life that Paul taught, and she wanted to learn as much as possible, as quickly as possible. Although she was accustomed to "taking charge," Lydia was also able to put herself under authority, and she did this readily: "If you agree that I am faithful to the Lord, . . . come and stay at my home" (Acts 16:15, TLB). Obviously, as a woman of great discernment and openness of heart, she had complete trust in Paul and Silas, and she wanted to make that very clear to her friends and neighbors. Lydia had finally found the truth for which she had been searching.

Lord, Your Word says that as the heavens are higher than the earth, so Your ways are higher than our ways. Thank You, Lord, for Your omniscience—Your thoughts are so much greater than mine.

41 – Saturday

PLATES HEAPED HIGH WITH ENCOURAGEMENT

"After Paul and Silas came out of the prison, they went to Lydia's house, where they met with the brothers and encouraged them." (Acts 16:40)

Read 2 Corinthians 11:24-33

I am beginning to believe
that our God works
in quite mysterious ways.
I never would have thought
that people would be won to Him
in the ways He seems to choose.
I've learned that He is in control
and I am not.

—Lydia

Public humiliation—stripping and beating—and a night in jail is not usually considered a good way for "out-of-towners" to make an impression on the townsfolk. What was Lydia's reaction when she heard that Paul and Silas were in almost-solitary confinement? Instead of checking the status of their stocks and bonds, these two men were spending the night looking at their feet, fastened in the prison stocks!

But God desires to use every circumstance that comes into our lives for His glory. At midnight, undisturbed by their discomfort, Paul and Silas were praying and singing hymns.

God sent justice in the form of an earthquake so violent "that the foundations of the prison were shaken" (Acts 16:26). The jailer saw the open prison doors and the broken chains and was about to kill himself before the Romans did. But Paul shouted, "Don't harm yourself! We are all here!" (16:28). The jailer was so amazed that he asked, trembling, "What must I do to be saved?" (16:30). And he and his whole household were saved that night.

You're amazing, Lord! As we praise You, You turn tragedy into triumph.

Week 42

"The Pythoness"

We've discussed the night in jail—but why were Paul and Silas there in the first place? The background story is fascinating.

> One day when we were going to the place of prayer, a female servant met us. She was possessed by an evil spirit that told fortunes [and] she made a lot of money for her owners by telling fortunes. She used to follow Paul and shout, "These men are servants of the Most High God. They're telling you how you can be saved." She kept doing this for many days. Paul became annoyed, turned to the evil spirit, and said, "I command you in the name of Jesus Christ to come out of her!"
>
> As Paul said this, the evil spirit left her. When her owners realized that their hope of making money was gone, they grabbed Paul and Silas and dragged them to the authorities in the public square. In front of the Roman officials, they said, "These men are stirring up a lot of trouble in our city. They're Jews, and they're advocating customs that we can't accept or practice as Roman citizens."
>
> The crowd joined in the attack against Paul and Silas. Then the officials tore the clothes off Paul and Silas and ordered the guards to beat them with sticks. After they had hit Paul and Silas many times, they threw them in jail and ordered the jailer to keep them under tight secu-

rity. So the jailer followed these orders and put Paul and Silas into solitary confinement with their feet in leg irons.

Around midnight Paul and Silas were praying and singing hymns of praise to God. The other prisoners were listening to them. Suddenly, a violent earthquake shook the foundations of the jail. All the doors immediately flew open, and all the prisoners' chains came loose.

The jailer woke up and saw the prison doors open. Thinking the prisoners had escaped, he drew his sword and was about to kill himself. But Paul shouted as loudly as he could, "Don't hurt yourself! We're all here!"

The jailer asked for torches and rushed into the jail. He was trembling as he knelt in front of Paul and Silas. Then he took Paul and Silas outside and asked, "Sirs, what do I have to do to be saved?"

They answered, "Believe in the Lord Jesus, and you and your family will be saved. They spoke the Lord's word to the jailer and everyone in his home.

At that hour of the night, the jailer washed Paul and Silas' wounds. The jailer and his entire family were baptized immediately. He took Paul and Silas upstairs into his home and gave them something to eat. He and his family were thrilled to be believers in God. (Acts 16:16-33, GOD'S WORD)

BACKGROUND READING: Acts 16

42 – Monday

A SPIRIT OF DIVINATION

"As we were on our way to the place of prayer, we were met by a slave girl who was possessed by a spirit of divination—claiming to foretell future events and to discover hidden knowledge—and she brought her owners much gain by her fortune-telling." (Acts 16:16, Amplified)

Read Isaiah 14:12-20

I'd known of her existence,
signs boasting of her powers everywhere:
She tells your future
to the very hour and minute!
But I'd ignored them until now.
Today there was no way to pass this girl!
—Lydia

Controlled by a spirit of divination, a slave girl practiced fortune-telling. The Greek word for divination is the word from which we get our English word "python," and so she was called a "pythoness." (This name was used when referring to persons supposedly indwelt by the spirit of the Greek god Apollo, the Python god at the shrine of Delphi in central Greece, the home of the famous Greek oracles.)

Since the girl's utterances were regarded as the voice of Apollo, she was much in demand. Perhaps her owners, having located her in a small room on a busy street in Philippi, advertised the talents of this young woman possessed by the famous Apollo Python spirit. When inquired of—for a price—she would go into a semi-trance, giving a personal word to the inquirer, answering questions concerning his or her personal, social and business life.

But their big business was about to show a sharp decline!

Lord, You do not desire for me to be fascinated by the study of demons. Nor do You desire for me to be excited by sensational happenings. But please, Lord, give me the courage I need for spiritual warfare.

SHE KEPT FOLLOWING PAUL . . .

"She kept following Paul and [the rest of] us, shouting loudly, These men are the servants of the Most High God! They announce to you the way of salvation! And she did this for many days." (Acts 16:17-18, Amplified)

Read Ezekiel 28:11-19

As soon as she saw Paul and Silas
she began to scream:
These men are servants
of the Most High God!
These men announce to you
the Way!
She screamed . . .
and screamed . . .
and screamed.
—Lydia

The girl's repeated announcement can be interpreted in different ways. The expression "Most High God" was commonly used by both Jews and Gentiles to refer to the Supreme Being. At that time, the Greek mystery religions and other cults also offered salvation, so the girl's message did not necessarily refer to the salvation paid for on the cross by Jesus Christ. She may have identified pagan cults in the same way.

"At one time the girl was over-mastered by the evil spirit who was her real lord; at another time she felt a longing for deliverance from her bondage."[1] And so the girl's constant cry could have represented her personal, overwhelming desire to know the Most High God.

In any case, Paul's annoyance was caused by and directed at the demonic spirit of divination, not the girl. Demons recognized the Lord Jesus when He lived here on earth and identified Him as the Most High God. In James 2:19, we are told that even the demons believe that there is one God—"and shudder"!

Lord, since even demons "shudder" when they recognize Your presence, let me not take lightly the privilege of coming into Your courts—with praise!

"AND IT CAME OUT THAT VERY MOMENT"

"Then Paul, being sorely annoyed and worn out, turned and said to the spirit within her, I charge you in the name of Jesus Christ to come out of her! And it came out that very moment. But when her owners discovered that their hope of profit was gone, they caught hold of Paul and Silas and dragged them before the authorities in the forum." (Acts 16:18-19, Amplified)

Read Luke 8:26-39

The girl was tortured
that was plain to see.
She'd no control of what she said.
The voice was not her own.
The spirit used her body,
voice and mind.

—Lydia

The Greek word used to describe the slave girl means "a young girl or female slave." This poor little girl was doubly a slave—not only to the men who owned and exploited her, but also to the demons which controlled her. Her condition was pitiful, and Paul was very emotionally disturbed by the situation. The forceful Greek word translated "annoyance" combines the intertwined emotions of grief, pain and anger.

When Jesus was confronted by demons who identified Him, He was not pleased by their declarations of His status. The apostle Paul, as well, refused to allow the demonized girl to continue advertising his presence. Paul commanded the spirit to leave the girl's body, in the name of Jesus—the biblical "formula" used all through Acts by the representatives of Jesus.

The girl's deliverance was immediate, instantaneous.

But the exodus of the demons left the girl an ordinary young woman—perhaps just a girl who was terribly shaken by what had happened, a girl without any power or desire to predict the future or to make money for her owners. Naturally, her masters were enraged with her, and with Paul and Silas, who had destroyed their flourishing business.

Thank You for reminding me, Lord, that not everyone will react favorably to what Your disciples do in Your name.

DEMONIC ILLUSIONS

"The Spirit says clearly that in later times some believers will desert the Christian faith. They will follow spirits that deceive, and they will believe the teachings of demons."
(1 Timothy 4:1, GOD'S WORD)

Read 2 Corinthians 11:14-15; Luke 4:31-37

Her masters were enraged—
they'd lost their source of gain.
Their evil powers gone, as well,
the girl no longer subject
to their will.

—Lydia

As we mentioned earlier, the Greeks were fascinated by the Oracle of Delphi, where strange and mysterious messages were given to those who frequented the area. The Greeks also admired ventriloquism, the ability to project one's voice so that it appears to come from another person or object. Since ventriloquism was often misused for the purposes of magic, the Greeks associated this talent with pythonism, attributing it to demonic power.

In demonization, however, another being, an evil personality, speaks out of the mouth of a human being, often producing strange sounds or a different voice than that of the individual. Probably the voice which so upset Paul was a very unnatural one for a young woman. We might ask, "Why did he wait so long to bring deliverance to the young woman?"

Possibly Paul realized that, once the deliverance had taken place, his time in Philippi might be limited. Paul's example suggests that there are right and wrong ways, right and wrong times and places to handle deliverance from demonic activity. In many churches the topic is so threatening that it is never discussed. Many others have been deluded by "professional liars" who have "lost their capacity for truth" and are "chasing after demonic illusions."

Thank You, El Elyon, Lord of Hosts, for taking away our fear—because "greater is he that is in [us], than he that is in the world" (1 John 4:4, KJV).

"BEING CONFIDENT OF THIS . . ."

"In all my prayers for all of you, I always pray with joy because of your partnership in the gospel from the first day until now, being confident of this, that he who began a good work in you will carry it on to completion until the day of Christ Jesus." (Philippians 1:4-6)

Read Ephesians 6:10-18

I am beginning now to realize
the battle we are in.
It is not humans that we fight
but principalities and powers
not flesh and blood
but unseen rulers of this world.
—Lydia

George B. Eager, founder of the children's Mailbox Club, writes in their newsletter:

> I have been shocked and dismayed at many things, but something which I saw recently is the most evil thing I have ever seen in my entire life. A children's worker showed me a three-page, full-color ad which ran in a magazine for children and teens.
>
> This ad . . . pictures Satan as a cute little fellow with a smiley face and a funny looking pitchfork. On page one, he says, "Let's make a deal." The deal is that he wants the children and young people to sell their souls to him. . . .
>
> Then this same smiley-face devil proceeds to tell them that hell is a fun place where the only rule is that there are no rules. . . . In the background he shows something like an amusement park. The demons surrounding him are all scantily dressed young girls. He urges the readers to ensure their permanent place in hell by selling their soul to him. There is a contract at the end which they are to sign and send to a company in California marked Attn.: Devil Man. The contract reads: "I, the undersigned, do hereby give possession of my soul to the Devil, for eternity, for ever and ever and ever and ever and ever and ever."[2]

42 — Saturday

"YOUR ATTITUDE SHOULD BE THE SAME . . ."

"Do nothing out of selfish ambition or vain conceit, but in humility consider others better than yourselves."
(Philippians 2:3)

Read Philippians 2:1-16

I feel compassion for that girl,
new feelings I have never felt before.
At one time I would simply block her out,
discard her like a pile of ruined cloth.
But now I cannot get her from my thoughts . . .
God, are you telling me
to open up my home
to this deluded girl?

—Lydia

"Have the same attitude," Paul pleaded, "that Christ Jesus had. Although he was in the form of God and equal with God, he did not take advantage of this equality. Instead, he emptied himself by taking on the form of a servant, by becoming like other humans, by having a human appearance. He humbled himself by becoming obedient to the point of death. . . ." (Philippians 2:5-8, GOD'S WORD)

Servanthood involves different things for different people. Some, like Lydia, have the gift of hospitality. Joyce and Morgan Ilgenfritz enjoy God's blessing on a private ministry as they invite single moms to stay in their home. But not everyone's temperament is suited to having people live with her; other servants of God need to preserve their home as their "castle," a private place to study, write or prepare for public ministry.

It's important to understand how God has made us and for what He has suited us and to work within those boundaries. "For you created my inmost being; you knit me together in my mother's womb" (Psalm 139:13).

Thank You, Lord, that my frame was not hidden from you when I was made in the secret place, that You are familiar with all my ways.

Week 43

Phoebe, Tryphena and Tryphosa

Phoebe the Postperson, the "special deliverer" of Paul's epistle to the Romans! Since the imperial post of Rome was not available for private correspondence, Paul's letters had to be sent by a private messenger. Who better than his trusted friend, the woman he referred to as "our sister" Phoebe? In choosing Phoebe, Paul was conferring a great honor upon her. Paul himself had not yet visited Rome, and so Phoebe acted as his personal representative as well as the representative of Christ.

Paul called Phoebe "a servant of the church in Cenchrea," a seaport near Corinth. Scripture tells us that Paul had a haircut in Cenchrea to fulfill a vow he had taken. But barbers were not the only vendors waiting to offer their services to tourists. You may remember that the temple of Aphrodite—"the temple of love"—served by 1,000 priestess-prostitutes, was in nearby Corinth. To be a Christian at Cenchrea, or any seaport swarming with sailors, was no easy matter.

An advantage to living near Corinth, however, may have been the opportunity to meet Aquila and Priscilla during their stay there. Perhaps the couple became role models in ministry. Phoebe may have welcomed the trip to Rome as an opportunity to see her old friends once again.

In addition to calling Phoebe a servant, Paul also described her as "a succourer of many, and of myself also" (Romans 16:2, KJV). The old word "succour" had a variety of meanings: comfort, help, support, blessing, nourish, strength, calm, cheer, consolation, encouragement. The word "servant" comes from the Greek *diaconos,* from which the words "deacon" and "deaconess" are derived. What a job description! Phoebe was truly God's servant—one who comforted the discouraged, fought for the oppressed and unprotected and also nurtured those in ministry.

When Paul left Corinth, via Cenchrea, for Ephesus, he traveled by boat (Acts 18:18). When Phoebe left for Rome, she may also have traveled by sea but, at the time, the preferred manner of travel for a woman was overland, by caravan. Perhaps Phoebe traveled north, through Macedonia, and stayed in Lydia's home when she reached Philippi. And by that time, the former "Pythoness" may have been an established member of the Church! (Historians tell us that in the early Christian Church, there were two requirements: exorcism—perhaps a better term today would be "deliverance"—and catechism, in that order.)

Phoebe the Postperson would have had the opportunity to stop at many places where Christian churches had been established, bringing greetings and a message directly from Paul. When she reached her destination, Paul urged the Roman people to receive Phoebe as a key representative of the church at Cenchrea. "Help her in every way you can, for she has helped many in their needs, including me" (Romans 16:1, TLB).

Paul sent special greetings to Tryphena and Tryphosa, faithful workers in the early Christian Church at Rome who may have welcomed Phoebe on her arrival. And imagine Phoebe's delight, at the end of a long journey full of new places and people, to see her old friends Aquila and Priscilla once again!

BACKGROUND READING: Romans 16

43 — Monday

REALITY CHECK

"Since earliest times men have seen the earth and sky and all God made, and have known of his existence and great eternal power. So they will have no excuse [when they stand before God at Judgment Day]." (Romans 1:20, TLB)

Read Acts 9:1-19

If only those around me
would recognize
their desperate need for healing
from their sin!
Paul once was Saul
who hunted Christians down
but God saw what he could become . . .
The "Hound of Heaven" hunted Saul
and turned him into Paul.
Yes, all have sinned—and there is hope for all.
—Phoebe

A funny thing happened on the way to Damascus, where Saul was heading to take Christians as prisoners to Jerusalem. He encountered what John Trent, in his book *LifeMapping,* would call a "flash point."

Prior to that day, Saul had gone from house to house dragging off to prison people accused of being Christians. Saul stood by while Stephen was stoned, mercilessly giving consent to his death. But on his way to Damascus, a light from heaven flashed around him.

The tables had been turned. Paul the Persecutor fell helplessly to the ground.

Thank You, Lord, that You also pursued me.

43 — Tuesday

"PLACE OF HIGHEST PRIVILEGE"

"When God promised Abraham that he would become the father of many nations, Abraham believed him. . . . And Abraham's faith did not weaken. . . . Abraham never wavered in believing God's promise. . . . He was absolutely convinced that God was able to do anything he promised."
(Romans 4:18-21, NLT)

Read Acts 9:20-31

God's message to the world
is written in the stars:
the Lion of Judah is there,
The Virgin Birth so fair.
God's love shines through creation
for all the world to see.
Though He receives no honor
from many He's created,
God has a plan.
He holds the cure for sin.
—Phoebe

God hates sin. Sin requires a penalty—death—in order for God's righteous demands to be satisfied; the ransom must be paid. Jesus Christ fills that role to perfection. And that is why the cross is so significant. It became the place of judgment. It was there that the price was paid in full.

When, like Paul, we have recognized the wretchedness of our condition and the need for a cure; when, increasingly, we realize our plans just don't work; when, finally, we are ready for God to reorganize our lives—Paul points to the peace and joy of trusting God's plan. When we have confessed our sin and believe the promises of God, He will accept us in the same way He accepted Abraham. Not only that, but God promises to bring us into a "place of highest privilege" (Romans 5:2, TLB), where we can look forward to becoming all that God has in mind for us to become. In the meantime—in the waiting room—we learn patience, strength of character and trust.

You're teaching me, Lord, that the waiting room precedes the place of highest privilege.

43 — Wednesday

SAVED BY FAITH

"What can we boast about doing, to earn our salvation? Nothing at all. Why? Because our acquittal is not based on our good deeds; it is based on what Christ has done and our faith in Him. So it is that we are saved by faith in Christ and not by the good things we do." (Romans 3:27-28, TLB)

Read Ephesians 2:1-10

Some use "grace" as an escape,
avoid all rules and laws—they sin.
Others are so bound by rules and laws
they miss the joy of their new life.
We are no longer bound to sin,
we are no longer tied to law.
We're free to serve because we love.
—Phoebe

Grace is not license to do as we please. Freedom has limits. Love has biblical restrictions.

But can we earn our salvation? Isn't that asking if we need to add to Christ's work? The answer is NO!

When your friend brings you a birthday gift out of love for you, do you unwrap it, thank her, then get out your wallet and ask how much it cost so you can repay her? Wouldn't she be offended if you did? Love motivated her giving. Suggesting you'd pay for it would be a slap in the face.

Salvation is a gift of love. "It's free, but it wasn't cheap. It's simple, but it wasn't easy. It's yours, but it isn't automatic. You must receive it. And when you do, it's yours forever!"[1]

Thank You, Lord, for your amazingly free gift.

43 – *Thursday*

OFFSPRING OF FAITH

"The law no longer holds you in its power, because you died to its power when you died with Christ on the cross. And now you are united with the one who was raised from the dead. . . . Now we can really serve God, not in the old way by obeying the letter of the law, but in the new way, by the Spirit."
(Romans 7:4, 6, NLT)

Read Romans 7:1-14

I feel it's such an honor
to be the bearer of the news
that Jewish law no longer is our master,
that we're no longer married to the law.
We are the bride of Christ!
And those of us who never married
look forward to a wedding feast
where we'll be cherished
by our Bridegroom.
—Phoebe

God didn't deal with this dilemma of the human race as a distant or unimportant problem. So intent was He on His goal of letting humanity know He understood that He shrink-wrapped His own Son in human flesh—and placed that tiny package in the virgin womb of a teenaged girl.

POINT TO PONDER: That tiny package became a Man who was tempted in every way that we humans are tempted. He was rejected by the very men He had helped to plan and create. And He felt abandoned by the very Father who had sent Him to earth. Yet He still sought to gather His beloved ones to Himself.

Thank You, Father, for sending Your Son to be my Elder Brother as well as my Mediator.

43 – Friday

THIS LIFE OF CONTRADICTIONS

"I don't understand myself at all, for I really want to do what is right, but I can't. I do what I don't want to—what I hate. . . . Who will free me from my slavery to this deadly lower nature?" (Romans 7:15, 24, TLB)

Read Romans 7:15-8:4

We all deal with this war within.
It rages on within our souls.
But because our God became a man
we now have access to
the mind of Christ . . .
the love of Christ . . .
the joy of Christ . . .
the peace of Christ . . .
—Phoebe

Do you struggle with what it means to experience the Spirit-filled life? Does "the abundant life" seem to escape you? Romans 7 and 8 may sound so familiar you almost think you wrote it yourself.

Have you ever watched a caterpillar struggle to emerge from its cocoon? If I were the caterpillar inside, freedom from that binding restriction wrapped around me would seem a tantalizing but elusive dream. These chapters in Romans provide a realistic description of our similar struggle with sin.

Romans 7 and 8 also give perspective and understanding—and the secret to overcoming our sinful nature! The indwelling presence and power of the Holy Spirit is to our lives what electricity is to an all-electric home. Nothing will happen unless the Spirit flows through us!

Your Spirit alone, Lord Jesus, can free me from the struggle. Thank You for reminding me once again that being filled with Your Spirit is a process of breathing out—emptying myself of sin, accepting forgiveness—and breathing in Your infilling.

43 — *Saturday*

ENCOURAGEMENT FROM ABOVE

"And in the same way—by our faith—the Holy Spirit helps us with our daily problems and in our praying. For we don't even know what we should pray for, nor how to pray as we should." (Romans 8:26, TLB)

Read Romans 8:5-39

My grace is sufficient,
our Master said to Paul.
When you are weak,
then I am strong.
My strength shows up best
when set in frames of
people who are weak
who then become
living demonstrations
of Christ's power.
—Phoebe

Satan wants to rob us of love . . . of joy . . . of peace. He robs us of love through oppressing us with feelings of resentment toward others. He robs us of joy with his messages of guilt. (Satan gets his jollies in accusing us, causing false guilt. True guilt comes not through condemnation, but through conviction of the Holy Spirit.) Satan robs us of peace through anxiety, discouragement, discontent.

These messages of Satan, these "thorns in the flesh," hinder the Holy Spirit from bearing witness with our spirits. The last thing Satan wants is for us to exercise the gifts of the Spirit within the Body of Christ, with the fruits of the Spirit evident in our lives. Satan wants us to be so obsessed with "the struggle," feeling that our lives are full of contradictions and hypocrisy, that we are nonfunctional. Or we may even think, *Wouldn't it be better to die and be with the Lord?*

Lord, help me to differentiate between the thoughts put into my mind by Satan and the thoughts that are of You. Help me to think about the true, the right, the pure. . . .

Week 44

Syntyche and Euodias

Philippians, the epistle of joy! Paul wrote this thankful letter to encourage the believers in their suffering and also to warn them about "those men who do evil" (3:2), who would try to steal their joy.

Not only unbelievers, however, are "joy-stealers." Apparently Euodias and Syntyche, who had once been the best of friends—whose names, Scripture tells us, were both written in the book of life—had stolen each other's joy.

What or who precipitated the joy-stealing? What *was* the "sin" of Syntyche? Or was it Euodias who was becoming "odious" in the relationship?

Both women, evidently, had worked right alongside of Paul. There was no doubt in his mind that both lives were genuinely committed to Christ and the spreading of the gospel. Did their friendship split apart because of jealousy? Miscommunication? Different understandings of theological issues? Children who competed with each other? (One child always has to win, of course, and one has to lose.)

Perhaps one had a beautiful singing voice and the other was a great cook—but the singer got all the rave reviews. Perhaps one had children and the other longed for children—or perhaps one of them had well-behaved children and the other had strong-willed, non-compliant children.

Perhaps one spoke in tongues and the other did not.

How many church splits have begun through the souring of a relationship? The closer the pair was originally, the deeper the hurts . . . the greater the need to share the hurts with just one person, then to feel vindicated by just one, maybe two, other people . . . the wider the ripples of misunderstanding . . .

A picture in a magazine showed a young man on his knees. The caption was this comment: "Even when they disagree, Christians should share the same position. Where there's disagreement, there's reason for prayer."

When we humble ourselves in prayer, we search for God's answers rather than our own. We find "the mind of Christ"—and understanding of others.

So before you take a strong stand for what you believe, spend some time on your knees.

BACKGROUND READING: Philippians 1

44 – *Monday*

JOY VS. ANXIETY

"And now I want to plead with those two dear women, Euodias and Syntyche. Please, please, with the Lord's help, quarrel no more—be friends again." (Philippians 4:2, TLB)

Read Philippians 4:4-8

Ah, when I think how close we were!
And now we haven't spoken
a word
in months.
There was that difference
of discernment,
that disagreement,
and then a gradual parting of the ways.
—Syntyche

In the same chapter where Paul mentions our friends' names, he also talks about *anxiety*. As mentioned earlier, one definition of anxiety is "the fear that something I need will not be provided." That *something* can be an emotional, physical or material need. Whatever the cause, anxiety can dominate our thoughts and actions so much that we become very difficult to live with.

Perhaps Syntyche was the kind of woman whose conversations with her friend were her way of finding out what she was thinking, of dealing with her anxiety, of mapping out her plan to handle life. But perhaps one day Euodias got a little tired of being used as a sounding board—she had her own anxieties to deal with that day—and maybe she quoted the words of Paul to her friend: "Tychie, Paul says, 'Do not be anxious about anything, but in everything, by prayer and petition, with thanksgiving, present your requests to God. And the peace of God, which transcends all understanding, will guard your hearts and your minds in Christ Jesus' (Philippians 4:6-7). Why don't you spend some quiet time meditating on those thoughts today?

"And, Tychie, I need a little space . . . to think through some problems of my own. I'm going to let the answering machine get the phone. So . . . if you call again today, you'll get the machine. I'm not going to answer my phone anymore today."

Lord, I know that often my anxiety is simply a lack of trust in You. Please forgive me.

44 – Tuesday

JOY VS. RESENTMENT

"Have the attitude the Lord wants [you] to have."
(Philippians 4:2, God's Word)

Read Matthew 18:15-20

Since Syntyche no longer speaks to me
I've lost not only her voice
but also the sense of His voice
as well.
It seems as though a wall's been built
that can't be penetrated.
Oh, how I miss her friendship!
—Euodias

Anxiety is often accompanied or followed by resentment: "believing that my needs are threatened by something which God has allowed to happen to me." This strong feeling may appear to float aimlessly through our minds; if we analyze it, however, it may actually be targeted toward God. On the other hand, just as kids often take out the frustrations of their day on a younger brother or sister, we adults may blame someone who "has it better than I do" for our problems.

Perhaps Euodias had a loving husband who provided well for her, but maybe Syntyche's husband found it difficult to put in five consecutive days of work. Syntyche may have initially chosen Euodias as a friend because of her security, confidence and giving ways, but perhaps the comparison of their husbands and their economic situations got in the way of their friendship.

> Forgetting what is behind and straining toward what is ahead, I press on toward the goal to win the prize for which God has called me heavenward in Christ Jesus.
>
> All of us who are mature should take such a view of things. And if on some point you think differently, that too God will make clear to you. Only let us live up to what we have already attained. (Philippians 3:13-16)

Father, I so often struggle with feelings of resentment. You know the dynamics of each situation. Please cleanse my heart.

44 – Wednesday

JOY VS. GUILT

"And I ask you, my true teammate, to help these women."
(Philippians 4:3, TLB)

Read Titus 2:1-8

If only there were someone
to talk to
to listen like a mother
to judge between us like a father
instead of this—
this sibling rivalry!
I miss our friendship so
but I don't know how to say it
without backing down.
—Syntyche

Who was Syzygas? An elder in the church? A mutual friend? A friend of Paul who knew both women? Looks like he had quite a job on his hands! Mentors with the gift of discernment—and patience—are greatly needed in the Church today. Many people have grown up without parents at home to intervene in fights and to model constructive ways of handling conflict. Or, if parents were physically present, they may not have "been there" emotionally for their children.

When we are hurting emotionally and we feel that no one cares, it is easy to turn to wrong ways of satisfying our needs: fornication, adulterous affairs, drugs, overeating, workaholism.

Guilt comes from believing that what God provides is not enough and then going outside of God's will to secure what He has not provided.

Jesus said, "Do not store up for yourselves treasures on earth, where moth and rust destroy, and where thieves break in and steal. But store up for yourselves treasures in heaven. . . . For where your treasure is, there your heart will be also" (Matthew 6:19-21).

Lord, I can trust You to provide—emotionally, physically, materially—so that there is no need for me to go outside Your will to get my needs fulfilled.

"MAKE MY JOY COMPLETE . . ."

"They worked side by side with me in telling the Good News to others." (Philippians 4:3, TLB)

Read 1 Corinthians 6:1-11

This wall that's grown between us
has separated others too.
It seems that if
someone's her friend
she can't be mine.
Perhaps I've said too many things
about our disagreement
to too many people.
—Euodias

Jesus said, "How can you say to your brother, 'Brother, let me take the speck out of your eye,' when you yourself fail to see the plank in your own eye? You hypocrite, first take the plank out of your eye, and then you will see clearly to remove the speck from your brother's eye" (Luke 6:42).

POINT TO PONDER: *Anxiety, resentment* and *guilt* begin in just one relationship between two people, but inevitably they create ripples in the body of Christ. The ripples develop into waves of awkwardness and tension that sweep through entire churches, developing storms of distrust and fear. Often the initial problem in the initial relationship is forgotten or obscured as Christians unite—against each other. How these "family feuds" must grieve the heart of our heavenly Father!

Paul advised his old friends in Philippi: "If you have any encouragement from being united with Christ, if any comfort from his love, if any fellowship with the Spirit, if any tenderness and compassion, then make my joy complete by being like-minded, having the same love, being one in spirit and purpose" (Philippians 2:1-2).

Lord, I know it grieves Your heart when Your children fight. Help me to resolve my feelings toward ____________ *before those feelings spread to others in Your body.*

44 – Friday

WORK IT OUT!

"Let everyone see that you are unselfish and considerate in all you do. Remember that the Lord is coming soon."
(Philippians 4:5, TLB)

Read Luke 17:1-10

I wonder what would happen
if we met one day
and I asked forgiveness
for talking to others
about her.
Could we just agree
to disagree?

—Syntyche

Jesus said, "If a believer does something wrong, go, confront him when the two of you are alone. If he listens to you, you have won back that believer."

He went on to say, "But if he does not listen, take one or two others with you so that every accusation may be verified by two or three witnesses. If he ignores the community, tell it to the community of believers. If he also ignores these witnesses, deal with him as you would a heathen or a tax collector" (Matthew 18:15-17, GOD'S WORD).

Then Jesus followed this "Showing-him-his-fault Formula" with the parable of the unmerciful servant. Although his great debt was canceled by his master, this servant did not forgive those who were indebted to him in a small way. "In anger his master turned him over to the jailers to be tortured, until he should pay back all he owed. This is how my heavenly Father will treat each of you unless you forgive your brother from your heart" (18:34-35).

Thank You, Lord, for these insights. I need to deal directly with people, not talk about them behind their backs. Help me to put this into practice today.

44 – Saturday

DEEP-SPIRITED FRIENDS

"Is there any such thing as Christians cheering each other up? Do you love me enough to want to help me? Does it mean anything to you that we are brothers in the Lord, sharing the same Spirit? Are your hearts tender and sympathetic at all? Then make me truly happy by loving each other and agreeing wholeheartedly with each other, working together with one heart and mind and purpose." (Philippians 2:1-2, TLB)

Read 1 Samuel 18:1-4; 20:16-17, 41-42.

I'm almost ready
to go to her,
to let bygones be bygones.
Does she hate me?
Is there any love still left
between us?

—Euodias

Current counselors might tell Euodias and Syntyche that they had made the mistake of falling into a codependent relationship. Paul urges us to be "deep-spirited" friends. What is the difference?

POINT TO PONDER: In a deep-spirited relationship, there is give-and-take on both sides. *Neither one does all the giving or all the taking.* They take turns pouring out their heart. They take turns listening to each other—active listening, which is hard work. They are honest with each other, even when it hurts. They are free to let each other know when they "need space." They admonish each other when forgiveness is needed—from the Lord or from each other—for bad attitudes or sinful actions. They pray for each other and may pray together.

We should be aware of the dangers. Even same-sex "deep-spirited" friendships can become so close that spouses, family members or other friends can feel threatened or left out. Opposite-sex "deep-spirited" friendships between married people (but not married to each other) should be handled with great caution—and given to the Lord to direct as He chooses.

Sometimes, Lord, when my friend has poured wine on my wounds, the alcohol in the wine stings, and I resist. But thank You for the healing oil of prayer that binds us together again.

Week 45

Eunice and Lois

Perhaps you are a single parent, struggling with the problems of raising children in today's world on your own. The sections with an emphasis on marriage in this book may have hit a sore spot with you.

What help can you derive from women in the New Testament?

Eunice and Lois were the mother and grandmother of Timothy, who became a spiritual son to the childless Paul. Eunice was a Jewess, but she had married a Greek who was not sympathetic to Jewish customs. It seems probable that he died or disappeared early in Timothy's life. Eunice was left to raise her son alone, with her mother's help, and God's.

"Is tonight today?"
My three-year-old seeks to reconcile
confusing entities in his mind.
He has been promised a visit
To his favorite friend's house
Tonight.
Is that today?
Yes, but still tonight.
But—tonight is miserably far away.
Too distant to anticipate in his young mind.
He only understands the now of life.

I find an echo of his confusion
In my adult mind.
Do I understand a life hereafter?
Or heaven? or eternity?
Or is my mind too finite to comprehend
God's promises to me?

Father, I too am but a child,
So limited in understanding,
Earth-anchored in thought.
Teach me
To let go the moorings of my unbelief.
Help me
To realize as much as I can absorb
Of Your great love—
A love that sent Your Son to die for me,
A love with no beginnings and no end.

And yet
All that the human eye can see is now—
And those about me, Lord, may only see
Your power through me.
What grave responsibility,
An awesome task,
To be the channel of Your love
Right now.

BACKGROUND READING: 2 Timothy 1:3-5; Psalm 71

45 — Monday

MISSIONARY OR MISFIT?

"If any do not obey the Word [of God], they may be won over not by discussion but by the [godly] lives of their wives."
(1 Peter 3:1, Amplified)

Read 1 Corinthians 7:12-16

Alone—what a terrible word!
It hangs like a threatening sword
by night and by day
at home or away
and hinders the song of the birds.
—A contemporary Eunice

I am part of a unique group at our church. I am qualified for membership because I fit into the last of the following categories: single, separated, divorced, widowed . . . married without spouse at church. (My husband is on the road most weekends.) We joke about calling ourselves the "Oddballs" or the "Misfits," but often it's not funny *or* fun to spend a lot of time alone as temporarily or permanently single, especially when one is responsible for children.

There have been times when I felt cheated, tied down and resentful of the freedom I saw in others' lives. Having spent many hours at private "pity parties," I can readily understand others who experience similar pain. Much more complicated problems than mine, however, are encountered by Christians with non-Christian spouses. Paul's directions are explicit here, however: the Christian's presence in the home is the greatest testimony possible and may result in the salvation of the spouse and the children. The greatest goal in this situation, then, is a family united in Christ.

Timothy's mother, Eunice, must have experienced the problems of a divided household, having married a Greek who did not share the Jewish concern for circumcision (Acts 16:1-3). I am sure that she would heartily reinforce Paul's statement in Second Corinthians 6:14, where he warns believers not to become "unequally yoked" (KJV).

Thank You, Father, for the warnings in Your Word.

45 – Tuesday

LET A WOMAN LEARN . . .

"A woman should learn in quietness. . . . I do not permit a woman to teach or to have authority over a man."
(1 Timothy 2:11-12)

Read James 3:1-18

The tongue is a man-eating thing!
Like a vulture who's swift on the wing
It flies here and there
Leaving sounds in the air
And waiting destruction to bring.

Lois and Eunice probably understood Paul's meaning in this passage much more readily than contemporary women do. They had spent fifteen years training Timothy thoroughly in the Scriptures; was Paul saying that they did not have the right to teach Timothy and others?

Why did Paul make this enigmatic statement? In the story of Mary of Bethany we discussed the lack of religious instruction for Jewish women; they were even excluded from men's religious discussions in the home. In response to this, Paul is saying, "Let a woman learn. . . ."

Unfortunately, women who were aware of the roles of temple priestesses and of the Delphi Oracle may have abused their new liberty in Christ by attempting to teach others before they had mastered the basics themselves. Perhaps this is why Paul says (in the Greek present active indicative): "I am not presently permitting a woman to teach or have authority over men." Perhaps in the future they could teach, but at that point in time they needed to learn—in silence!

So often, Father, I have been guilty of allowing my mouth to be in motion before I put my brain in gear. Thank You for the "waiting rooms" in our lives that slow us down and in the process teach us so many valuable lessons.

45 – Wednesday

EVE'S SECOND CHANCE

"For Adam was first formed, then Eve; and it was not Adam who was deceived, but [the] woman who was deceived and deluded and fell into transgression. Nevertheless (the sentence put upon women [of pain in motherhood] does not hinder their [souls'] salvation), and they will be saved [eternally] if they continue in faith and love and holiness, with self-control; [saved indeed] through the Child-bearing, that is, by the birth of the [divine] Child." (1 Timothy 2:13-15, Amplified)

Read 1 Timothy 3:1-15

Said the tempter to Eve, "That's a lie!
If you eat that good fruit, you won't die!
Your eyes now are closed
'Cause to me you're opposed . . .
Just relax and enjoy a new high!"

Eunice and Lois may have been taught that because woman had been created second, she occupied a secondary position of subjection, and because Eve had been deceived by the serpent, gullible womanhood had been doomed to eternal silence.

The preceding passage from First Timothy 2:15 has been used to support the theory that women should stay "barefoot and pregnant" because it has been translated (KJV) "she shall be saved in childbearing." Obviously this cannot mean that labor pains are eternally redemptive. The Amplified Translation explains that woman will be saved by the birth of a special Child—namely, the Messiah.

Although Eve was deceived and did become a sinner, she and all women after her share in salvation through the Messiah, who was "born of a woman." Despite the pain and suffering that has come into women's lives as a result of sin, trust in their Creator-Redeemer will produce the fruits of salvation in their lifestyle: faith, love and holiness, with self-control. Redemption triumphs over the fall!

Thank You again, Father, for forgiving and restoring me when I confess my sins to You, just as You forgave Eve and restored her to fellowship with You.

45 – *Thursday*

THE SERPENT'S SIGNIFICANCE

"Train the younger women to love their husbands and children, to be self-controlled and pure . . . to dress modestly, with decency and propriety . . . with good deeds, appropriate for women who profess to worship God."
(Titus 2:4-5; 1 Timothy 2:9-10)

Read Titus 2:1-8

"Do you want to stay here all your life?
You're content just to be a housewife?
Oh, eat it, it's good!
You'll learn what you should!
C'mon, I'll loan you a knife!"
—the Tempter

As a girl I often wore my hair in pigtails or braids (how I hated them!) and wondered about the meaning of "braided hair" in First Timothy 2:9. I found out later, of course, that braided hair and "costly attire" were the signs of a prostitute. Therefore, Paul is not condemning gold or pearl jewelry, but saying that faith in action is much more important than fashion. Every woman realizes that styles are constantly changing, but Lois and Eunice recognized that a change in lifestyle is of utmost importance.

My heart aches for the many young mothers who are forced to leave their children prematurely to help support the family or buy a home. Many times women in this situation are in need of significance as much as financial security, and they find significance, at least temporarily, in more and more time spent away from their families. A constantly rising divorce rate is the result. The serpent is still sly, and Eve is still listening.

A single woman also faces a need for significance and perhaps a greater need for security (financial *and* emotional). Competition on the job demands that she look her best, and she finds it very easy to dress in a way that encourages undesirable responses. How easy it is to listen to the serpent and settle for God's second best!

Help me to remember, Father, that even what appears to be good can be the enemy of Your best for me.

45 – Friday

QUALIFICATIONS FOR MINISTRY

"[The] women likewise must be worthy of respect . . . not gossipers, but temperate and self-controlled, [thoroughly] trustworthy in all things." (1 Timothy 3:11, Amplified)

Read 2 Timothy 3:1-9

So gullible Eve ate the fruit
Not knowing she'd swallowed, to boot,
the devil's advice.
Before she thought twice,
Sin's misery had planted its roots.

Paul's counsel in First Timothy 3:11 may have been addressed directly to Lois and Eunice, since it is probably not meant for deacon's wives (as commonly translated), but for women deacons. The New Testament Greek does not assign a female gender to the word used for deacon.[1] (This was the same word used in describing Phoebe in Romans 16:1; Phoebe was to be received graciously and helped, because she had helped and would continue to help many others, including Paul.)

Notice what Paul says: in order to be worthy of an office in the church, women must think before they speak and avoid gossip at all costs. Paul was aware that people's tongues are often their own worst enemy. Temperance and faithfulness were also essential qualities for a deacon or deaconess.

Paul points out in Second Timothy 3:6-7 that women who are easily swayed by their emotions and "various impulses" can become "silly" and "sin-burdened" (TLB) and therefore more susceptible to false teachers, who, Paul says, will be prevalent in "the last days." (Beware!) This is certainly not a put-down of women in general, but a much needed warning; we can all learn from Eve's example.

Thank You also, Father, for the example of Eunice and Lois and their strong, sincere faith in You.

45 — *Saturday*

WOMAN TO WOMAN

"The older women . . . are to give good counsel and be teachers of what is right and noble, so that they will wisely train the young women to be sane and sober-minded."
(Titus 2:3-4, Amplified)

Read 1 Timothy 5:1-16

Some days you feel misunderstood
And forbidden things look very good;
Remember the snake
And stay wide awake
So you're able to do what you should!

I feel sure that God used Paul's relationship with Timothy's mother and grandmother to impress on him the need for the church family's inclusion of those who had been cast-offs in society, especially the orphans and the widows. Since women were so dependent on men economically, women without husbands were often forced to resort to prostitution as a means of support. (The Old Testament story of Tamar and Judah in Genesis 38 is an illustration of this).

Widows who had children or grandchildren were to be cared for by their family members. Childless widows, however, left without family, were to be cared for by the Church. Those who qualified (minimum age, sixty) would form a special group having specific duties in the ministry of the Church (prayer and acts of mercy) and occupying a place of honor and dignity rather than having the useless feeling so discouraging in old age.

I have been helped greatly by a woman counselor, my friend Ruth Dourte, and I feel very strongly that woman-to-woman counseling is a real need within the Church. Many potential problems could be avoided if the wisdom and experience of Christian women could be utilized in this way. We need you, "mother[s] in Israel" (Judges 5:7).

Just as You gave Paul a son and a mother (Romans 16:13) "in the faith," so You have given me a spiritual family as well. Thank You for "filling in the gaps" with these needed relationships, Father—just another way of showing Your love for me.

Week 46

Drusilla

Have you ever done a genogram of your family? This interesting form of the traditional "family tree" is often used in counseling to trace patterns in families—patterns of hereditary diseases, incest, alcoholism, adultery. Patterns of denial or deceit may emerge, as in the Old Testament family of Jacob.

As we study these often surprising patterns, it is important to remember that as we confess these family sins to God and acknowledge their effects on us, He stands ready to help us break the patterns!

After a spiritual "flash point" in his life, a man named Saul became the apostle Paul, a strong leader of the Christians he had once violently persecuted. God led him to evangelize and disciple Gentiles in many areas new to the gospel message, including the countries now called Turkey and Greece. Upon returning to Jerusalem after his third missionary journey, however, he was targeted by rabble-rousers, who accused him of bringing Gentiles into the temple and telling everyone to disobey the Jewish laws.

In Acts 26, we find Paul being brought to trial before Felix, governor of Judea, and his beautiful young wife, Drusilla. (Historians tell us that Felix had employed a magician to seduce Drusilla away from her first husband, a nearby king.)

If we could see a genogram of Drusilla's family of origin, a pattern of terrible cruelty, adultery and incest would emerge. . . .

Her father, Herod Agrippa I, went down in history as the first royal persecutor of the early Christian Church.

Her great-grandfather, Herod the Great, was responsible for the "Massacre of the Infants" in his paranoid attempt to kill the Christ child. Because of his overwhelming fear of betrayal, he also had his wife Miriamne and one of his own sons, Antipater, executed.

Herod Antipas, Drusilla's uncle, had John the Baptist beheaded at the request of his wife Herodias and her daughter (by another marriage), Salome. (Salome's father was Antipas' brother, Herod Philip. Salome later married her great-uncle, Herod Philip II.)

The Herodian family tree—full of rotten and damaged fruit!

BACKGROUND READING: Acts 21:15-26

46 – Monday

IS BEAUTY ONLY SKIN-DEEP?

"The high priest Ananias went down to Caesarea with some of the elders and a lawyer named Tertullus, and they brought their charges against Paul before the governor [Felix]. . . . Several days later Felix came with his wife Drusilla, who was a Jewess." (Acts 24:1, 24)

Read Acts 21:27-40; 1 Peter 3:1-6

Many eyes will be on me today . . .
Shall I choose the emerald or the sapphire?
Which flatters my complexion best?
Or should I wear, perhaps, the simple Rose of Sharon?
Its understated beauty will enhance my own.
—Drusilla

At age fourteen, already famous for her beauty, Drusilla was married to King Aziz of Emesa. But when Governor Felix, married twice before (to two other queens), set eyes on her, he was so entranced by her beauty that he employed a Cypriote magician to seduce Drusilla away from her husband.

In defiance of Jewish law, Drusilla, a Jewess, divorced King Aziz and left Emesa for her new residence in the governor's mansion in Caesarea. Eager to please and entertain his young wife, who was probably curious about this "follower of the Way," Felix sent for Paul to come before them in the judgment hall. (This was Paul's second appearance before Felix.)

Felix did not realize that Paul's testimony would bring him under conviction and forever affect his life—and perhaps that of his young wife as well. In the same way, we may never know the effects of our lifestyle or words of testimony on those around us who are watching and listening.

Father, through Your Holy Spirit, show me any unconfessed sin in my life that could block my witness. I want to be more concerned about inner beauty than outer beauty.

WELL AQUAINTED WITH THE WAY

"He sent for Paul and listened to him as he spoke about faith in Christ Jesus." (Acts 24:24)

Read Acts 22:1-30

This man is not impressive, as I thought he'd be.
I'd hoped for someone handsome,
pleasing to the eye,
at least dynamic in his speech.
There's no charisma in his face.
His body does not hold my eyes.
He's but a lone fanatic, nothing more.
—Drusilla

When Drusilla left her husband and married a Gentile, she defied Jewish law—but she was still a Jewess. What was her reaction to Paul's earnest testimony of belief in Jesus Christ? Despite her disobedience of Jewish law, was she still tied into Jewish teaching, contemptuous of this "follower of the Way"? Or did she wish for Paul's peace and serenity in the midst of difficult circumstances?

At Felix' first meeting with Paul, the apostle emphasized that he served the very same God who was worshiped and served by his ancestors. Paul also stated that he had been minding his own business while worshiping in Jerusalem—not arguing in the temple, disturbing the peace or stirring up riots, as he had been accused by Tertullus. Felix, who was "well acquainted with the Way" (Acts 24:22), could have settled the case then and there, had he chosen to do so. Since he was uncertain what his best move was politically, however, Felix "waffled."

Waffling . . . shilly-shallying . . . playing for time. . . . Are those our game plans as well, when God wants us to make a decision for Him or against Him?

Father, I've had enough of being a people-pleaser. My heart's desire is to please only You.

"THAT'S ENOUGH FOR NOW!"

"As Paul discoursed on righteousness, self-control and the judgment to come, Felix was afraid and said, 'That's enough for now! You may leave.' " (Acts 24:25)

Read Acts 23:1-35

I see my husband getting edgy
I haven't listened close enough
to know the reason why
But I have no desire to understand his words.
What can this old man know
of power or fame?

—Drusilla

As the courtroom conversation with Felix continued, Paul did not stop with his own testimony of conversion. "As he reasoned with them about righteousness and self-control and the judgment to come, Felix was terrified. 'Go away for now,' he replied. 'When it is more convenient, I'll call for you again' " (Acts 24:25, NLT).

Whether or not Paul was aware of the governor's corrupt administration and his unlawful marriage to Drusilla, Paul was simply saying, without fear of consequences, the words that God's Spirit nudged him to speak.

POINT TO PONDER: Often we hold back because of fear or intimidation when God wants us to look to Him and follow His leading. As we do so, we may be addressing problems of which we are totally unaware. God has promised us "the mind of Christ" (1 Corinthians 2:16), which means we have access to Christ's discernment and Christ's wisdom, as long as our own opinions—or pride—do not get in the way. Have you appropriated that promise?

Father, You know I have a recurring weakness in this area. But I love You so much that I don't want that sin to come between us. I am now giving it to You.

46 – Thursday

"WHEN I FIND IT CONVENIENT"

"When I find it convenient, I will send for you." (Acts 24:25)

Read Acts 24:1-21

It's over . . . .
I'll gather my robes about me,
concentrate on holding my head high
and walking like a queen.
Yes, many eyes are on me—
They think I'm young!
I'll show them I can reign.
—Drusilla

Afraid of what Paul was saying, Felix dismissed Paul rather abruptly. This fearless, outspoken follower of the Way may have been an entertaining diversion at first, but now Felix was feeling uncomfortable.

What about Drusilla? Had her interest in Paul been just a passing fancy, a childish curiosity? Was her real passion focused on pomp, power and position?

It seems that both Felix and Drusilla listened only when it was "convenient" for them. Is that the way we listen to God? Do we read His Word only when we have time? Do we go to His house to worship only when nothing else seems more interesting? Do we pray only in emergencies—when it is convenient for us?

Lord, I confess that I'm often an emergency pray-er. I commit myself to a regular plan of reading Your Word—and of praying it back to You.

THE POWER OF A TYRANT

"At the same time he was hoping that Paul would offer him a bribe, so he sent for him frequently and talked with him."
(Acts 24:26)

Read Acts 24:22-27

Ah, Felix sees that man again today
but I've no interest
in a second hearing.
I'd rather find my entertainment
in the jester of the court
or learn to dance
in ways unknown to Jews.
—Drusilla

Had the prisoner's words captivated the procurator? Was that the reason—or was it only because Felix was hoping Paul would offer him a bribe—that Felix called for Paul frequently?

Obviously money was extremely important to Felix, as well as power and prestige. Felix had originally been a slave, then a freedman, then a high official in government. The historian Tacitus said of him: "He held the power of a tyrant with the disposition of a slave."

Can we be trusted with the freedom God grants us? Can He trust us to be good stewards of the money and possessions He gives us? Can we be trusted with positions of leadership? Have we learned that the best leader is a servant-leader?

Show me, Lord, how to be a better steward. Please send someone to disciple me.

46 – Saturday

IT HAD NEVER BEEN CONVENIENT

"When two years had passed, Felix was succeeded by Porcius Festus, but because Felix wanted to grant a favor to the Jews, he left Paul in prison." (Acts 24:27)

Read Proverbs 5

My husband's losing his position. . . .
Should I have stayed with King Aziz?
Had I not left him,
I would still be queen.
Perhaps I'll sweet-talk my dear Felix
into taking me to Rome.
I still am young and beautiful—
who knows what I'll find there?
—Drusilla

Two years later, Festus replaced Felix as governor. And Paul was still in prison. Had Drusilla desired to put in a good word for Paul, she would have had many opportunities—and possibly a good deal of influence over her husband's decisions. It seems, however, that she chose not to intercede for Paul. Perhaps her days were filled with other, more exciting or fashionable pursuits.

Or perhaps Paul had made her conscious of her own sins, and she hated him for it.

Tradition says that, years later, Drusilla died with her son by Felix beneath the lava in the great eruption of Mount Vesuvius. The city of Pompeii was destroyed, and Drusilla along with it. Probably she had never found the time—it had never been "convenient"—to listen to and act upon Paul's words of truth.

Lord, please show me through Your Holy Spirit any other areas of unconfessed sin in my life. Does my behavior or attitude in any way question Your faithfulness and dependability?

Week 47

Bernice

Bernice was Drusilla's older sister, and historians tell us that great hate existed between the two sisters. Drusilla was beautiful, and plain women rarely love beautiful sisters. But if Bernice felt inferior to Drusilla, she did not allow her feelings of inferiority to cramp her style.

When only thirteen, Bernice was married to her uncle, Herod of Chalcis. He died, leaving her with two sons. History records that after her husband's death Bernice lived with her brother, Agrippa II, in an incestuous relationship. Naturally, the court gossips loved to speculate about them.

After his hearing before Felix and Drusilla, Paul was sent to Caesarea to be examined by Agrippa II. Bernice, as her brother's official consort, was present at that trial.

At another time, before another trial, Pilate's wife had warned him, "Have nothing to do with this just man." It seems, however, that neither Drusilla nor Bernice made any effort to intercede for Paul.

We have observed the "damaged fruit" on this family tree. As we learn more about these women's personal track records, we wonder if these women were capable of compassion. Perhaps there are women like Bernice or Drusilla in your family.

BACKGROUND READING: Proverbs 6:20-35

47 — Monday

THE ROOT OF BITTERNESS

"King Agrippa and Bernice arrived at Caesarea to pay their respects to Festus. Since they were spending many days there, Festus discussed Paul's case with the king." (Acts 25:13-14)

Read Hebrews 12:1-17

So once again I follow
in my sister's train
—my little sister!
Compared to her,
I'm old and plain
and tired of always taking second place.
—Bernice

Did Bernice have a "root of bitterness" (Hebrews 12:15, KJV)? Some girls grow up in the shadow of an older sister whose act is too hard to follow. Bernice, on the other hand, may have been the older sister who felt constantly compared to a beautiful—or smart or athletic—little sister.

With no hope of competing with the baby of the family, an older sister may assume a tough, "I-don't-care" front in order to deal with the hurt. She may well go on to fulfill her parents' gloom-and-doom prophecies for her life: "Why can't you get along with people like your sister does? Everybody just loves her! And why can't you cooperate with your parents like she does? You don't hear *her* mouthing off at us! You won't amount to anything in life if you don't. . . ."

Was Bernice's love of "great pomp" simply an effort to fill an aching hole in her heart?

Lord, sometimes only You are aware of my motivation. Make the unconscious conscious. I place myself under Your loving gaze.

47 – Tuesday

AN INCESTUOUS COUPLE

"The next day Agrippa and Bernice came with great pomp and entered the audience room with the high ranking officers and the leading men of the city. At the command of Festus, Paul was brought in." (Acts 25:23)

Read 1 Corinthians 5:1-12

I read their minds,
their beady eyes ask questions
that their lips disdain to frame.
They think themselves too holy
to pronounce my name
but they speak worse than "harlot"
in their hearts.
Who do they think they are
to scorn the sister of the king?
—Bernice

Raised in the Jewish faith, Bernice had to be aware that incest was strictly taboo in Jewish circles. And yet she became known in Rome and Caesarea for her scandalous conduct with her brother. As a result, everybody who was anybody in Caesarea, along with the top military brass, had made their way to the Great Hall to see Agrippa and Bernice's flourishing grand entrance.

Festus prefaced Paul's defense by stating that all the charges made by the Jews were fabricated. He had uncovered nothing else, in the nature of a charge, that would hold water.

Paul had grown up in Jerusalem as a strict Pharisee, the most demanding branch of the Jewish religion.

Perhaps Bernice was sitting on a gilded chair as she listened, wearing her most regal brocades and her finest jewels—but no royal gowns or precious jewels could beautify the sin of rebellion in her heart. Was her conscience pricked as she listened to Paul? And did she hate him because of it?

Lord, my Adonai, have I resented those in my life who spoke truth I did not want to hear?

47 – Wednesday

A LITTLE TOO CLOSE FOR COMFORT

"And now it is because of my hope in what God has promised our fathers that I am on trial today. This is the promise our twelve tribes are hoping to see fulfilled as they earnestly serve God day and night. O king, it is because of this hope that the Jews are accusing me. Why should any of you consider it incredible that God raises the dead?" (Acts 26:6-8)

Read Acts 25:24–26:5

I see his plan,
I read his mind as well.
He seeks to pit this crowd
against my brother—
Yes, draw Agrippa in against his will.
I'll warn him
lest he weaken.
I cannot let this trickster wear him down.
—Bernice

"Why is it a criminal offense to believe that God raises the dead?" Paul wasted no time in drawing Agrippa into the conversation, knowing that the king was well-acquainted with Jewish ways, and with Jewish quarrels as well.

Did Bernice appreciate the great privilege she experienced, as a woman, to witness such a memorable theological discussion? Jewish women were usually excluded from discussions of the law. One rabbi even said it was better to burn the law than to give it to a woman.

Bernice had wandered far away from her Jewish heritage. Perhaps she regarded the Jewish people simply as a group of quarreling, narrow-minded people. Certainly she must have known that they had rejected her and her way of life. Perhaps she told herself that she just didn't care.

Thank You, Lord, for the privilege to discuss and study Your Word. Forgive me for taking those privileges for granted.

WHY DO YOU PERSECUTE ME?

"About noon, O king, as I was on the road, I saw a light from heaven, brighter than the sun, blazing around me and my companions. We all fell to the ground, and I heard a voice saying, . . . 'Saul, Saul, why do you persecute me? . . . I am Jesus, whom you are persecuting.' " (Acts 26:13-15)

Read Acts 26:9-23

He waxes eloquent . . . .
My brother is seduced by him.
He is too easily drawn in
but I'll not lose this battle.
I've too much to lose.
—Bernice

Paul left the discussion of theology to tell his own personal testimony of confrontation by Jesus Christ. In the Great Hall, not even a whisper competed with Paul's words.

> I asked, "Who are you, sir?"
> The Lord answered, "I am Jesus, the one you're persecuting. Stand up! I have appeared to you for a reason. I'm appointing you to be a servant and witness of what you have seen and of what I will show you. I will rescue you from the Jewish people and from the non-Jewish people to whom I am sending you. You will open their eyes and turn them from darkness to light and from Satan's control to God's. Then they will receive forgiveness for their sins and a share among God's people who are made holy by believing in me." (Acts 26:15-18, GOD'S WORD)

Bernice was hearing the opportunity for sins forgiven, the offer of a place in the family of God. The offer applied to her, and to everyone in the Great Hall—but Bernice's heart and mind were closed.

Thank You, Lord, for Your wide-open offer of grace.

47 – Friday

"ALMOST PERSUADED . . ."

"Then Agrippa said to Paul, 'Do you think that in such a short time you can persuade me to be a Christian?' "
(Acts 26:28)

Read Acts 26:24-32

Ever since our childhood
my brother's heart was soft
and mine was hard . . .
Yet now I am amazed
that even my cold conscience
urges me to think again
of what this man has said.
—Bernice

Paul's "flash point" on the way to Damascus had been life-changing. The three days of physical blindness that followed sharpened Paul's perception of the heavenly vision.

Paul continued:

> I did not disobey the vision I saw . . . King Agrippa. Instead, I spread the message that I first told to the Jewish people in Damascus and Jerusalem and throughout the whole country of Judea. I spread the same message to non-Jewish people. . . . I told them to do things that prove they had changed their lives. (Acts 26:19-20, God's Word)

Festus' response to all this talk about life change was to shout: "Paul, you're crazy! Get a grip on yourself!"

But Paul was not deterred by the interruption. Instead, he threw one more shot at Agrippa: "The King knows what I'm talking about . . . . You believe the prophets, don't you, King Agrippa? Don't answer that—I know you believe."

The familiar old song, "Almost Persuaded," originates from Agrippa's answer: "Almost thou persuadest me to be a Christian" (KJV).

Lord, I need wisdom and strength to honestly confront the "almost-Christians" in my area of influence.

"IF HE HAD NOT APPEALED . . ."

"The king rose, and with him the governor and Bernice and those sitting with them. They left the room, and while talking with one another, they said, 'This man is not doing anything that deserves death or imprisonment.' Agrippa said to Festus, 'This man could have been set free if he had not appealed to Caesar.' " (Acts 26:30-32)

Read Acts 27

It's over—finally!
We can go back
to settled ways of life
to our nonconforming lifestyles.
Almost . . . almost I turned my back
on freedom's door.
—Bernice

The king had had enough. Conviction was breaking down his defenses. If he listened to much more of this, the light that shone on Paul might seek out and discover all his sinful secrets!

Agrippa and Bernice left the hall in pomp and ceremony, agreeing that Paul had done nothing worthy of death or bonds. They did nothing, however, to release him from those bonds.

The court gossips continued to whisper that Bernice was Agrippa's consort. To silence rumors, she married Ptolemy, king of Cilicia. She soon left him to return to her relationship with her brother. At some point she became the mistress of Emperor Titus, but that also was a short-lived affair.

Paul was not released. Instead, he was sent to Rome, and Acts 27 tells the story of the incredible storms he encountered on the way to Rome. But in the epistles written from a Roman prison, he preached a triumphant message.

POINT TO PONDER: Whose bonds were more binding—Paul's physical bonds or the royal couple's spiritual ones?

Lord, may I use Your powerful sword, Your Word, with wisdom and discernment, to cut through the bonds that shackle those around me.

Week 48

Apphia

Since the second century, tradition has handed down the story that Apphia was the wife of Philemon, a minister, and the mother of Archippus. Together Philemon and Apphia opened their home in Colossae (in what is now called Turkey) to the early Christian Church. Busy people, they may have depended heavily on their slave, Onesimus. Or perhaps he was just a boy—and perhaps they felt they spent more time trying to train him to do a job than it would have taken to do the job themselves.

The eighteenth-century historian Edward Gibbon tells us that in the Roman empire there were 60 million slaves. In those days, even among Christians, a slave was not a person, but a living tool. Any master had absolute power over his slave, the right of life and death. Brutal treatment of slaves was expected.

Was Onesimus treated brutally? Was he overworked? Possibly. Or perhaps he was young and wanted to see the rest of the world. All roads led to Rome, and that's where Onesimus ended up. There he could blend into the blurred backdrop of the thousands of other slaves—another nameless face in the crowd.

Although the young slave didn't realize it, God's Spirit was at work in his life. By the time he reached Rome he had probably put aside the fear of being found by his master, Philemon. He no longer worried about having the "scarlet letter"—**F** for the Latin *fugitivus*—branded on his forehead, or about being executed. Philemon had not tracked him down . . . but the "Hound of Heaven" was on the trail of the fugitive.

Paul was imprisoned in Rome, and God brought a prisoner and a fugitive together. And then He bonded them together.

Although it was a friendship God knew they both needed, it was a friendship "only for a season." Soon Apphia and her family became the recipients of a tender letter from the apostle Paul. That postcard-sized letter pled for Apphia, Philemon and Archippus to receive with leniency their runaway slave, Onesimus, who was coming home. Paul was not asking them to "tie yellow ribbons on the old oak tree" in honor of Onesimus, but he *was* asking them to treat their slave as a brother in Christ—a whole new concept for slaveowners.

Tradition holds that Apphia and the rest of her household, including Onesimus, were stoned to death during Nero's persecution.

BACKGROUND READING: The little book of Philemon!

48 – Monday

EVERY CHRISTIAN—ONCE A FUGITIVE

"All have sinned and fall short of the glory of God." (Romans 3:23)
"We love because he first loved us." (1 John 4:19)

Read 1 Corinthians 13

Where is our slave? He's run from us.
Will he survive?
He knows so little of the outside world.
He's just a boy . . . he's grown up in our home.
I worry about him.
—Apphia

Love opens up one's life, unconditionally, to a personal relationship with another. The kind of love we call *agape* love is not given or expressed based on prerequisites or guidelines. Loving with *agape* means we don't necessarily expect a response from our loved one—though we wait and long for it. When the waiting grows wearisome, it helps to remember that every one of us was once a runaway slave. We escaped from the One who formed us, the One who gave us life, the One who sustains us each day. We ran away willfully and disobediently, perhaps also from people who cared for us.

When Ben Franklin realized that the lighting of streets would not only add beauty to the city of Philadelphia, but would also make it safer, he didn't start a "lights on for safety" campaign. Instead, he simply hung a beautifully polished lantern on his own door, diligently lighting the wick each evening at dusk. The light was so attractive and helpful that people began following his example throughout the entire city.

Just as God continued to love us through our runaway days, He desires for us to continue to love the unlovely . . . "in order to offer ourselves as a model . . . that you might follow our example" (2 Thessalonians 3:9, NASB).

Help me, Lord, to be a lighthouse keeper, even when the work seems monotonous and the lighthouse feels lonely.

LONG HOURS IN THE WAITING ROOM

"Onesimus (whose name means "Useful") hasn't been of much use to you in the past, but now he is going to be of real use to both of us." (Philemon 11, TLB)

Read Romans 5:1-5; 2 Corinthians 4:17-18

I know God knows just where he is—
this boy who seems like our own son.
God's timing's good
and even if we never see Onesimus again
God has a place for him.
—Apphia

Patience means waiting for God's timing, being obedient to *His* course of action. The patient person does not try to resolve matters according to his or her own anxieties, preferences or whims. Instead, he or she discerns God's lessons from the situations of daily living, through consistent study of His Word, prayer, wise counsel and the fellowship of believers.

POINT TO PONDER: Do not confuse patience with procrastination! They are not in the same family. The patient person is able to act swiftly and decisively when she hears God's go-ahead. Patience, Endurance and Perseverance are sisters who work together to give us "PEP" when our own strength runs out, to help us remain faithful in the face of seemingly unresolved situations. The triplets act as cheerleaders to remind us that God is at work, accomplishing His purposes—whether or not we are aware of the final score.

> We can rejoice, too, when we run into problems and trials, for we know that they are good for us—they help us learn to endure. And endurance develops strength of character in us, and character strengthens our confident expectation of salvation. And this expectation will not disappoint us. For we know how dearly God loves us, because he has given us the Holy Spirit to fill our hearts with his love. (Romans 5:3-5, NLT)

Please remind me, Lord, that from heaven's viewpoint, these long days will seem like a few short moments in the waiting room . . . .

OUR PENALTY AS A FUGITIVE WAS SEVERE

"The life which I now live in the flesh I live by the faith of the Son of God, who loved me, and gave himself for me."
(Galatians 2:20, KJV)

Read Hebrews 13:1-8

You've given me this faith, my God, in You . . .
the faithfulness to keep on praying for this boy . . .
the attitude, the mind-set that
all things will someday work together for our good
and his as well.
—Apphia

Faith creates faithfulness, "a long obedience in the same direction," the ability to trust God daily for every moment. Faithfulness leads to consistency in our walk with God, our talk with others and a lifestyle which others can follow.

Be aware—those around us will still "work on our nerves" at times! Each of our personalities, through the complicated circumstances and interactions of our lives, has become extremely complex. If my self-image feels very fragile some days, that's also true of the person I'm dealing with, no matter how tough or confident he or she may seem. When I am faithful, God gives me discernment with which I can recognize the delicate needs of others. Then He enables me to orchestrate my own abilities so that I can meet their needs in kindness and sensitivity.

Often in a counseling session I sense the need for a client to be freed from the iron bars of bitterness. If I say to her, "Oh, you must forgive ___________," the pronouncement may leave her saying to herself, *She's never been where I was, where I am. She simply doesn't understand the depth of my hurt.*

If, however, I can share a similar story from the life of another—or out of my own past hurt—and follow that story with a prayer for continuing healing for both of us, my client will often respond in a totally different way. And she will often, down the line, become a friend.

Lord, help me resist the temptation to preach when, as the Indians used to say, I have not walked in that person's moccasins.

GRACE OPENED TO US THE WAY OF APPEAL

"Be kind and compassionate to one another, forgiving each other, just as in Christ God forgave you."
(Ephesians 4:32)
"For there is one God and one mediator between God and men, the man Christ Jesus, who gave himself as a ransom for all men—the testimony given in its proper time."
(1 Timothy 2:5-6)

Read 1 Timothy 1:12-19

I can forgive him, God.
Although the laws would schedule death
for a deserter,
We could not bear to see him killed
or branded like a steer,
a wounded animal.

—Apphia

Apphia and Philemon could have said, "Look at all the years and money we invested into that boy, and he left us without a word. We feel abandoned, betrayed. Why should we forgive him just because he says he's turned over a new leaf? How can we know his new behavior will continue?"

To personally deny my forgiveness to someone else is to make a mockery of what Christ has done on my behalf, and of His words: "Forgive us our debts, as we forgive our debtors." Because of you, because of me, Jesus came to the throne of God, where justice and holiness and righteousness reign, and said to the Father, "This person is under My forgiveness. She has come to me in faith, and on the basis of My blood she is cleansed. I come, as her advocate, on her behalf."

POINT TO PONDER: Just as forgiveness and acceptance are basic to our relationship to God in Christ, so forgiveness is critical to the development of any and all relationships. My fellowship with God is directly affected by my forgiveness—or my lack of forgiveness—toward others.

Help me to remember, Jesus, that if I deny someone access to my life by an unforgiving spirit, I deny You.

48 – Friday

ARE YOU ON THE RUN?

"Brothers, if someone is caught in a sin, you who are spiritual should restore him gently. But watch yourself, or you also may be tempted." (Galatians 6:1)

Read Galatians 6:1-10

Suppose Philemon had been tempted
when he was but a boy
to run away as our Onesimus has?
My husband never knew the torture
of the mind-set of a slave—
nor I.

The lad just may have feared
that someday
we would sell him to another.

—Apphia

Remember the television show "Gentle Ben," the continuing saga of a large—no, huge—lumbering bear who inspired terror in the hearts of those who saw only his "incredible hulk" and not his heart?

Have you allowed God to bless you with the fruit of gentleness? How do you relate to the problems of others? How do you handle expressing your own feelings when that expression would be at the cost of another's rights, feelings or reputation? Do you dominate conversations? Or have you learned to listen actively, drawing out the other's opinions and feelings?

Gentle Bens are firm, even bold, at God's bidding, but in the process they seek to minister to others. Self-centered attitudes of survival and conquest are not on Gentle Ben's agenda.

Convict me, correct me, Lord, when I begin to be critical and catty and conquest-oriented.

WHAT IS YOUR PLACE OF ESCAPE?

"I am sending him—who is my very heart—back to you. I would have liked to keep him with me so that he could take your place in helping me while I am in chains for the gospel. . . . Perhaps the reason he was separated from you for a little while was that you might have him back for good—no longer as a slave, but better than a slave, as a dear brother." (Philemon 12-13, 15-16)

Read Hebrews 12:1-17; Colossians 1:25-27

And now we have him back!
O God,
may we live out our faith before him
so gentle, kind and good
in our forgiveness
so patient in our expectations
so loving in our day-to-day exchanges
that we will never be the reason
he thinks of running, God,
from us—
or You.

—Apphia

Had Onesimus learned self-control, the ability to direct his desires toward God's purposes, not his personal gratification? Had Onesimus gained hope, the inner confidence in God's ability to carry out His plans and purposes?

Have you learned that running away, whether by bodily escape or mental fantasy, is only a temporary escape from reality?

Hope is that quality of the Spirit-controlled mind which opens my eyes to see beyond the problems and pressures of today into the wider panorama of God's plan.

Forgive me for the times when, like Onesimus, I've run away from responsibility. Or just from reality. Please cleanse my mind, conscious and unconscious, of wrong fantasies. Thank You for putting hope into my heart.

Section 8:

Preparing My Heart for Christmas: "... when the fullness of time was come ..."

Week 49

Elizabeth

You've read about the death of John the Baptist at the hands of Herodias. You may be asking, who *was* this man whom Herodias hated with such a violent passion?

John certainly was not vying with Herodias to gain supremacy in her kind of power structure; he was invested with a different type of authority, an authority from God Himself. Yet John was a very humble man. He described himself as being unworthy even to loosen his cousin Jesus' sandals.

Herodias, as wife of the ruler of Galilee, was entitled to whatever luxury was available in her day. John was no threat to her in this area either; self-denial was his creed. He wore animal skins and ate whatever food was available in the wilderness of Judea.

Humble and self-denying? Yes. Submissive to Herodias' power? Never! John was courageous, zealous, a powerful preacher. Jesus later described him as a burning, shining light. Herod recognized that John's power was rooted in his reliance on God rather than the control he exercised over people.

We are well acquainted with the Herodian family. John the Baptist came from a completely different environment. His father, Zechariah, was a priest and his mother, Elizabeth, was a descendant of Aaron, Israel's first high priest.

As in any profession, there were good priests and bad priests. Both Elizabeth and Zechariah, however, were "upright in the sight of God, observing all the Lord's commandments and regulations blamelessly" (Luke 1:6). But, although they were both well along in years, until John's birth, Elizabeth was childless.

BACKGROUND READING: Luke 1:5-25

49 – Monday

NOW, LORD?

" 'For my thoughts are not your thoughts,' . . . declares the LORD." (Isaiah 55:8)

Read Hebrews 11:1-6

I never will forget the time,
I know the very day
I heard the news, I saw the words
That took my shame away.
My husband could no longer speak
Because of unbelief
And yet our souls were flooded
With a sense of great relief.

—Elizabeth

Zechariah was a devout man; he had spent his life as a priest, in the service of the Lord Jehovah. When the messenger of the Lord actually appeared before him, however, Zechariah was uncertain and fearful. Zechariah had spoken to the Lord countless times in praying for his congregation, but when the Lord's messenger spoke to him, Zechariah asked how he could be sure the message was genuine. He wanted a sign.

Zechariah was obviously a cautious man. He was solid and dependable. Perhaps he always liked to have his course completely mapped out before he made the first move. It can be difficult to have Someone else making the plans.

POINT TO PONDER: Sometimes we get into such a rut that God has to give us a nudge in the direction He wants us to travel. God understood Zechariah's fear of new beginnings in his old age: "Do not be afraid, Zechariah; your prayer has been heard. Your wife Elizabeth will bear you a son" (Luke 1:13). Perhaps Zechariah had not prayed that prayer for the last twenty years, but God had heard the prayer when it was first uttered. God was answering, in His own time.

Thank You, Father, for the faith which encourages us to hope when all seems hopeless, to continue believing when results are not visible. Thank You for being the God of the impossible.

49 – Tuesday

"NO" TO "YES"

"Neither are your ways my ways." (Isaiah 55:8)

Read Hebrews 12:5-12

You see, we both were up in years,
Beyond the age of bearing
The child for whom we both had longed,
For whom we had stopped praying
And yet my husband still served God,
We still believed in Him;
He simply had said no to us . . .
And our eyes were growing dim.
—Elizabeth

Was God expressing anger at old Zechariah by temporarily taking away his speech? We can answer that question by asking ourselves a parent's purpose in temporarily suspending a child's privileges: it is to aid the child in maturing, to refine his or her character, to help the child toward better understanding of responsibilities as well as privileges. This is love, not anger.

Perhaps each of us has a particular problem that we continue to battle over the years—a weak spot, a chink in the armor. Zechariah probably had a logical, inquiring mind that wanted everything to be rationally worked out, all in order, but God was emphasizing his need for a childlike faith.

Zechariah had learned patience and humility over the years as it seemed that God was saying *no* to his prayer for a son. Now those same lessons were being relearned as God was saying *yes*.

Thank You, Father, for the chastening which reminds me of Your love—Your concern that I mature into a better person. Thank You that I am never too "big" for a spanking when it is needed.

49 – Wednesday

"IT'S MINE!"

"As the heavens are higher than the earth, so are my ways higher than your ways." (Isaiah 55:9)

Read Romans 12:3-13

And as my husband went about
The work to which he's called,
The angel Gabriel came to him.
My husband stood enthralled
"Be not afraid, good man; you'll be
The father of a son
Who will be one of God's great men—
And you must name him John."
—Elizabeth

> Elizabeth did not mount a spiritual pedestal when suddenly she learned that she was going to be the mother of a baby who would be filled with the Holy Spirit from birth. She did not go about exhibiting her specialties and downgrading Zecharias' weaknesses, as some women are so prone to do. Her visitation from God only increased her humility—before God, before Mary, and before her husband.[1]

Have you been guilty of this? I have! Especially if we have had our bouts with inferiority in the past, it is so easy to become "puffed up" when we find something we can do well. It was there as God's gift to us all along, just waiting for discovery, but when we put our anxious, grubby little paws on it, we herald it as *ours*!

POINT TO PONDER: Have you ever listened to children fighting over something that has been given to them? "It's *mine!*" Is God asking you to use one of His gifts to you in His service? Are you holding back?

Thank You, Father, for the gift You have given me. Help me to put it to work so that it benefits others. If I'm not sure what my gift is, help me to identify it and then to improve it.

49 – Thursday

ARE YOU AN ENCOURAGER?

"As the rain and the snow come down from heaven, and do not return to it without watering the earth and making it bud and flourish, so that it yields seed for the sower and bread for the eater, so is my word that goes out from my mouth: It will not return to me empty, but will accomplish what I desire and achieve the purpose for which I sent it." (Isaiah 55:10-11)

Read Isaiah 40:28-31

Great joy and gladness will be yours
And many will rejoice!
The vine's fruit he must never touch
But he will be the voice
Announcing the great coming King
In power and in spirit.
He'll soften hearts and change men's minds!
—Elizabeth

Zechariah heard these words from the very lips of the angel Gabriel, but he doubted. Elizabeth was not present when the angel spoke, but she seems to have been one of those rare persons who harbored few doubts. She had formed the habit of rejecting negative feelings and attitudes in her own mind and in the minds of others. Elizabeth was an encourager.

Positive thinking is not the only qualification essential to an encourager. Although we may be attempting to think positively, there are some days of the month when it is difficult to see good in anyone or anything. These are the times when it is essential that we have built up a pattern of simple trust in a loving, caring heavenly Father.

Too simplistic, you may say! Perhaps you feel you have been too disillusioned by earthly parents to trust a heavenly Father. Is it fair to judge God by the humans created, humans with a free will of their own?

Father, I'm being honest when I say that I have many problems and doubts. I want to say "I trust You," but some days I feel dishonest mouthing the words. Thanks for understanding.

49 – Friday

FREE OF JEALOUSY

"You will go out in joy and be led forth in peace."
(Isaiah 55:12)

Read Genesis 30:1-24

And Mary, you are blessed by God
Above all other women.
My child leaped in my womb for joy—
A visitor from heaven!
Because you did not doubt the Lord,
Believed the angel's words,
God's chosen to reward your faith
Because His voice you heard.
—Elizabeth

Elizabeth was not only untroubled by doubts; she was also free of jealousy. It probably never occurred to her to feel slighted that her younger cousin was to be the mother of the Messiah, while she, Elizabeth, would be the mother only of His forerunner. Instead of being jealous of Mary, she was a true friend when Mary needed it most—Elizabeth the encourager!

The Old Testament story of the sisters Rachel and Leah, who both loved Jacob, tells us a lot about jealousy. Jealousy tears away at the deepest roots of consciousness. It begins when I see someone as having more worth than I sense in myself. Perhaps that person seems to be more important to someone I love than I am. Perhaps that person is accomplishing great things while I sit by unnoticed. Perhaps that person seems to draw others to herself with a magnetism that I may try to imitate, but at which I fail.

POINT TO PONDER: Perhaps that person crossed my life to nudge me out of a rut, to make me realize that I have been a spectator for too long, to stir me into action. God may be telling me things about myself through the emotion of jealousy.

I think You are telling me, through the story of Rachel and Leah, Father, that You love everyone equally. Thank You for the ways in which You express Your love to me.

49 – *Saturday*

NOTES OF PRAISE

"The mountains and hills will burst into song before you, and all the trees of the field will clap their hands." (Isaiah 55:12)

Read Luke 1:57-80

My husband cannot speak just now
But his tongue will soon be loosed,
And we will sing God's praises then
With new notes introduced!
Our child will be God's prophet
To prepare Messiah's way.
The rising of the Sun will come
With light for each new day.
—Elizabeth

The story is so familiar to us that we tend to read it without emotion, but certainly we would have reacted had we been standing in Zechariah's sandals! The old priest, however, was unable to express his emotions, except in writing, for nine long months.

Rev. Fred Fowler, the man who was our pastor and spiritual father for over fourteen years was rendered unable to speak by a severe stroke. Our first visit with him after his hospitalization left us frustrated with our inability to communicate, but we understood the meaning of the first chapter of John in a new way.

Words
Bursting to come forth
But held back
By an invisible guard,
Strangled in mid-air . . .
A stroke victim's frustration.

The Word
Bursting with love
Became flesh
And dwelt among us
But still
It goes unheard—
God's heartbreak.

Thank You, Father, for keeping Your promises.

Week 50

Mary: Hearing from God

"The Word became flesh" . . . in the womb of a young peasant girl from Nazareth, a Hebrew virgin who was engaged to marry Joseph, a carpenter who also lived in Nazareth. Very little is actually known about Mary, but according to ancient tradition, she was the daughter of Joachim and Anna, descendants of Israel's King David.

This week will be devoted to gaining a better understanding of what it means to have God speak to each of us in a personal way, as He did to that village girl so long ago.

As in many biblical passages, the story of the Annunciation can become so familiar that it loses much of its meaning for us. So turn with me to the Old Testament book of First Kings and let me interface Mary's story with that of another biblical character, the prophet Elijah. Elijah had done great things in God's service, but in First Kings 19 he was going through a period of severe discouragement. Jezebel, the queen of Israel, had put him on her black list. Elijah was hiding because he was afraid for his life, yet he didn't even know if he wanted to go on living.

But God wanted him to go back and face the music. The story of Elijah shows how much God cares about us, even when *we* don't care. God provided food and a place to rest for the "burnt-out" prophet, and then gave him a great audiovisual lesson.

A howling windstorm, a breathtaking earthquake and a raging fire passed before him, but God was not in any of these. Finally, when God spoke, it was in a gentle whisper.

So what is the point of all this? Why discuss Elijah in a section about Mary? Because God had to get a message through to both of them. Although the messages were completely different in nature, both of them were hard words to comprehend. Both assignments were difficult, daring, dangerous; both assignments called for full cooperation with a Partner, a Partner whose name was Jehovah.

Both Mary and Elijah felt alone. Both were frightened, and neither of them completely understood God's message. But both gave their all.

> Therefore, I urge you . . . in view of God's mercy, to offer your bodies as living sacrifices, holy and pleasing to God—this is your spiritual act of worship. Do not conform any longer to the pattern of this world, but be transformed by the renewing of your mind. Then you will be able to test and approve what God's will is—his good, pleasing and perfect will. (Romans 12:1-2)

BACKGROUND READING: Luke 1:26-56

50 — Monday

RECOGNIZING GOD'S VOICE

"And the word of the LORD came . . . 'What are you doing here . . . ?' " (1 Kings 19:9)

Read 1 Kings 19:1-18

When Gabriel first came to me
I was confused, afraid,
Misunderstood the meaning
Of the words that he had said.
How could I be a mother,
Give birth to God's own Son?
I didn't have a husband
Yet was I the chosen one?

—Mary

People ask: "How does God speak? In an audible Voice?"

I remember a confusing day in my own life several years ago. While on an out-of-state camping trip, our oldest son was hospitalized with a dangerously ruptured appendix. After almost two hours of surgery, he began the slow climb back to his usual good health. With the crisis behind me, however, I began to disintegrate. Having spent my long-anticipated vacation in a hospital room, I was suffering from the aftermath of surgery tension, the worry of insurance inadequacy and thoughts of a ten-hour trip home with a convalescing child (and two healthy ones). Feeling slightly claustrophobic, I wandered through the rain outside the hospital, in need of a comforting touch.

I felt confined in the mud and mire;
I begged for a touch or a tongue of fire.
The earth didn't shake when I cried out in pain,
But God sent His love in the gentle rain.
God didn't reply with a rushing wind
In my hour of need He spoke through a friend.

The still small voice Elijah heard
Still echoes today in the song of a bird,
In the laugh of a child,
In the whispering pines . . .
God speaks today to our hearts and minds.

MY AVAILABILITY TO GOD

"I have been very zealous for the Lord *God Almighty."*
(1 Kings 19:10)

Read Psalm 8

The Holy Spirit, he explained,
Would come upon me when
The power of the Highest
Was visited on men.
The holy sinless Child
Whose mother I would be
Would save my soul from hell.
With God all things can be.
—Mary

Often we do not recognize the hand of God in our lives, moving "in mysterious ways," until a much later time. Sometimes we do not recognize God's voice, but He suits His message to each individual need.

The familiar story of the old cobbler who dreamed that Christ would visit him is a good illustration of our own lack of discernment. The man turned away several needy visitors because he was saving his time and hospitality for the Master. Jesus did come, but in the forms of a child, a poor mother, a tired old man—and the cobbler did not recognize Him.

POINT TO PONDER: Elijah was hiding from Queen Jezebel in a cave when God told him to go out and stand on the mountain—certainly a point of high visibility! Mary, on the other hand, was probably in her backyard when the angel appeared, but completely available to God, even though the angel's words created a maelstrom of emotions in her heart.

What about you? Have you been hiding from God? What is your cave of refuge? Have you missed hearing God today?

Lord, help me to be sensitive to Your voice, from whatever direction it comes.

50 — *Wednesday*

WHAT IS GOD ASKING?

"The LORD said, 'Go out and stand on the mountain in the presence of the LORD, for the LORD is about to pass by.' " (1 Kings 19:11)

Read Psalm 2

I still didn't understand
Words so mysterious.
I thought of Joseph, feared results
So very serious.
Disgrace could come to me,
Desertion by my friends,
Or even death itself . . .
Would anyone understand?
—Mary

With the vibrant intensity of youth, Mary loved God with all her heart, soul and mind. Although human, her motivations must have been as unselfish as her actions and words, else God would not have chosen her for this great honor. Though she wanted to understand, she did not.

I believe that Mary also loved the kind, soft-spoken carpenter, Joseph. Along with love went concern for his feelings and his reputation. What would Joseph think of her? Would he be cruelly disappointed in her, shocked by this unexpected turn of events that could ruin their future life together?

In the story in First Kings 19, God also asked Elijah to do something he was afraid to do, something he did not want to do. Has God ever asked you to do something that sounded difficult, even dangerous? What was your response?

Lord, make me willing to be willing.

MY RESPONSE TO GOD

"And after the fire came a gentle whisper."
(1 Kings 19:12)

Read Psalm 73:21-28

Yet there was just one answer
That I could freely give:
I am Your own handmaiden,
My life for You I live.
I am Your servant, O my Lord,
You tell me what to do
Whate'er the consequences
I give them all to You.

—Mary

After she asked the normal questions and recovered from the first shock of seeing and hearing a messenger from God, Mary felt at ease in his presence. Why? Because she was accustomed to being in God's presence.

Do you find yourself so accustomed to noise that you switch on the TV, radio or CD player automatically when you are alone? We need to be very careful to have quiet times in our lives, quiet times in which we acknowledge the presence of only one Other.

POINT TO PONDER: Even good music or messages—or devotional books like this one—must not be allowed to take the place of God's voice. We need to slow down our hectic pace so as to be able to hear. Elijah, when alone, did not sense God's voice in the sound of the windstorm or the earthquake or the fire; he had to listen very carefully for a gentle whisper, the still small voice that only the ears of the heart can hear.

Lord . . . I'm listening.

THE JOY OF KNOWING HIS WILL

"Then a voice said . . . , 'What are you doing here?' "
(1 Kings 19:13)

Read Numbers 5:11-31

My heart is overflowing
My heart is full of praise!
To think I am the chosen one!
I stand in awe, amazed.
His mercy's everlasting
(Though how mighty is His rod!)
And every generation
Will call me blessed of God.
—Mary

In the story of Elijah, God asked Elijah twice what he was doing in the desert. When God repeats a question (as Jesus did with Peter in John 21), He has a purpose. God was emphasizing that He wanted Elijah to be available for service, not hidden away moping in a cave somewhere, although the time of discouragement was a valuable postgraduate course.

Mary could have been apprehensive; as a matter of fact, she had good reason to develop a severe case of bleeding ulcers. In that day, a woman suspected of unfaithfulness (even to her fiancé) was subjected to the ordeal of bitter water. Numbers 5 describes the way in which the suspected woman was brought to the tabernacle (or temple) and forced to drink "holy water" mixed with dust from the temple floor. If she became sick, she was judged guilty. Certain guilt was punishable by stoning, after she had been dragged by the neck of her robe to an appropriate spot, usually outside the city walls.

Knowing all this, still Mary's heart was full of praise. Her life now had definite direction. God had spoken, and she was His servant!

I want to do Your will, Lord, but I'm scared.

50 – Saturday

THE JOY OF SERVICE

"The LORD said to him, 'Go back the way you came. . . .' "
(1 Kings 19:15)

Read Psalm 118:22-29

He satisfies the hungry hearts
And sends the rich away.
He helps His servant Israel
And proves His strength each day.
We are His chosen people
And holy is His name!
From ages everlasting
His truth remains the same.
—Mary

What were the options for Mary? Disgrace was certainly a very real possibility, for herself and her family. Desertion by her fiancé, Joseph, must have loomed ominously on the horizon. Death by stoning, as already mentioned, could have abruptly cut off her young life. It would have been easy for Mary to run away from the kind of responsibility God was asking her to take onto her young shoulders—to say, "I'm not the one, God; please find someone else."

It wasn't easy for Elijah, either. He told the Lord, twice, that he was the only believer left in Israel, but God said He had reserved 7,000 who had not bowed to Baal. So Elijah went back and did what God asked him to do, with a fresh anointing.

POINT TO PONDER: "Go back the way you came!" Wow, what a lesson! God has spoken, and life has taken on new direction, but now go back to where you were—the place you ran away from—and bloom where you are planted. No transplanting allowed! (In Elijah's case, God did the transplanting—later, in His own time! That's when transplanting is effective.)

As Mary said and as Joni Eareckson Tada, a quadriplegic, sings from her wheelchair, "I am Your servant," Lord.

Week 51

Mary, Did You Know?

A contemporary Christmas song addresses a series of questions to Mary, the mother of Jesus. The song asks if Mary foreknew the things her Son would do—walk on water, give sight to a blind man, calm a storm. The song also asks if Mary was fully aware of Jesus' identity.

Scripture tells us that "Mary treasured up all these things and pondered them in her heart" (Luke 2:19).

What does it mean to *ponder?* These are some of the possibilities the thesaurus offers: brood over, consider, contemplate, debate, dwell on, evaluate, examine, explore, meditate, mull, pore over, probe, reason, review, weigh, wonder . . .

Ponder this part of Mary's story:

> Now there was a man in Jerusalem called Simeon, who was righteous and devout. He was waiting for the consolation of Israel, and the Holy Spirit was upon him. It had been revealed to him by the Holy Spirit that he would not die before he had seen the Lord's Christ. Moved by the Spirit, he went into the temple courts. When the parents brought in the child Jesus to do for him what the custom of the Law required, Simeon took him in his arms and praised God, saying:
>
> "Sovereign Lord, as you have promised,
> you now dismiss your servant in peace.
> For my eyes have seen your salvation,

which you have prepared in the sight of all people,
a light for revelation to the Gentiles
and for glory to your people Israel."

The child's father and mother marveled at what was said about him. Then Simeon blessed them and said to Mary, his mother: "This child is destined to cause the falling and rising of many in Israel, and to be a sign that will be spoken against, so that the thoughts of many hearts will be revealed. And a sword will pierce your own soul too." (2:25-35)

Mary did *not* know the future! Over the next thirty years she must have spent countless hours pondering Simeon's prophecy. Would the sword destined to pierce her soul be wielded by a Roman? Would her body feel a blade of steel? Or did the old man's words predict a different kind of piercing?

Joseph, did you know?

No, Joseph was completely in the dark when he was given brief directions from an angel in a dream. Certainly not a plethora of information involved here!

Jesus, did You know?

Yes. Jesus knew.

At the age of twelve, Jesus looked into His mother's eyes and asked: "Didn't you know I had to be in my Father's house?" (2:49).

I doubt that Mary fully understood the words of her Son. The path that lay before the young woman "who had found favor with God" was as unknown to her as our futures are to us. But Mary trusted her Father.

We can trust Him too.

BACKGROUND READING: Psalm 22

51 — Monday

JOSEPH, A GRACIOUS MAN

"This is how the birth of Jesus Christ came about: His mother Mary was pledged to be married to Joseph, but before they came together, she was found to be with child through the Holy Spirit." (Matthew 1:18)

Read Deuteronomy 22:13-30

Joseph, did you know
that the girl you love
is carrying the God-child?
Joseph, did you know
that this pregnancy
will strike a blow to your pride?

We tend to picture the "holy family" as haloed, sanitized icons stamped on gold foil. Perhaps this is a leftover from old paintings in which Mary seems to receive Gabriel's life-changing news quite calmly, as though she were accustomed to seeing angels in her backyard, as though Gabriel were simply pronouncing a benediction or blessing on a job well done.

But the Gospel of Luke describes Mary as "afraid" and "greatly troubled." And Matthew states that an angel admonished Joseph not to be "afraid" to take Mary as his wife.

Today in the United States, where a million teenage girls become pregnant out of wedlock each year, Mary's predicament has lost its poignancy. In the first century, however, in a closely knit Jewish community, betrothal was as binding as marriage. As discussed earlier, an engaged woman found to be promiscuous was subject to death by stoning.

Joseph was gracious, then, in planning to privately divorce Mary rather than press charges. "Because Joseph her husband was a righteous man and did not want to expose her to public disgrace, he had in mind to divorce her quietly" (Matthew 1:19).

Help me, Lord, to show a Joseph kind of kindness to my family members—and my in-laws.

51 — Tuesday

THE SHAME OF SMALL-TOWN SCANDAL

"But after he had considered this, an angel of the Lord appeared to him in a dream and said, 'Joseph son of David, do not be afraid to take Mary home as your wife, because what is conceived in her is from the Holy Spirit.' " (Matthew 1:20)

Read Luke 1:39-56

Did you know that the Child she bears,
who'll sit upon your knee,
this Son of small-town scandal
will set all mankind free?

Why did Mary go to visit Elizabeth? Luke tells of Mary hurrying off to confide in the one person who might possibly understand what she was going through—her cousin Elizabeth, who was also experiencing a miraculous pregnancy.

Rev. Jim Bollback comments: "Elizabeth does indeed believe Mary's story and shares her joy, and yet the scene poignantly underscores the contrast between the two women. The whole countryside is talking about the miracle of Elizabeth's healed womb; meanwhile, Mary has to hide the shame of her own miracle."

When Mary left for the town "in the hill country," did she tell Joseph where—or why—she was going?

How did Joseph deal with his initial feelings of disbelief? His agony of betrayal?

Joseph did not put himself or his own feelings first. He though first of what God had said, and then of Mary. And later, during the early months of their marriage, Joseph continued to show remarkable restraint and self-discipline. "He had no union with her until she gave birth to a son. And he gave him the name Jesus" (Matthew 1:25).

Joseph had listened carefully to God's message, and he obeyed. The angel said, "She will give birth to a son, and you are to give him the name Jesus, because he will save his people from their sins" (1:21).

Thank You, Lord, for reminding me that not everyone will understand the ways You work in my life.

NAZARETH—A NO-PROPHET TOWN

" 'Nazareth! Can anything good come from there?' Nathanael asked. 'Come and see,' said Philip." (John 1:46)

Luke 4:14-30

Jesus, did You know
they say nothing good
can ever come from Nazareth?
Jesus, did You know
that Your friends will leave?
They couldn't face Your cross-death . . .

Did Mary's parents, much less the people of Nazareth, *ever* believe her story?

After Jesus began to minister, "in the power of the Spirit . . . news about him spread through the whole countryside. He taught in their synagogues, and everyone praised him" . . . until He went home to Nazareth, "where he had been brought up" (Luke 4:14-16). In Nazareth, when He stood up to read in the synagogue—"as was his custom"—Jesus read from Isaiah 61:1-2: " 'The Spirit of the Lord is on me, because he has anointed me . . . to release the oppressed. . . .' Today this scripture is fulfilled in your hearing," Jesus continued (4:16-21).

Amazed at the graciousness of His words, the people asked, "Isn't this Joseph's son?" (4:22). But their amazement quickly turned to anger. Jesus went on to cite the Old Testament examples of Elijah's ministry to Naaman and the widow of Zarephath—outsiders to Israel—as typical of the way in which a prophet ministers to people outside his hometown because he is not accepted or believed there.

The anger of the people of Nazareth drove them to throw Him out of the town. The jostling crowd pushed Him to the brow of the hill on which the town was built, meaning to throw Him off the cliff there. But His time had not yet come. The hill was not Calvary. "He walked right through the crowd and went on his way" (4:30).

You've reminded me, Lord, that a prophet is often without honor in his hometown. Thank You for reassuring me that You'll help me to handle this situation I'm facing.

"ISN'T THIS JOSEPH'S SON?"

"But you, Bethlehem Ephrathah, though you are small among the clans of Judah, out of you will come for me one who will be ruler over Israel, whose origins are from of old, from ancient times." (Micah 5:2)

Read Isaiah 53:1-12

Did You know You'd be mocked by men,
The very ones You made?
Did You know You'd be rejected
As salvation's price you paid?

Did you know that the old greeting "Merry Christmas" actually admonishes us to enjoy ourselves—to be merry—in the worship ("mass") of Christ, the Messiah born in Bethlehem, as predicted by the ancient prophets? But today's Christmas, though it may spotlight the Babe in the manger, often ignores the God-man that the Baby became.

We prefer singing Santa songs over meditating on the Man of Sorrows. He was a Man who knew suffering well, who fraternized with tax collectors, prostitutes and lepers. A King with no majesty, no beauty, to attract His subjects to Him. Such a king would be rejected by people of self-interest, people who were afraid of becoming unpopular or unclean.

He is still despised, rejected. Because we, disloyal subjects, traitors that we are, have gone astray. Each one of us wants to be king. Each of us has turned to his or her own way.

And the Lord has laid on Him the iniquity of us all.

All that iniquity! Imagine it. All that sin, all that suffering, on the shoulders of One who Himself was sinless.

"Yet it was the LORD's will to crush him and cause him to suffer, and though the LORD makes his life a guilt offering . . . after the suffering of his soul . . . I will give him a portion among the great . . . because he poured out his life unto death. . . . For he bore the sin of many, and made intercession for the transgressors" (Isaiah 53:10-12).

It's overwhelming, Lord, to think that You were crushed—physically, spiritually and emotionally—for me.

51 – Friday

IMMANUEL—"GOD WITH US"

"All this took place to fulfill what the Lord had said through the prophet: 'The virgin will be with child and will give birth to a son, and they will call him Immanuel'—which means, 'God with us.' " (Matthew 1:22-23)

Read Isaiah 9:1-7

But do not fear,
God's with us—here!
Grace is the face He wears,
Jesus His name, to a cross He came,
The Child the virgin bears.

Shame is much worse than guilt. Guilt is something I have done. Guilt can be good if it makes me feel the conviction of the Holy Spirit, then confess my sin. I am forgiven by God.

But shame is like an old piece of plastic, buried in a musty basement corner for years, fastened around me so tightly that it feels like forever. It covers me, shutting out any traces of light, smothering my senses, permeating my clothes with its odor.

Guilt is about what I have done. Shame is about who I am.

But *the people who formerly walked in darkness have seen a great light!* Because the Sun of Righteousness was willing to bear the sin and shame of the world, a light has dawned, a healing light, a cleansing light. "For to us a child is born, to us a son is given, and the government will be on his shoulders" (Isaiah 9:6).

He is a wonderful Counselor who will listen carefully to our stories of sin and shame.

He is a mighty God powerful enough to take away our sin and shame.

He is an everlasting Father who will always be there for us.

And He is the Prince of Peace, who will reign in justice and righteousness.

Thank You, Prince of Peace, for taking away my guilt and shame.

51 — Saturday

"A SWORD WILL PIERCE YOUR OWN SOUL TOO"

"The Word became flesh and made his dwelling among us. We have seen his glory, the glory of the One and Only, who came from the Father, full of grace and truth. John testifies concerning him. . . . 'This was he of whom I said, "He who comes after me has surpassed me because he was before me." ' " (John 1:14-15)

Read Luke 2:25-35

Jesus, did You know
that a carpenter
would be Your earthly father?
Jesus, did You know that a tree would be
the piercing of Your mother?

Did You know
only Word-made-flesh
Could convince us that You cared?
Did You know there'd be such pain
As eternal life You shared?

Yes, Jesus knew.

"Your attitude should be the same as that of Christ Jesus: Who, being in very nature God, did not consider equality with God something to be grasped, but made himself nothing, taking the very nature of a servant" (Philippians 2:5-7).

Having the same attitude as that of Jesus means asking: *What would Jesus do in this situation?*

Jesus was God, yet He was willing to give up the privileges of royalty. Incredibly, He was willing not only to leave His throne and remove His crown, but to wear the shackles of a slave, to live in handcuffs.

Our Lord . . . handcuffed by love.

But reaching out to us in grace.

Lord, if You made Yourself nothing for me, how can I offer You less?

Week 52

Anna

Anna: a woman of simple, straightforward faith, more interested in unseen things of the spirit than in material, tangible possessions. Like many of the New Testament women, very little is said about her. Some commentators interpret Luke's brief description of Anna to mean that she was eighty-four years old, others that she had been a widow for eighty-four years. (With seven years of marriage added to the latter total, she would have been over 100 years old when she saw the Baby Jesus.)

The most important fact about this elderly saint from the tribe of Asher, however, is that she worshiped God night and day. She made her home in God's house.

Although it appears that Anna had no children, she reminds me very much of my mother, who lived in a mobile home on our property before she became a resident at Chapel Pointe in Carlisle, Pennsylvania. Since my mother's greatest joy was to be in the "house of the Lord," I'm sure her favorite place was the beautiful chapel in the home.

Years earlier we were abruptly awakened to the unmistakable imprint of cancer on her slim body. I vividly remember the morning I fled from an unbearably noisy hospital coffee shop to a quiet hospital chapel to find an outlet for my jumbled emotions.

Here I sit in this hospital coffee shop again,
Listening to the idle chatter,
bad jokes
and laughter

With which people are trying to
wake up.
It's very early in the morning.

Five floors up
My mother is donning a
gown—
Those horrible creations—you
know the kind.
She doesn't mind.
Her thoughts are not on
approaching surgery
Or of death
(Death holds no fear for her).
She's thinking only of some-
thing she could say
To turn the minds of those
around her
To her living Lord.

I have seen beautiful women,
Stylishly, expensively dressed,
Reflecting wealth and elegance.
I've heard learned women speak
With precise terminology and
tense.
My mother tends to ramble on
and on,
Sometimes forgetting why she
started.
And plaid housedresses are her
favorite clothes
(They're "comfortable!").

At one time she embarrassed me
With her plain clothes
And constant words of witness.
But picturing her now in that
cotton gown,
Her long hair spread around her
face
(No hairpins allowed during
surgery!)
I know I would not trade her for
a queen.
Come to think of it, she's always
said
She is the daughter of the King.

Oh, Father, if it be Your will,
Spare her to me yet a little
while.
I need to learn so many things:
kindness,
patience,
love,
And her life teaches me so well.

BACKGROUND READING: Luke 2:36-38

FAITH MEANS FAITHFULNESS

"Now faith is being sure of what we hope for and certain of what we do not see." (Hebrews 11:1)

Read Hebrews 11:32-40

"Old woman of the temple," I am called.
I do not mind the title—it is true!
I know each inch and corner of the court;
I know each curtain's texture, thickness, hue.
The young ones chafe to see behind this court,
But I'm content to linger here and pray.
I feel no need to prove myself . . . and yet
Perhaps I felt that urge in earlier days.
—Anna

During the month of December 1983, I was privileged to speak to a weekly Bible study group of about 100 women at the Hagerstown Union Rescue Mission. The lessons had to be very basic for the benefit of some who could hardly read and write. In one lesson I tried to reduce faith to its "lowest common denominator"—and raised many questions in my own mind in the process.

"Faith is being sure of what we hope for. . . ." Did that mean that faith was the realization of my teenagers' lengthy Christmas lists? If faith were a fairy's wand or a Samantha-like nose twitch, making the impossible tangible, one would have to stand in line to apply for this magical insurance against all ills. What is faith?

We used a simple acrostic to define faith. The *F* stood for faithfulness, for commitment, for a "bloom-where-you're-planted" kind of living. Elizabeth was "blameless" in the sight of God; Mary faced the consequences for her decision to serve God, whatever the cost; Anna served and worshiped God night and day. What a "faith-full" trio! Do those descriptions apply to you?

Your Word tells me, Father, that without faith I cannot please You . . . and I do want to please You. Please show me how.

FAITH MEANS AWARENESS

"Carry each other's burdens, and in this way you will fulfill the law of Christ." (Galatians 6:2)

Read Romans 12:9-21

I know some widows who feel cheated of
A normal life, a home and children's cheer.
I have no lack of any one of these;
I'm happy as I serve and worship here.
Security is to be found in love;
I have the love I need and more besides!
I find significance in serving God
And in His temple, with me, He resides!
—Anna

Have you ever noticed how an insecure person continually draws attention to him- or herself? A person secure in Christ's love is much freer from internal pressures and much more aware of the needs of others.

Awareness is the "A" in the FAITH acrostic.

POINT TO PONDER: The '70s and '80s have been called the "me decades": "Look out for Number One!" In the '90s we hear, "If it feels good, do it!" How much has the "please me" philosophy influenced your lifestyle?

Anna did not waste time pitying herself because she deserved a break today (or any other day). She did not continue to puzzle over why she should be alone while others had happy family lives. Anna simply kept on worshiping God, secure in His unfailing love, while serving others in a significant way.

Forgive me, Father, for being so me-centered.

FAITH MEANS INDIVIDUALITY

"Your Maker is your husband—the L*ORD Almighty is his name—the Holy One of Israel is your Redeemer; he is called the God of all the earth." (Isaiah 54:5)*

Read Romans 12:2-8

I am so old that I must stop and think
To count the years the temple's been my home.
God's worship has become my very life;
I serve Him, and I find I'm not alone.
My husband died so many years ago
But God has been my judge and husband too,
And all my needs have always been supplied!
My God is faithful, just and wholly true.
—Anna

Have you ever watched a high school choir and noticed, as Dr. James Dobson points out, that eighty to ninety percent of the girls wear their hair almost exactly the same way? The urge to conform is very strong in teenagers and can be just as dominating in adults.

It was obvious to everyone that Anna lived in a different world from most women. Rather than being centered in a home and family, her life revolved around the temple and the One she worshiped there. Cooking skills were outranked by the priority of fasting, and the gossip of the marketplace was superseded by the intercession of prayer.

POINT TO PONDER: God tells us that individuality (the *I* in the FAITH acrostic) is very important. He has made each one of us unique, and we need to actively resist letting the world squeeze us into its mold. Individuality should affect our thinking, our attitudes, our activities, our Christmas lists, our Easter shopping, our summer calendars. . . .

Thank You, Father, for Your unique plan for my life. Help me to resist the pressure to conform.

FAITH MEANS TRUST

"I know whom I have believed, and am convinced that he is able to guard what I have entrusted to him for that day."
(2 Timothy 1:12)

Read 2 Timothy 4:1-8

I know it in my heart, the time will come
When I will see the One we're waiting for!
Old Simeon won't die until he sees the Christ;
He has this certain promise from the Lord.
The time is soon! I too will see the Light
That brings salvation to the Gentile world,
The glory of our people Israel
Flag of all nations, He will be unfurled!
—Anna

Anna began to thank God as soon as she saw the Baby Jesus—she had an expectant faith. God had promised Israel a deliverer; what God had promised, He would fulfill!

So trust is the *T* in the FAITH acrostic. The apostle Paul expressed this kind of trust when he wrote to his fellow Christians at Philippi: "Being confident of this, that he who began a good work in you will carry it on to completion until the day of Christ Jesus" (Philippians 1:6).

Trust does not hit the panic button in an emergency. It does not become hysterical and irrational when frustrated. It does not become negative when overwhelmed by piles of dirty wash, muddy footprints on a newly waxed floor or a sick child on my "free" day. Trust says, "I know whom I have believed, and am convinced that he is able to guard what I have entrusted to him." I am not able, but He is!

Thank You, Lord, that You are *able!*

52 – Friday

FAITH MEANS THANKFULNESS

"Be joyful always; pray continually; give thanks in all circumstances, for this is God's will for you in Christ Jesus."
(1 Thessalonians 5:16-18)

Read Psalm 100

Yes, even today could be the day of days,
The earthly highlight of my sojourn here,
The day I look upon my Savior's face,
Rejoicing in His presence! I've no fear!
Yes, even now I see old Simeon run,
Unmindful of his weak, uneven gait;
He seems to have his eyes on someone now.
I must see too! I hope I'm not too late!
—Anna

Faith is spelled with only one ***T***, but there is a second ***T*** that is very much a part of faith, a quality evident in the lives of Mary, Elizabeth and Anna. We have already mentioned it: Anna's thankfulness.

I awoke this morning full of praise, but later in the day I was anything but thankful. My mood changed because my husband and youngest son were traveling north during a winter storm, and I found it difficult to trust Him with that which I had committed to Him.

Expectation can be the enemy of thankfulness. Expectation says: "I should have had a phone call by now! He should have stayed where he was when the roads got bad . . . he shouldn't have attempted that last leg of the trip . . . he should be more concerned about our son's safety." Thankful trust says: "I am so grateful, heavenly Father, that I can talk to You about the fear that is clutching at my heart."

Help me, Father, to let go of my expectations.

FAITH MEANS HUMILITY

"Humble yourselves before the Lord, and he will lift you up."
(James 4:10)

Read Romans 14:1-21

It is a Baby in its mother's arms,
A sweet-faced mother and an earnest man
Who've come to offer up their sacrifice,
For purification is the custom of the land.
Old Simeon's taken the Baby in his arms,
Blessed Child and parents too as in a daze.
I know Messiah's come, at last He's come!
I must tell everyone! I must give praise!
—Anna

Earlier I mentioned our need to learn individuality, the art of standing alone even when under pressure to conform (Romans 12:2). The next verse of that passage tells us to maintain an honest estimate of ourselves, which, it seems to me, is increasingly difficult in today's world.

POINT OF PONDER: Well-known Christian leaders urge us to "love yourself," to varying degrees of that expression. Whatever we read or hear, we need to keep in the perspective of Jesus' injunction: "Love your neighbor as yourself" and "whoever wants to be first must be your slave" (Matthew 20:27). Humility is a necessary ingredient of FAITH.

Romans 12 explains that just as there are many parts to our bodies so there are many parts to Christ's body, and it takes each one of us to make it complete. Anna's ministry in the temple must have provided encouragement and edification to many who, like her, were eagerly awaiting the coming of the Messiah. Each one of us can be an "Anna" to someone else. The Messiah has come, and there is good news to share!

Help me, Father, to be an Anna, an others-centered person.

ENDNOTES

Week 4

[1] Lawrence J. Crabb, Jr., *Effective Biblical Counseling* (Grand Rapids, MI: Zondervan, 1977), p. 61. Used by permission.

Week 7

[1] Karen Burton Mains, "Infidelity," *Decision* (March 1984). Used by permission.

[2] Ibid.

Week 8

[1] Edith Deen, *All the Women of the Bible* (New York: Harper & Row, 1955), p. 203.

[2] Karen Burton Mains, "Infidelity," *Decision* (March 1984). Used by permission.

[3] Evelyn and Frank Stagg, *Women in the World of Jesus* (Philadelphia: Westminster Press, 1978), p. 106. Used by permission.

Week 13

[1] Joan Winmill Brown, *Corrie: The Lives She's Touched* (Old Tappan, NJ: Fleming H. Revell Company, 1979), p. 20.

[2] Ibid.

Week 20

[1] Joni Eareckson (Tada) and Steve Estes, *A Step Further* (Grand Rapids, MI: Zondervan, 1978), pp. 176-178. Used by permission.

[2] Ibid., p. 179.

[3] Ibid., p. 182.

[4] Ibid., p. 183.

Week 22

[1] Keith M. Bailey, *The Children's Bread* (Camp Hill, PA: Christian Publications, 1977), p. 35. Italics added.

Week 24

[1] Vivian Anderson Hall, *Be My Guest* (Chicago: Moody, 1979), p. 14. Used by permission.

[2] Ibid.

Week 25

[1] Evelyn and Frank Stagg, *Women in the World of Jesus* (Philadelphia: Westminster Press, 1978), pp. 118-119. Used by permission.

[2] Lois Gunder Clemens, *Woman Liberated* (Scottdale, PA: Herald Press, 1971), pp. 25-26. Used by permission.

Week 27

[1] Oswald Chambers, *My Utmost for His Highest* (New York: Dodd, Mead & Company, 1949), p. 246.

Week 28

[1] Blair and Rita Justice, *The Broken Taboo: Sex in the Family* (New York: Human Science Press, 1977), p. 16. Used by permission.

[2] Ibid.

[3] Ibid., p. 168.

[4] Ibid., pp. 170, 188.

[5] Ibid., p. 182.

[6] Ibid.

Week 30

[1] Maitland A. Edy, *The Sea Traders* (New York: Time-Life Books, 1974), pp. 106-107.

Week 31

[1] David McCasland, *Oswald Chambers: Abandoned to God* (Grand Rapids, MI: Discovery House Publishers, 1993), 84.

[2] Ibid.

[3] Ibid., p. 85.

[4] Ibid., p. 87.

Week 33

[1] Amy Carmichael, *Edges of His Ways* (Fort Washington, PA: Christian Literature Crusade, 1975), p. 159.

Week 35

[1] Edith Deen, *All the Women of the Bible* (New York: Harper & Row, 1955), p. 210.

[2] Albert Benjamin Simpson, *When the Comforter Came* (Camp Hill, PA: Christian Publications, 1991), pp. 7-8.

[3] Ibid.

[4] Ibid., pp. 47-48.

[5] Ibid.

[6] Ibid.

Week 36

[1] Lawrence J. Crabb, *Effective Biblical Counseling* (Grand Rapids, MI: Zondervan, 1977), p. 61.

[2] Ibid.

[3] S.I. McMillen, *None of These Diseases,* revised ed. (Old Tappan, NJ: Fleming H. Revell, 1984), p. 71. Used by permission.

[4] Ibid.

Week 37

[1] Walter Wangerin, *The Book of God* (Grand Rapids, MI: Zondervan), pp. 633-34.

[2] Jean Livingston, *Tears for the Smaller Dragon* (Camp Hill, PA: Christian Publications, 1997), p. 197.

[3] Amy Carmichael, *Edges of His Ways* (Fort Washington, PA: Christian Literature Crusade, 1975), p. 53.

[4] Ibid.

[5] Ibid, p. 191.

Week 38

[1] Don Williams, *The Apostle Paul and Women in the Church* (Ventura, CA: Regal Books, 1977), p. 37. Used by permission.

Week 39

[1] Emle Bradford, *Paul the Traveler* (London: Allen Lane, 1974), p. 194.

[2] Reginald E. Witt *Isis in the Graeco-Roman World* (Ithaca, NY: Cornell University Press, 1971), p. 14.

Week 40

[1] Don Williams, *The Apostle Paul and Women in the Church* (Ventura, CA: Regal Books, 1977), p. 50. Used by permission.

[2] Ibid., p. 64.

[3] Joy Jacobs and Deborah Strubel, *Single, Whole and Holy* (Camp Hill, PA: Horizon Books, 1996), pp. 170, 172-173.

Week 42

[1] Ed Murphy, *The Handbook of Spiritual Warfare* (Nashville, TN: Thomas Nelson Publishers, 1992), p. 325.

[2] George B. Eager, *Ideas and Things* (Vol. 1, No. 1), The Mailbox Club, 404 Eager Road, Valdosta, GA 31602-1399, p. 8.

Week 43

[1] Charles R. Swindoll, study editor, *The Living Insights Study Bible* (Grand Rapids, MI: Zondervan, 1996), p. 1199.

Week 45

[1] Don Williams, *The Apostle Paul and Women in the Church* (Ventura, CA: Regal Books, 1977), p. 42. Used by permission.

Week 49

[1] Eugenia Price, *God Speaks to Women Today* (Grand Rapids, MI: Zondervan, 1964), pp. 141-142. Used by permission.

Titles by Joy Jacobs

One I Love (with Ruth Dourte)

Single, Whole and Holy (with Deborah Strubel)

They Were Women Like Me

They Were Women, Too

When God Seems Far Away